CrossRoads

A SOUTHERN CULTURE ANNUAL

2004

Edited by Ted Olson

MERCER UNIVERSITY PRESS | MACON, GEORGIA | 2004

ISBN 0-86554-866-8
MUP/P248

© 2004 Mercer University Press
1400 Coleman Avenue
Macon, Georgia 31207
All rights reserved

First Edition.

Book design by Burt & Burt Studio

∞The paper used in this publication meets the minimum requirements
of American National Standard for Information Sciences—Permanence of Paper
for Printed Library Materials, ANSI Z39.48-1992.

Library of Congress Cataloging-in-Publication Data

CrossRoads / edited by Ted Olson.
p. cm.
ISBN 0-86554-866-8 (pbk. : alk. paper)
1. American literature--Southern States. 2. Authors, American—Homes and haunts—
Southern States. 3. Southern States—Literary collections. 4. Southern States—Biography. 5.
Southern States. I. Olson, Ted.

PS551.C76 2004
810.8'0975—dc22
2004009006

Front cover art: *Tallulah Falls*. George Cooke. c. 1834-49. Oil on canvas.
Georgia Museum of Art. University of Georgia. Gift of Mrs. Will Moss. Photographed by Michael McKelvey.

CONTENTS

The book you now have in your hands, *CrossRoads: A Southern Culture Annual,* is dedicated to the interdisciplinary study and artistic appreciation of the American South (broadly defined) and of Southern culture. Mercer University Press has made a commitment to publish this book as an annual anthology featuring writings and illustrations that offer new perspectives on and new expressions of Southern culture. In most respects, this book series will continue the editorial approach of *CrossRoads: A Journal of Southern Culture,* a semi-legendary periodical originally published in the early- and mid-1990s by a dedicated group of graduate students (including the editor of *CrossRoads: A Southern Culture Annual)* then affiliated with the University of Mississippi and that school's Center for the Study of Southern Culture, a leading regional studies organization.

Beginning publication at the same time as a better known Oxford, Mississippi-based periodical (*The Oxford American*) and predating another journal (*Southern Cultures*) that entered the same territory, *CrossRoads: A Journal of Southern Culture* eventually went the way of most projects undertaken by graduate students (this particular project depended largely upon volunteer labor, and graduate students by definition must move on to live life and launch careers). Nonetheless, readers who happened upon the relatively unpublicized and sporadically distributed journal produced at Ole Miss apparently enjoyed *CrossRoads* and learned about the South from it, for we graduate students received a number of letters that said as much. During its short lifespan of five years (1992–1997) and of seven irregularly published, thematically focused issues, *CrossRoads: A Journal of Southern Culture* featured previously unpublished material by many of the leading scholars, writers, and artists committed to interpreting and celebrating the South, including work from (in alphabetical order): Rob Amberg, A. R. Ammons, Mary Ulmer Chiltosky, Jim Clark, James Dickey, Robert Drake, Ann W. Fisher-Wirth, Wayne Flynt, Ernest Gaines, David Galef, Eugene Genovese, Kathryn Gurkin, Alex Haley, Fred Hobson, David Huddle, Patricia Spears Jones, Jack Temple Kirby, Jeff Daniel Marion, Ed McClanahan, Walter McDonald, Errol Miller, Ethelbert Miller, Jim Wayne Miller, Robert Morgan, Marilyn Nance, Tom Rankin, John Shelton Reed, Sheryl St. Germain, Jeanne Shannon, Jon Michael Spencer, Joel Williamson, and Steve Young. *CrossRoads* also provided a forum for lesser known scholars, writers, and artists.

The Ole Miss graduate students who participated in the production of *CrossRoads: A Journal of Southern Culture* were, in chronological order of their participation in the periodical: Ted Olson, Susan Bauer Lee, Michelle Callaway, Barbara Lowe, Jon Parrish Peede, Eric Cash, Jeff Weddle, Joseph Dumas, Lynn McKnight, Steven Jarvis, Tina Ma, Orin Carpenter, John Cox, Nougzar Kopadze, James Lilley, Bland Whitley, Kris Zediker, Sarah Sanders, Matthew Brothers, Allison Finch, Dan Fountain, Maury Gortemiller, Anne Mueller, and Jean-Mark Sans. Numerous faculty and staff associated with the University of Mississippi were supportive of *CrossRoads: A Journal of Southern Culture*, including Charles Reagan Wilson, William R. Ferris, Ann J. Abadie, Tom Rankin, Colby Kullman, Robert H. Brinkmeyer, Ted Ownby, Lisa N. Howorth, H. Dale Abadie, Michael R. Dingerson, Donald C. Peters, Thomas D. Wallace, Gloria D. Kellum, James F. Payne, David S. Hargrove, David Warren Steel, Joseph B. Atkins, Daniel E. Williams, Larry Debord, Sarah Dixon Pegues, and Richard Howorth. The University of Mississippi's support of *CrossRoads: A Journal of Southern Culture* allowed the periodical to accomplish its goal of increasing awareness of a widely misunderstood and romanticized American region. The periodical fulfilled that particular task rather well, if with relatively little fanfare.

The folks at Mercer University Press learned about *CrossRoads: A Journal of Southern Culture* the Southern way: by word of mouth. One of the people whose work had been published in the periodical— Howard Dorgan—and I were standing by the Mercer University Press table at an academic conference in 2002, looking at new book releases, when Mercer's Marsha Luttrell asked Howard if he knew of any worth-while literary or scholarly projects that Mercer might pursue. Howard immediately pointed at me and told her about *CrossRoads*. A couple of weeks later, I received a phone call from Marc Jolley, the Director of Mercer University Press, who told me he was interested in reviving *CrossRoads* in some form. Initially, we discussed my editing that publication again as a periodical, but he and I soon decided that since we were starting over we should truly start over. We settled upon another idea— rather than pursue a shorter, more frequently published periodical on Southern culture, we would produce a larger, annual book. Dr. Jolley volunteered that we might launch the book series with an inaugural volume containing an anthology of works previously published in *CrossRoads: A Journal of Southern Culture* (since that periodical was never widely distributed). After thinking about options for a few days, I decided that, in order to truly distinguish *CrossRoads* the book from *CrossRoads* the periodical, we might as well begin with a book featuring mostly never-before-published materials. At this point I wrote Charles Reagan Wilson, Director of the Center for the Study of Southern Culture at the University of Mississippi, to gain his Center's support for Mercer University Press's plan to revive *CrossRoads* (since during its final two years of publication at Ole Miss the periodical had been granted a Center-sponsored graduate assistantship and had been listed as an official Center publication). Dr. Wilson quickly sent blessings for our going ahead with the new/old project. Calls for submission for *CrossRoads: A Southern Culture Annual* were subsequently posted in various locations, and word was also spread more informally. This book is the result of those written and spoken invitations to participate. The exciting and varied work included here, contributed by people from most of the Southern states and subregions, bears witness to the fact that the South continues to inspire, fascinate, confound, and horrify people (whether such people live within or beyond the region's long-contested boundaries).

We hope that *CrossRoads: A Southern Culture Annual* will continue to receive deeply felt and sensitively reasoned submissions for subsequent volumes. These submissions can include—but are not limited to—creative writing, artwork, photo essays, oral histories, memoirs, profile essays, and analytical academic essays. Regarding the latter, we are interested in considering for *CrossRoads* relevant, well-written scholarly essays from any of the following academic disciplines: history, literature, folklore, music, art, cultural geography, cultural theory, politics, journalism, education, psychology, sociology, anthropology, women's studies, and environmental studies. Our goal with *CrossRoads: A Southern Culture Annual* is—through publishing work that makes connections and that examines aspects of Southern cultural life not normally explored or even easily understood—to enhance general awareness of Southern culture and to enliven discussions about the South. The main criteria ensuring consideration of submitted materials for subsequent volumes of *CrossRoads* will be that all materials should (to borrow William Faulkner's famous phrase) "tell about the South" and that they should do so memorably.

For more information on *CrossRoads: A Southern Culture Annual*, please consult the Mercer University Press website or write to the editor of *CrossRoads* in care of East Tennessee State University, Box 70400, Johnson City, TN 37614.

Ted Olson

Measure for Measure

BY BRENDA WITCHGER

I grew up in a small Alabama community with music all around me. Cadence and interval, scale and syncopation, timbre and tone. There were no instruments, no melody as such, for the music came from the everyday language of people I encountered each day, especially the old folks. I worry these days that the music of our language—our own unique orchestration of the mother tongue—has about played out. As the South becomes more homogenized, we are in danger of losing some of the speech patterns, idioms, and accents that make our language sing. It gives me the weary-dismals, as Aunt Tessy used to say.

Southerners are a diverse and complex lot, which is why Hollywood and New York almost always get it wrong. It's why so many depictions of the South and its inhabitants have been reduced to cornpone—*The Beverly Hillbillies*, *Hee-Haw*, and *The Dukes of Hazzard*. If we could only glad-eye some of those folks and get them down here, we could school them a little, as my Uncle Kin might opine.

Traveling 100 miles from any given point in the South can bring marked changes in folkways, customs, terrain, politics, mores, traditions, and religious practices. And when it comes to the Southern accent—there isn't one, there are more varieties than you can say grace over.

Where I grew up in north Alabama, in the foothills of the Appalachians, we worked our *r*s, hammering them like iron on an anvil (to change a flat tar, you've got have the tar arn). But where my father's side of the family lived just 150 miles south, the tone was soft from the round vowels of the Deep South, where *r*s are rendered useless except for beginning words (Motha and Fatha are in the gahden).

The variables are thick on the ground: there's the Texas twang (and the larger question of whether Texas should even be considered Southern at all); both the low country and highlands accents that evoke different strains of speech from the British Isles; Gullah; Cajun patois; Creole and African influences; and numbers of other linguistic quirks and whimsicalities within socio-economic strata and individual families.

What we all seem to have in common is a love of color and flummery. Why play the scales when you can go eight to the bar? Nowhere is this more evident than when Southerners take on weights and measures. We pack a full complement of handy terms for how much, how far, or how long. On this subject of quantifying words and phrases, most Southerners understand one another full well, though we often confuse and befuddle outsiders—those from somewhere else. Virtually every Southerner—at least those of a certain age—understands how much a mess of peas is. It's more than a piddly and less than a slew, and it varies depending on the number of people in the family, the weather conditions in any particular year, and whether it's early or late in the growing season.

The current crop of Southerners is in danger of losing a goodly number of quantifiers. These people are developing a tin ear for dialect and a loss of regional identity. They don't hear the spoken word much anymore, except as it's relayed through the TV or stereo, produced and narrated by those not from around here. It seems to me we are—right now—on the cusp of a shift. As Great Uncle Clive would say, our ox is in the ditch. Perhaps it's time to codify some of our measuring words— like Sequoyah's syllabary, which preserved the Cherokee language through the generations.

When we're talking amounts of anything, Southerners can get right down to the nitty-gritty. There's a difference between a mite, a tad, and a smidgen (a smidge if you've got the right sass to carry that one off).

And all those are different from an itty-bitty, a dab, or a swink. Still smaller is a t-niny—or a t-nincy if you want to parse it on down. Eventually you get down to nothing, then proceed to what Cousin Leland described as "no bigger than the little end of nothing whittled down to a sharp point."

We like to parcel out time in our own way as well. That's another thing Hollywood gets wrong, portraying us as slow—in cranial activity as well as in speech. There's a big difference between leisurely and lazy. Various studies have shown that Southerners speak roughly the same number of words per minute as folks from other parts of the nation. We may stretch individual words here and there and sometimes create two syllables where only one exists, but we get to the point about the same time as anyone else. We just enjoy ourselves more while we're getting there.

There are lots of words for marking and measuring time down here. Everyone knows when people say they'll get to something by and by that you don't hold your breath. On the other hand, if they promise to get to it directly—or more accurately, d'rectly—you've been promised some immediacy.

Although it seems antithetical, a good long while is generally not perceived to be as long as a long while. But a great long while is considerably longer. "Afterwhile" is a slippery one and has to take into account the context and the reliability of the speaker. More often than not it's meant to put someone off until they forget the whole thing. "Yes, I'll mow the yard afterwhile." A "spell," as in "come sit for a spell," has already gone out of common usage, but most Southerners still understand the term and would never think of overstaying their welcome.

Another term headed for the linguistic attic is "nigh on." Used in place of "nearly," it carries a poetic resonance. "We've been married nigh on twenty years" sounds much happier and more hopeful about that circumstance than "we've been married nearly twenty years."

We like a little meter in our measurement of the days, too. Uncle Riley used to claim he worked his cotton crop in season from kin to cain't—from first light to full dark. Dawn is daybust, or day clean, or comin' light. Twilight is dusky dark, or the pink of evening, or the shank of day. After that comes good dark, which—paradoxically—is when all kinds of bad business usually happens.

"Along about" sounds a whole heap friendlier than "at approximately." "We got to the beach along about two o'clock" sounds like people enjoying life. "We got to the beach at approximately two o'clock" sounds like a military maneuver.

A visit to Aunt Honey and Uncle Dear—an overbearing aunt and her hopelessly henpecked husband—was always rich with quantifiers. Aunt Honey was a renowned cook, and she tried to teach those comin' up—us young ones—her special secrets. We all learned pretty quickly the nuances of measures, such as a good handful, a dollop, a pinch, a tad, and a gracious plenty of any given ingredient. Aunt Honey didn't own measuring spoons. An old chipped teacup she kept in the flour bag was the closest she came to a measuring instrument aside from her own two hands and her sharp eye.

When Aunt Honey had laid the table there was "not much wood showing," a compliment to a woman who put on a good spread. As the plates and bowls circled the table, Uncle Dear would eventually demure, "No thanky; I've reached." Great Aunt Myrtle preferred the more lady-like phrase, "No thank you kindly, I've had my ample sufficiency." Kids would rub their bellies and declare them "thick as a tick."

Outsiders sometimes get misled by Southerners' expressions for distances. Within hollerin' distance is just what it sounds like, and can be extrapolated into two hoots and a holler. Down the road a piece is farther than that. If it's a right smart piece, you should take a bottle of water, and if it's a far piece, plan bathroom breaks. When you've been doing quite a lot of traveling around—probably because you're lost from following directions such as those above—you've been "all over hell and half of Georgia."

When I was little, my father would refuse my request to visit a cousin's house on a Sunday afternoon by saying "Naw, it's too far and snaky," which had nothing to do with snakes but may well have originated back when pathways led people through snake-infested woods. In my day it just meant he didn't want to drive the fifteen miles of meandering county roads to carry me to my cousin's. And, yes, in the South we carry people places in the car. Groceries and small children we tote.

A country mile is a flexible distance, compressing or swelling depending on the intent. "They just live over here a country mile" means one thing. "You missed me by a country mile" means quite another.

When it comes to money matters, old-time Southerners knew just how to tell the whole story without resorting to numbers. Forget lower class, middle class, and upper class. In the South, people are too poor to paint and too proud to whitewash, people are fixed, or people are in high cotton. People who put on pretentiously are all hat and no cattle, or all vine and no taters. If you come into sudden wealth, like winning the lottery, you've gone and gotten Yankee rich. But to confuse matters, a Yankee dime has nothing to do with money. It's the same as "give me some sugar," which has nothing to do with food.

To be sure, the musicality of our language is subject to dissonance. Our creative penchant has been hijacked by Hollywood and turned into parody. Politicians have exploited the Southern language in an effort to appear folksy. They insult the very people they're trying to impress. They pepper their speech with phrases like "in a coon's age," "quick as greased lightning," "hell bent for election," or "fast as Moody's goose." They overuse the currency. Someone should give out the warning: do not try this at home. Speaking Southern should be reserved for authentic Southerners who talk this way all the time; it is not meant for amateurs or posers. You can detect the fakes as soon as their lips start moving. As Uncle Riley would say, "It doesn't take long to study a hot horseshoe."

Yes, in the South we've got more ways to say "how much" than Carter's got little liver pills. Unfortunately, we've got an equal number of threats to the distinctive tune of our speech. Language is a fluid thing. It changes in response to the times and circumstances, and that's generally a good thing. Many of the expressions I heard growing up have a decidedly anachronistic ring to them now.

The present generation of Southerners has little opportunity to hear adults swappin' stories like I did as a young girl. We're in a hurry to relay information, and more often these days we're doing it Jack Webb style—just the facts, ma'am. Gossip gets passed by telephone or over e-mail instead of at the feed store or at the Piggly Wiggly. Idioms and figurative expressions are purged. The range and tone and songfulness of Southern speech are forgotten or ignored. Today's teens know how fast a DSL line can transmit, but they might be bumfuzzled if given the task of picking a mess of peas.

Peas Please

That Good Ol' Pot Likker

BY LINDA BEHREND

I grew up in the South, and some of my fondest memories of that time concern the food we ate, the way it was prepared, and the dialect associated with the kitchen. Southern dishes and methods of preparation reflected the influence of a culture that made do or did without. For example, Mama used to fix greens a lot. Now, greens is one thing I just do not like. Whenever Mama fixed greens, she would say, "I want to get some of that good ol' pot likker." I didn't know for a long time what she was talking about. To me, it sounded like she was saying "lick-er," but I never saw her lick out the pot ("lickin' out the bowl" is what you did when someone made a cake). I was probably grown and cooking for others before I found out that "pot likker" was like "corn likker" and meant the dark-colored cooking water ("liquor") left in the bottom of the pot when you cooked greens. And, I have since learned that some people believe pot likker works like an aphrodisiac! Little did I know all those years I was turning up my nose at Mama's greens.

There are several different kinds of greens: turnip greens, mustard greens, or collards, swiss chard, kale, beet greens, and spinach…and some people even eat dandelion greens. "Creecy greens" is like watercress; you can eat the leaves of that, too. Sometimes Mama would pick a mess of poke to cook for greens. (A mess is just some amount, determined by however many you want to feed, of whatever it is you're going to cook.) Poke is a weed that grows wild in the fields and along the road—you can tell it by its deep purple berries. The stems are purple, too, when it grows tall. You can eat poke like a vegetable—but only the young, tender leaves. The berries are poisonous to people, but birds eat them. Sometimes when you hang your clothes out to dry—does anyone hang clothes out anymore?—you come back to find purple "blobs" on them where a bird has eaten poke berries and left its mark.

Poke weed (the leaves only) can be cooked like greens, but it can also be made into poke "sallit" ("salad"). Poke sallit is sort of like lettuce salad, which makes me think of something else Mama used to make. When we had leaf lettuce in the garden and the leaves were still young and tender, she would fix "wilted lettuce." To make this, Mama fried bacon and poured the grease, while it was still hot, over the lettuce leaves along with a little vinegar. Some people called it "killed" (or "kilt") lettuce, but Mama didn't think it was proper to call it that.

We always put vinegar on any kind of greens (I think most people put vinegar on theirs), but I had a cousin who put mayonnaise on hers! Our family even put vinegar on green beans. Now, green beans have lots of different names. Some people call them string beans, but while others call them pole beans, snap beans, or half-runners. When they get full, you've got shelley beans (shellies)—or, even, shucky beans.

On winter Saturdays, we always had white beans with chow-chow and catsup on top. White beans come in two varieties: little Navy beans (which doesn't make sense, does it?) and Great Northerns. "Chow-chow" is what some people would call relish. To make it, Mama would fasten a big food grinder to the edge of the kitchen table and grind up cabbage. Then she put in chopped-up onions and red and green peppers, and I don't know what else. And, of course, there were seasonings—vinegar and sugar and spices—all mixed together, poured over the ground-up vegetables, and packed into jars.

Many Southerners when they talk about soup beans mean brown beans. And there are two varieties of these, too: pinto beans and October beans. Most people put a piece of "fat meat" in with their beans while they're cooking—that can be fatback or ham hock or hog jowl or sow belly. But the main thing you have to do to make good soup beans is to cook 'em for a lo-o-n-g time. My mother-in-law was an expert at cooking soup beans, and I've heard her say you have to "cook 'em hard" to make good soup. That means you cook them on "high" until they start to fall apart (you have to add water while they're cooking on high heat); then you turn the heat down low and let them cook for the rest of the day.

Of course you can't have soup beans without corn bread. The way people say it around here, it's really one word: "soup beans-'n'-corn bread." Corn bread can be made different ways, too. Mama always made us corn sticks in a cast iron corn-stick pan. Her corn-stick pan was nice and black because she always poured a little oil in each section and put it in the oven to heat while she mixed up the batter. When the pan was good and hot, she poured the batter in with the oil, which made it sizzle. Corn sticks are good and crunchy. Some people bake their corn bread in a cast iron skillet. When you do that, the outside is crunchy, but the inside is soft. You can also make corn bread in a skillet on top of the stove—that's what people call corn pone. You put oil in the skillet, get it real hot, and drop the batter in by spoonfuls. These fry up nice and brown. "Spoon bread" and "Johnny-cake" are other kinds of bread made with corn meal. Of course, if you live in North Carolina you eat grits, also made from corn.

The other kind of bread that people in the South eat a lot of is the biscuit. "Biscuits" also makes a compound word, as in "biscuits-and-gravy." Several kinds of gravy are popular there, including brown gravy, white gravy, chicken gravy, and red-eye gravy. But what people eat most with biscuits is sausage gravy. When Mama made biscuits, she let us have the dough that was left over after she had cut out all she could with her biscuit cutter. We used it to make "fist biscuits." To do this, you roll the dough into a little ball between your palms and then flatten it with your fist. Or we would shape some dough into a bird's nest and make little baby eggs out of a tiny pinch of dough. Some mornings Mama would make us "soakie." For this, you take cold, leftover biscuits and split them open. Put the biscuits in a bowl, sprinkle some sugar over them and add a pat of butter. Then pour warm milk over all and let it soak in.

The same kind of dough you use for biscuits can also be used to make cobbler. You just leave out some of the salt and add sugar. To make a cobbler, you use whatever fruit you have on hand and put pieces of dough on top instead of making a crust, as for a pie. You can drop the dough on in dollops (it has to be pretty wet for this), or roll or pat it out and cut it into strips to make a lattice design.

Fried chicken is another food we had a lot when I was growing up. Mama always fried chicken in a cast iron skillet. She would put the skillet on top of the stove to heat while she floured the chicken. She always bought chicken pieces at the grocery store, but I can remember her telling how her mother would go out in the yard and get a chicken, pick it up by the head, and sling it around to break its neck. Then, of course, she had to pluck the feathers, clean it, and cut it up. Makes you want to quit eating chicken if you think about it very much.

Anyway, Mama floured the chicken in a brown paper bag (some people call that a poke). She would put flour in the bag and sprinkle in some salt and pepper. Then she would drop the chicken in, a piece or two at a time, hold the top of the bag shut with her fist, and shake it up until the chicken was coated with flour. This she dropped into the skillet, which was now good and hot. Mama fried chicken in butter or margarine, but many people fry theirs in lard.

Mama sometimes fixed rabbit like that, too. My daddy couldn't stand the thought of eating a poor little rabbit (he didn't hunt), so she would tell him it was fried chicken. You can imagine how upset he was when he found out what she had put over on him. Mama said, when she was growing up, her brothers used to go squirrel hunting and bring back squirrel for her family to eat. Every now and then, our family had beef tongue. Mama boiled it in a big pot with spices and seasonings. We ate it warm, or sliced it and put it on sandwiches after it got cold. I remember Mama fixing pork brains, too.

A long time ago, folks used what they had and didn't waste any part of it. Today, people want to be able to go to the store and buy whatever they want at the moment—either it's in season or not. Used to, you only had foods when they were in season. They weren't available all the time, but it seems like they tasted better then. Times sure have changed...but I still don't much like greens!

Weight of Sweetness

BY JEAN-MARK SENS

Round as a melon will ever be,
not so perfect as earth seen from a satellite,
spherical fruit gravid with life seeds,
small ribs of teeth inside waiting to burst pippins
beneath a green rind of corrugated moonscape.
Hundreds of rotund planets cool
under the store neon,
each with a gravity of its own.
Customers assess the sweetness of melons
by guessing the weight of its wet flesh inside.
All make the same gesture,
coveting vegetable bliss,
the hand lifts up a cantaloupe in two or three brief tractions—
nose almost touching its navel—
and either slings it back to the pile
or elects it, and carries it away
soon to reveal the prime of its prize:
smell and flesh exposed to the eye around a table.

The Horse's Sugar

BY DEIDRA SUWANEE DEES

"Otis, Otis! Come here, Otis!" she called. Otis climbed down from the skinny dogwood that barely supported his lanky frame. Running up the back steps, jacket flapping, he burst through the big door, slamming the screen door behind him. He entered the warm kitchen and held out his cupped right hand. Otis's mother Mama Bell piled on some lumps of sugar and said, "You take this sugar to Coosah, Otis, okay?" Looking straight into his dark Muscogee eyes, Mama Bell said, "You feed all this sugar to the horse, you hear me?"

"Yes, ma'am," Otis said, closing the kitchen door with his left hand, steadying the other hand so as not to let the screen door hit it and spill the sugar. As he walked to the barn in the fall afternoon, his nose caught a scent of the sugar. Otis thought, "How good that sugar would taste! Like the candy the white kids brought to school in their lunch pails. Like the lollipops in the big store that Indians couldn't afford." As he walked into the barn—into the shadows, out of Mama Bell's sight—he pushed his face into the pile of sugar, taking a big bite. The sugar was rocky and gritty at first, and then it melted like syrup and slid down his throat.

Otis shoved his right hand under the horse's mouth, saying, "Coosah, here's your sugar, ole boy." With the other hand, Otis rubbed Coosah's face while the horse nibbled and slobbered.

Coosah looked up, seeming to ask, "Where's the rest of my sugar?" The horse nudged the side of the boy's head. Otis ducked, then caught himself, thinking he really shouldn't be bothered by Coosah's slobber. After all, Otis thought, it was a small price to pay for stealing the horse's sugar.

⁂

My father told me this story many times when I was growing up. His voice would always falter at the story's end. "I believe that was the only time—the only time—I ever disobeyed my mother," he once acknowledged.

I always felt sorry for Daddy, not really knowing what to say. He never spoke of it, but I knew Mama Bell died shortly after she sent her son out to feed Coosah some sugar.

Daddy has long since died. Now I tell this same story to my children; and when I come to the story's end, my father's awkwardness returns.

A Far Cry

BY MENDI LEWIS OBADIKE

I make a wrong turn in the suburbs
and get lost in the backwoods of Tennessee
with nothing to protect my African body
but a Japanese car.

Trees night the sky. There's a man
driving behind me. I think he can tell by the nap
of my hair. I think he will follow me
into a driveway if I try to turn around.

How far is Alabama?
Which doorstep shall I dare
to darken? What makes them
tear our flesh sometimes?

A ghost of a woman stands roadside,
waving down cars. I follow her flashlight
to an old barn where some have gathered
for an unknown cause. Could be church

or a hanging, but all I trust
is the strangeness here, and this
blank-faced beacon is strange
as bush on fire. So I put on

my ancestors' armor. A smile,
a shuffle, a voice I lace with *please*
and a twang. Anything to remind them
of the ones who know how to bow their heads.

Only then do I heel-toe through the mud
to the barn, where three white men
wait in the doorway. Wait watching me, a small,
brown woman. A stranger, crossing their land.

The Ozarks and Dixie:
Considering a Subregion's Southernness

BY BROOKS BLEVINS

I am a Southerner. My father is a Southerner. His father was, too. We all knew it, just knew it. Perhaps, though, we've lived under a misconception. We're Arkansans, and everybody knows Arkansans are Southerners. Yet, we're also Ozarkers, and, like our kinfolk back in Appalachia, we have always been a little different.

At the age of twenty-two, I left home to have my Southernness challenged. I had never spent more than two weeks at a time outside the Ozarks—except for a summer of National Guard training in Texas and Illinois (drill instructors, whose keen sense of American regional stereotypes lends flavor and occasional irony to their blustery condescension, certainly know that Arkansas is a key component of the benighted South). But at twenty-two, I left for graduate school in Alabama—the *true South*, as I was about to discover.

Much to my surprise, my Southernness wilted in the face of such a test. Utterly unimpressed with my peripheral claim on the South, my apathy toward football, my disdain for grits and greens, and my inability to distinguish green cotton from soybeans, the Alabamians chewed me up and spat me out. Stripping me of my Southernness, these

Southerners rendered me a regional misfit, a native of a Southern state whose Southernness was suspect at best.[1]

Southerners have for generations participated in the exercise of self-definition. What is "the South"? Who are "Southerners"? How do we define "Southern"? Often the self-definitions have been more than mere regional descriptions—sometimes they truly are self-defining. Inherently confident in their Southernness, Southerners often describe themselves, their lives, or their experiences in the process of definition. Not surprisingly, there are almost as many different definitions or descriptions of the South as there are Southerners. A Cajun's definition of the South differs significantly from that of the Tennessee mountaineer.

Scholars have stepped in to weigh statistics, history, cultures, mindsets, and their own experiences in a general attempt to decide which definition, if any, comes closest to capturing the essence of the American South—the Cajun's or the mountaineer's, or perhaps the Carolina mill worker's, the Alabama coal miner's, or the Tidewater planter's. These scholars and pundits have defined the South in numerous ways using gauges as diverse as race, lethargy, workstock, kudzu, and even fireworks on New Year's. Some deal with the Southern mind, others with a physical South of gray borders.

The southeastern part of the United States is full of subregions that, depending on one's definition, may or may not fit neatly into the scholar's South. The Ozarks subregion is among these. Stretching from central Arkansas to central Missouri—with a sideways lop over into northeastern Oklahoma—this geographic entity straddles political boundaries imposed by a federal government unmindful of the area's physical

---

[1] This article is derived from a paper presented at the annual conference of the Arkansas Historical Association held in Batesville, Arkansas, in April 1998. Any similarity in content and spirit to Paul K. Conkin's presidential address at the sixty-third annual meeting of the Southern Historical Association in Atlanta in November 1997 (and later published in the February 1998 issue of the *Journal of Southern History*) is purely unintentional and simply underscores the demographic and social similarities between the Ozarks and Appalachia. The author was not present at the Atlanta conference and did not read the published version of Conkin's speech until well after the author's April 1998 presentation.

integrity. The imaginary line that separates Missouri from Arkansas has proved exceedingly important to the Ozarker's regional affiliation. Because most Missouri Ozarkers I have known do not consider themselves Southerners and because most people who identify with the South do not consider Missouri a part of it, I will consider here the question of the Southernness of the Arkansas Ozarks, the old Confederate Ozarks, using as guides or gauges the various definitions offered by scholars. Perhaps we will discover the Ozarks' rightful place in the panoply of American regions; perhaps the discussion will simply confuse the matter for those Ozarkers who know in their gut exactly who it is that they are. Furthermore, because I am a historian, the following observations will for the most part be couched in terms of historical descriptions of the South and the Ozarks, though I will address the issue of change over time and its relation to the discussion.

One of the first scholarly treatments of the central theme of the South was written by U. B. Phillips. In his 1928 *American Historical Review* article, "The Central Theme in Southern History," based largely on his observations of the plantation South, the historian described the "cardinal test of a Southerner and the central theme of Southern history" as the "common resolve indomitably maintained that it shall be and remain a white man's country."[2] Thus, the central theme of the South and its history is the subjugation of the black man. Here, we are immediately challenged by the fact that, throughout history in the greatest part of Ozark territory, there have been few if any blacks to subjugate. The hilly terrain and generally poor soil prevented the development of plantation-style agriculture, which, in turn, limited the number of slaves brought to the Ozarks before the Civil War. In the twentieth century, the black population of the fifteen core Ozark counties, those lying wholly within the upland plateau, has never exceeded .5 percent of the total population. In 1930, two years after Phillips's article was published,

[2] Ulrich B. Phillips, "The Central Theme in Southern History," *American Historical Review* 34 (October 1928): 31.

blacks accounted for at least one percent of the population in only three Ozark counties—Izard, Washington, and Van Buren—and these three counties were home to four in five black Ozarkers. Three Ozark counties—Boone, Fulton, and Newton—were the only ones in Arkansas with not a single black resident in 1930, and three additional counties counted only one black person in their census. Today, though the black population in the Ozarks has doubled since 1930, the black percentage of the total population is unchanged, and over 90 percent of black Ozarkers now live in the "Northwest Arkansas City" corridor from Fayetteville to Bentonville.

According to Phillips' interpretation, and the interpretations of other scholars who place race relations at the center of Southern history and culture, the Ozarks has no direct claim on Southernness. That is not to say that the Ozarks has been free from bigotry or that the subregion has been an oasis of racial harmony. In at least a few cases, Ozark communities were all white by design.[3] It is most probable that in Phillips's world of 1928, the great majority of Ozarkers shared the racist sentiments of lowland Arkansans, and consequently at least acquiesced to the white man's hegemony in the Old Confederacy. It should also be remembered that no less an Ozark mountaineer than Orval Eugene Faubus directed the state during one of the darkest hours of race relations and subsequently became a symbol for Southern resistance to racial integration and to the Civil Rights movement. Nevertheless, in most Ozark communities, from Siloam Springs to Mountain Home, the paucity of blacks obviated the need to turn racist sentiments into acts of violence or methods of oppression.

Somewhat intertwined with the notion of race is the identification of staple crop agriculture, particularly cotton raising, as a component of Southernness. The Ozarks' Southernness by this gauge is more ambigu-

---

[3] For an example of one Ozark town that became all white due to racial strife, see Jacqueline Froelich and David Zimmermann, "Total Eclipse: The Destruction of the African American Community of Harrison, Arkansas, in 1905 and 1909," *Arkansas Historical Quarterly* 58 (Summer 1999): 131–59.

ous. Before the 1960s, many Ozarkers raised the white fiber, though not as intensively as most other Arkansans. In the 1870s and 1880s, a wave of cotton cultivation swept up from the bottomlands south and east of the Ozarks and into the valleys and on to the rocky hillsides. By 1889 only three Ozark counties—Washington, Benton, and Madison in extreme northwestern Arkansas—produced fewer than 1,000 bales of cotton.[4] Nevertheless, falling prices and infertility forced many Ozark farmers out of the cotton business around the turn of the century. By World War I, the cotton wave had receded, leaving the South's staple crop only in the narrow fertile valleys of the interior and the gently sloping plateaus of the eastern and southern Ozarks. On the eve of the Great Depression, and at the peak of the South's dependence on cotton, almost 12,000 Ozark farmers devoted more than 130,000 acres to cotton cultivation. The majority of Ozark cotton was raised east and south of the Boston Mountains. More than 75 percent of the agriculturists in four counties—Cleburne, Izard, Sharp, and Van Buren—raised some cotton.[5] The most intensive cotton county in the Ozarks, Cleburne County, surpassed the non-Ozark state average in percentage of farmers growing the crop and equaled the average of just less than sixteen acres of cotton per farm.

But cotton production was far from monolithic in the Ozarks. Farmers in three northwestern counties grew no cotton at all, and 70 percent of the region's crop was produced in four counties representing the eastern and southern limits of the interior Ozarks. By using this test of Southernness, we face the prospect of classifying certain areas of the Ozarks as being more Southern than others.[6] In counties such as Cleburne, Izard, Sharp, Fulton, and Van Buren, and to a lesser extent Stone, Marion, and Baxter—or primarily those counties comprising the

[4] U.S. Department of the Interior, Office of the Census, *Eleventh Census of the United States, 1890: Agriculture* (Washington, DC: GPO, 1895).

[5] U.S. Department of Commerce, Bureau of the Census, *Census of Agriculture, 1935: Reports for States, With Statistics by Counties*, vol. 1, part 2 (Washington, DC: GPO, 1936).

[6] Ibid.

eastern and southeastern Ozarks—cotton growing approached a level of importance and intensity found elsewhere in this cotton state. If a culture of cotton cultivation connotes Southernness, then most communities, and by extension most Ozarkers, in these counties at one time qualified as Southerners. Conversely, the farther west a person traveled in the Ozarks, the fewer cotton patches he or she saw and the smaller those cotton patches became. Using the gauge of staple crop-cotton agriculture, northwestern Arkansas and the Boston Mountain highlands would not have measured up as being part of the South.

Of course, the cotton argument, at least as applied to the Ozarks, is a purely historical one, for no cotton has been produced there in more than three decades. But the decline of cotton cultivation in the Ozarks does not have to render this particular gauge of Southernness useless. With only a few exceptions, nowhere in the modern South is cotton growing as widespread as it was fifty or seventy-five years ago, and, now that California is the nation's leading cotton-producing state, one has to question the usefulness of cotton planting as a modern sign of Southernness. In much of the South, kudzu has replaced cotton. In the 1930s and 1940s, New Deal agricultural allotment programs, cooperative extension service agents, and the Soil Conservation Service convinced Southern farmers to plant the viney Asian plant in worn-out cotton fields, a development that most people would come to abhor and that would lend another mark of dubious distinction to the post-World War II South. Again, this is a mark that by and large the Ozarks do not share. If one uses the "where kudzu grows" test of Southernness, most of the Ozarks is safely outside the South.[7] Although kudzu can be found in the Ozarks, it is rare enough that it sparks interest when it is seen there. By contrast, kudzu is so common in areas of Georgia, Alabama, and other Deep South states that the passer-through may only become con-

---

[7] John Shelton Reed, "The South: What Is It? *Where* Is It?" in *The South For New Southerners*, ed. Paul D. Escott and David R. Goldfield (Chapel Hill: University of North Carolina Press, 1991) 21.

scious of the ever-present kudzu when confronted by a succession of pastures and groves not smothered by the vine.

A similar agricultural gauge of Southernness is the mule test.[8] This theory posits that the higher the mule-to-horse ratio in favor of mules as the workstock of choice in a given area, the more Southern that area probably is. Using this test we find results comparable to those generated by our cotton survey. Arkansas in 1929 was certainly a mule state. Statewide, mules outnumbered horses almost three to one. Only four Arkansas counties reported more horses: Benton, Boone, Carroll, and Washington—all Ozark counties and all in the northwest. But elsewhere in the hills, mules outnumbered horses, and in some areas the difference was striking. Izard County contained 2,000 more mules than horses; Van Buren County farmers favored mules three to one. Even in mountainous Searcy and Stone Counties, mules held a two to one advantage over horses.[9] This gauge appears to absorb a larger puddle of the Ozarks into the Southern pool; simultaneously, it continues our trend of dividing the Arkansas Ozarks into more and less "Southern" components.

In the background of Phillips's race argument and the impetus for the South's dependence on King Cotton was the weather. Clarence Cason defined the South as that part of the United States that reached 90 degrees in the shade at least 100 days a year.[10] That certainly limits the range of what is Southern. Cason's definition would at best limit the South to a sometimes-narrow swath of plantation land and piney woods stretching from eastern Georgia, just below the Piedmont, down into Florida's swampy hinterland, and across the Gulf Coastal Plain of

---

[8] Just about anyone who has ever written much about the South has written about mules at one time or another. For a scholarly examination of the place of the mule in Southern culture and history, see Charles F. Lane, "Southern and Quasi-Southern Cultural Landscapes," in *The South in Perspective*, ed. Francis B. Simkins (Farmville, Va.: Longwood College, 1959); and George Bolton Ellenberg, "Mule South to Tractor South: Mules, Machines, Agriculture, and Culture in the Cotton South, 1850–1950" (Ph.D. diss., University of Kentucky, 1994).

[9] Ibid.

[10] Clarence Cason, *90 Degrees in the Shade* (Chapel Hill: University of North Carolina Press, 1935). See also Ulrich B. Phillips, *Life and Labor in the Old South* (Boston: Little, Brown, 1929).

Alabama, Mississippi, and Louisiana into eastern Texas. Only the lower section of Arkansas could measure up to such a stiff standard. The Ozarks certainly would not. The highland elevation and the Great Plains weather system claim a corridor from Eureka Springs to Harrison for the Midwest. There, the temperature reaches 90 degrees fewer than sixty days a year.

The weather definition introduces us to another complexity in the quest for the essence of Southernness—that is, the possibility or probability of the existence of several Souths. Some scholars have used the terms "small South" and "large South" to denote the decreasing similarities among Southern people as one migrates away from an epicenter of Southernness—whether Clarksdale, Mississippi, or Lower Peach Tree, Alabama, or some South Carolina plantation. Again, our epicenters share the distinction of satisfying our stereotypes and definitions—they are, or were, staple-crop producing, black-majority, 90 degrees in the sultry shade, plantation examples of the South, and they so easily pass the tests of Southernness because most likely they were the models around which the gauges were constructed. The Ozarks could never have been included in this "small South." But the "large South" has room for the Ozarker and for others on Dixie's periphery.

Two additional gauges of Southernness reflect the notion of "small South" versus "large South"—fireworks and politics. After the Civil War, bitter ex-Confederates urged fellow Southerners to halt the practice of celebrating the Fourth of July, a Yankee holiday. But Southerners like their fireworks. Thus was born the tradition of fireworks as part of a New Year's Day celebration, with a quieter Independence Day.[11] If the South is that part of the nation whose New Year's fireworks sales surpass those of the Fourth of July, then we find once again a restricted Dixie. Although New Year's fireworks celebrations were not uncommon in the Ozarks as recently as the 1950s, today they are found almost exclusively

---

[11] John Gould Fletcher, *Arkansas* (Chapel Hill: University of North Carolina Press, 1947) 269, 368.

in the Deep South. Arkansas's largest retail fireworks dealer, headquartered in Batesville on the Ozark periphery, profits from New Year's sales in Cleveland, Mississippi, Shreveport, Louisiana; and Houston, Texas; but the dealer has never experienced success north of Tupelo.

In terms of politics, some political scientists and historians have argued that the South has been defined by a rigid, one-party system. Between the end of Reconstruction and the latter days of the Civil Rights Movement, southern Democrats exercised hegemonic control unparalleled in American history. Judging by the party affiliation of elected state and federal officials during the one-party era, most Ozarkers participated in or acquiesced to Democratic dominance. But when a Republican voice made it to the state capitol in Little Rock, that voice was almost invariably sent by a contingent of dissenting Ozark voters. The Ozarks had been home to the greatest number of Arkansas's anti-secessionists and Union sympathizers. For many in the Ozarks, as in Appalachia back east, resentment and hostility toward the antebellum Democratic elite and toward the Confederate-sympathizing bushwackers carried into Reconstruction and continued beyond that point for generations. Between 1919 and 1959, five different Ozark counties—Newton, Searcy, Van Buren, Carroll, and Madison—elected at least one Republican to the Arkansas House of Representatives. In twenty-one general assembly elections during that span, Searcy County sent a Republican to Little Rock eight times, including five consecutive sessions between 1945 and 1953, while her neighbor Newton County elected a Republican representative seven times. In 1945 alone, four Ozark Republicans served in the Arkansas house.[12] Although Arkansas sent no post-Reconstruction Republicans to Congress until 1967, it was not uncommon for Republican candidates to garner more than 40 percent of the votes cast in the third, or northwestern, district. In the closest race before 1966, 47 percent of northwestern Arkansas voters cast their

---

12 W. J. McCuen, *Historical Report of the Secretary of State, 1986*, ed. Steve Faris (Little Rock: Arkansas Secretary of State, 1986) 385–420, 237.

ballots for Republican John Worthington in his bid to unseat the Democratic incumbent John Tillman. And it is no coincidence that Harrison's John Paul Hammerschmidt was elected Third District representative in 1966, Arkansas's first Republican in Congress in almost 100 years, or that the state's first post-Reconstruction Republican Senator (Tim Hutchinson, elected in 1996) hailed from the Benton County town of Gravette.

Thus, as we were forced to do on the cotton test, we may have to differentiate between areas within the Ozarks when assessing political Southernness. An unmistakably active two-party system survived in selected areas such as Searcy, Newton, and Madison Counties, areas that appeared rather un-Southern in terms of race and cotton cultivation. But much of the Ozarks showed few signs of political opposition to the one-party Democracy of the first three-quarters of the twentieth century, and, therefore, reflected a very Southern political atmosphere.

And no discussion of Southernness would be complete without at least a mention of religion. Perhaps the only thing that could equal the dastardliness of a Republican in the eyes of many a "Yellow Dog" Democrat was a damned Catholic, or for that matter a damned Campbellite or Free Will Baptist. Outside of Louisiana and other such strange locales, the South has long been synonymous with evangelical Christianity. Through recent times, the region was dominated by Baptists and Methodists, particularly Southern Baptists and, until the Wesleyans reunited, Southern Methodists. In some ways, the Arkansas Ozarks' religious claim to Southernness is similar to its political claim—that on the surface the hill country suggests an alliance with the old Confederacy, but that a closer inspection of statistics forces qualification. The almost complete absence of blacks in the Arkansas Ozarks, both historically and currently, might suggest that the hegemony of Southern Baptists and Methodists would be even more overwhelming than in other parts of the South. Statistics fail to bear this out, however.

According to the 1926 religious census, more than 90 percent of Ozark church members belonged to one of the evangelical Protestant denominations, but less than half of these churchgoers attended congregations of the Southern Baptist Convention or the Methodist Episcopal Church, South. Although Baptists accounted for more than one-third of all Ozark adherents, less than two-thirds of Ozark Baptists were Southern Baptists, most of the remainder belonging to the splinter group known as the American Baptist Association. Only in Carroll and Cleburne Counties did Southern Baptists make up at least 45 percent of the religious populace. Furthermore, Episcopalians and Presbyterians, prominent in any lowland Southern town, were almost as rare as Catholics in the Ozarks. Even more striking than the relatively humble position of Southern Baptists was the strength of the nineteenth-century restorationist churches, the Church of Christ and the Disciples of Christ. Members of these churches were 2.5 times more common in the Arkansas Ozarks than in Arkansas as a whole. The spiritual descendants of Alexander Campbell and Barton Stone comprised nearly one-quarter of all religious Ozarkers on the eve of the Depression, and in the rural hinterland outside of Benton and Washington Counties 27 percent of all adherents were members of one of these two denominations. In mountainous Madison and Newton Counties, "Christians" claimed a majority of church members; they held pluralities in Baxter, Boone, and Fulton Counties.[13] These observations on Ozark religious affiliation inject a greater degree of nuance into our calculations. While most Ozarkers fit easily into the dominant religious culture of evangelical Christianity, denominational loyalties in the Ozarks reflect the settlement patterns connecting the Arkansas Ozarks to the upper South as well as the Ozarkers' unique responses to religion.

Thus far we have measured the Arkansas Ozarks using several different barometers of Southernness. Taken together, the results paint a complex and somewhat confusing portrait of the Ozarks set against the backdrop of the South. Using our chosen tests of Southernness, it would

---

[13] US Department of Commerce, Bureau of the Census, *Religious Bodies: 1926, Summary and Detailed Tables*, vol. 1 (Washington, DC: GPO, 1930) 580–83.

appear that the southern and eastern parts of the Arkansas Ozarks possess either a relatively solid or a middling claim to Southernness; northwestern Arkansas's inclusion in Dixie is somewhat less certain. If you're from Madison County, Arkansas, and your daddy named you Jefferson Davis, don't fret just yet. I'm not calling him a liar or you a Yankee. We'll summon the erudite Arkansan C. Vann Woodward to our rescue. In his classic essay "The Search for Southern Identity," Woodward, no Ozarker, argues that it is history itself that defines the South as a unique region. The South has experienced poverty in a land of plenty, failure in a land of perpetual success, and guilt in a land of innocence.[14] This common heritage of un-American experiences connects the mountaineer and the sharecropper, the mill worker and the landlord, the black man and the white man.

Using this now-common definition of Southernness, the Ozarks would appear to qualify as ably as most parts of the old Confederacy. Although a peripheral and largely forgotten part of the Confederacy, the Ozarks constituted a section of Arkansas and, therefore, were a member of the losing team. Arkansas Ozarkers, even those who refused to support the Confederacy, suffered through the poverty and shame that followed defeat, a plight exacerbated by generations of inept, racist politics. The same 36-degree, 30-minute line that had coaxed the majority of Arkansas's male Ozarkers into Confederate service and had influenced their Missouri cousins to eschew rebellion ultimately launched the two groups on separate trajectories of historical development and consciousness. The citizens of Mammoth Spring, Arkansas, became Southerners; across the state line, the Missourians in Thayer did not. While these people were quite similar culturally, ethnically, and economically, these two towns historically were forever divided by that one monumental event.

When pushed to identify the best definition of the South, sociologist and noted South chronicler John Shelton Reed turned to a map

---

[14] C. Vann Woodward, "The Search for Southern Identity," in Woodward's *The Burden of Southern History* (Baton Rouge: Louisiana State University Press, 1968) 3–25. Originally published in *The Virginia Quarterly Review* 34 (1958) 321–38.

showing the popularity of the entry "Southern," as opposed to "American," in phone books of the mid-1970s. According to this gauge—what might be referred to as the test of Southern consciousness—the Arkansas Ozarks subregion fit into a broader South by way of the fact that the term "Southern" was in the mid-1970s at least one-third more popular in phone books than the term "American." By this reasoning, if individuals or groups think they are Southern and call themselves Southern, then who's to argue?[15]

Ultimately, Reed's map, like Woodward's thesis, depends on conscious affiliation with some historical and cultural notion of the South. As historian David L. Smiley observed: "Those of whatever persuasion or tradition who believe themselves to be Southern are indeed Southern, and the South exists wherever Southerners form the predominant portion of the population."[16] It is this consciousness, more than physical or cultural attributes, that makes me a Southerner. Admittedly, from the standpoint of historical definition, the Ozarks, and for that matter the entire South, is less Southern today than at any time before. The growth of retirement communities and the increases in tourism have funneled tens of thousands of non-Southerners into northern Arkansas during the last half-century. In some areas today, outlanders outnumber natives; physically and culturally, these areas possess few characteristics that qualify them as Southern. Only history and heritage can justify many native Ozarkers' claims to Southernness. Yet, if we believe Woodward, that is enough.

When all the evidence is considered, maybe I really should not consider myself "Southern"…but I am "Southern." This stubborn clinging to a regional consciousness in the face of opposition and change is perhaps the most Southern attribute a person could have.

---

[15] Reed, "The South: What Is It? *Where* Is It?" in *The South For New Southerners*, 40.

[16] David L. Smiley, "The Quest for the Central Theme in Southern History," *South Atlantic Quarterly* 71 (Summer 1972) 325.

Going Quietly: The Making of a Documentary Project Among the Old German Baptist Brethren in the Virginia Blue Ridge

BY CHARLES D. THOMPSON JR.

Prophets, according to the Bible, have no honor in their own countries or even in their own households. In other words, prophets are better off pontificating where no one knows them. Can this adage be applied to documentarians who make and tell stories about communities in a variety of mediums? We might assume that oral historians, documentary photographers, and filmmakers, unlike prophets, are better off working close to home; that home folks are better equipped to get to the heart of a story and are more likely to be safe while doing so. If this is the case, we also probably presume that these projects are of the positive variety, the type of documentary work that avoids controversy.

Elizabeth Barret in her recent documentary film *Stranger with a Camera* retells the story of Canadian Hugh O'Connor, who in 1967 went to an eastern Kentucky community to make a film about people left out of the American Dream and was killed there, essentially for being an outsider and appearing to meddle in someone else's business. That story is sobering for any of us who have gone into less-than-familiar places to try to get a story or an image. Certainly the documentarian going to another country was not a good idea in that case. But would the fact that we happen to be "from around here" guarantee that we are safe in doing documentary work about our own community? What if a local documentarian wants to shed light on local poverty? Would that fact guarantee that there would be fewer ramifications? Are local field-workers therefore condemned to show and tell only the stories people want to hear in order to protect themselves?

Beyond questions of safety, who is best situated to obtain an accurate story, the insider or the outsider? Outsiders have to go through the difficult process of having people size them up, talk about them suspiciously when they're not around and essentially decide if they can stay and work or not—or worse, decide whether to kick them out. So, perhaps insiders are best situated as documentarians because people already have a pretty good idea of who they are. This saves a lot of explaining. However, while they can't easily kick an insider out, neighbors make judgments about insiders that can never be reversed, coloring an insider's work in ways that an outsider would not have to overcome. This is essentially what the biblical passage about prophets is talking about. A person can never quite shake off the problems associated with being known, and if that person attempts to say something prophetic, then he or she will be judged all the more harshly. On top of this, when a project happens to concern religion, as prophets have revealed, things get even more complicated. Start stirring up something sensitive and the tide begins to shift quickly away from support to suspicion.

Is that reason enough to avoid a project? Regardless of who does work in a community, truth inevitably is many-faceted and fleeting and always hard to pin down. Yet, who can better tell a story of a community than one who knew that story before it became a project, or who saw that community through a lens not yet clouded by grant proposals and timelines? There is no replacing the long-term view one gains from having family in a place, from having seen that place as a child. Nevertheless, looking through such a childhood-influenced lens is often a recipe for nostalgia. Some distance is necessary, but can people ever really separate themselves from their own experiences of their native place once those experiences have been ingrained in them as children?

There are problems with knowing a place so well that one can't see it for what it is, only through lens of past experiences—like one's own family being so close that we don't really notice their changes. Sometimes we're afraid of asking difficult questions of our own people because we in fact do know who'll have a problem with our boat-rocking. We also know stories of the troubles that similar explorations have caused. It's a heavy burden to carry the hard facts of one's own people to a wider public. It would be easier to leave out any critique and to preclude the syndrome of the unacceptable local prophet altogether. The outsider avoids having to stick around to see the consequences of his or her critique. The life of the traditional fieldworker who is able to leave and never look back might be easier and safer, but such a life is also a lot more shallow. Many outsiders have completed projects and left communities thinking the results of those projects were accurate, never learning that they got the story wrong. Another biblical aphorism applies here: woe to the prophet who bears false witness. Thus, in documentary work, neither strangers nor home folk have a corner on truth, and neither are necessarily categorically the wrong ones to do such projects.

My project "The Old German Baptist Brethren and Agricultural Change in the Virginia Blue Ridge," which I began in 1994, has been my attempt to gather a story about the community of my origin, yet I was working as an outsider. Although I lived in Franklin County, Virginia, until I was two years old and have returned there often for family visits ever since (including living with my grandparents for a year), and though I continue to have countless relatives living there, I still do not know the community as someone would who has always lived in that one place. I grew up 100 miles away because my father found a factory job in another town; this made me an outsider—even though I was born in Franklin County. At the same time, I was able to rely on family to help me make contacts with their neighbors. This also meant that because of their help I had family obligations over and above the usual set of ethics required of a fieldworker. Although I am an outsider in Franklin County, I am an insider there, too.

The fact is, a person's background of having been raised in a given community is not the only criteria for understanding that community. Just because a person knows one part of a community does not mean that that person knows another part, much less the whole, of that community. This was one of my challenges with my project on the Old German Baptist Brethren. As I was growing up, nearly a dozen full-time family members owned working farms in Franklin County, though since then the number of farms has slowly dwindled to just one or two (depending on the definition of "farm"). So, my concerns regarding agricultural change were personal, and I knew those parts of the county—those farms, at least—about as well as anyone could who did not live there. However, even though I can trace my ancestry to the Old German Baptist Brethren tradition in the county (many of my distant relatives are still members), I am not a member of their faith myself, nor are any of my closest relatives. In other words, I am an outsider to members of the Old German Baptist Brethren because I have not joined their congregation. Although I know and am known, I need introductions as well. I must ask questions that would be obvious to insiders. So, I am neither of here nor of there, neither insider nor outsider. I am in a liminal position, betwixt and between communities; like so many people around the world today, I am a hybrid. Granted that many people share my state of being in-between, in the unique place where I worked I had to explain and situate myself continually, both in terms of how I was related to the community and in terms of why I was there in their community. People who are in-between have to explain twice as much.

I explained my project at its beginnings to my 90-year-old aunt, and she understood its importance and agreed to help. Aunt Ethel called her German Baptist neighbors on the telephone to explain to them that I wanted to talk to people about their church and their way of life as farmers. Then she handed me the phone. I stammered a little, but I got the message through to her neighbors that I wanted to do a project about their community. They invited me to visit them later that afternoon and even to eat supper with them. As I discovered, it really didn't matter what I said so much as who called first. Needless to say, Aunt Ethel was a godsend for this project. The German Baptists were always gracious and welcoming, even if leery of any sort of media attention. They preach that they are "in the world, but not of the world," and this means that they want no publicity about themselves. They avoid evangelism altogether. They have no radios, televisions, or Internet. I knew that from the beginning I had to be extra careful with their stories and how I presented them.

The opportunity to work in Franklin County with the German Baptists also required some self-examination. Since I had used my aunt's help to enter the community and was related to many people there, my representation of the people and my own conduct during and after the project would affect my family's reputation as well as my own. Whatever I did would reflect back on Aunt Ethel, who as far as I could tell was loved by everyone who knew her.

I listened a lot and claimed little. I wrote a master's thesis on the group, gave copies to some of the German Baptist members and to Aunt Ethel and moved on to do other projects elsewhere, some of them far from home. People who read my thesis told me they liked what I wrote. As far as I know, the damage was nil, though the stakes were low.

In 2001, I returned to Aunt Ethel's neighbors with a new idea for a project. This time I would delve deeper into their lives through oral history interviews, and then I would write about agricultural change in Franklin County, incorporating the words of the German Baptists themselves. I had funding from the Virginia Foundation for the Humanities and backing from the Center for Documentary Studies at Duke University. This meant the stakes were higher for the project and for me. I thought that by building on my earlier work I would be able to hit the ground running. But this time Aunt Ethel's neighbors said no.

Their refusal to participate was not my fault, they said, but was the fault of a project conducted by the *Roanoke Times* in the interim between my two projects. It was a photojournalism piece that depicted this particular family in a variety of settings, including a scene at a Burger King where they stopped while taking their mother to a doctor, as well as a scene at a swimming hole in the nearby creek where girls in the family swam in their dresses and prayer coverings. Everyone in the community saw the article. Elders in the church reprimanded this family, asserting that the article portrayed the family as being too much in the eyes of the world; the article seemed a little lewd to the community since the photos had shown the girls swimming. It wasn't so much that anyone in the community felt this way, the elders said, but that they were concerned about the representation of German Baptists ignore the article projected to those outside the faith. So, my closest confidants from the thesis project could not join in my oral history project, even if my work would be very different from that of the photojournalist. My personal perspective did not matter—all documentary projects were out of the question, whether by outsiders, insiders, or those in-between.

After worrying that I should abandon the whole project and send the money back to the Virginia Foundation for the Humanities, I met with University of North Carolina-Chapel Hill Professor Emeritus Daniel Patterson, an authority on folklore and religion in the South, to ask him how I should proceed. He said, rather than avoiding starting altogether, I simply needed to explain my project, my motives, and my connections to the community, and to ask the community itself what they thought. I knew he was right, but this did not make the task any easier. I did not approach the church elders as a group formally to ask them what they thought because I would be asking for an official statement that would likely resemble the reprimand to Aunt Ethel's neighbors—a formal proposal of my project would bring solemn deliberation and perhaps yield a denial because of possible problems. Instead, I began approaching each individual family on my list of German Baptist farmers, including some of the Elders, one at a time. While explaining my purpose for being there, at times I would even mention that I knew about the *Roanoke Times* debacle. I told these people that I didn't want to repeat the same mistake. I asked them for guidance on how to ask questions without causing problems. People agreed to participate, giving me specific advice on what was appropriate and what was not. Some did not want photographs taken of themselves, particularly of their faces, though some did not mind as long as the pictures were in the context of farm work and would help illustrate the agricultural community. I was asked to avoid anything inappropriate at all costs as well as to keep out any semblance of "publicity" about particular individuals. Understanding that the intentions and results of oral history are quite different from those of publicity, people began to open up to me. Needless to say, Daniel Patterson's advice helped me salvage the project, though it was a challenge to overcome the problems resulting from one newspaper article by a seemingly innocent young woman who moved to Florida shortly thereafter. That photojournalist did not bear false witness exactly, but by leaving the area so quickly after she finished her piece for the *Roanoke Times*, she left any consequences of her actions behind her.

As I started on the project, I soon realized that my mention of people I had previously talked with was always a good way to put people at ease. Then, people would recommend that I talk with specific individuals they knew. In a few instances, some people made calls to their friends for me. When people began doing this, I felt that I had gained their trust. In the process, I had become somewhat of an insider because of my family connections, but I was also someone people talked about when I wasn't there. Thus, my being an outsider generated interest, but my being related to insiders—and my being an insider of sorts myself— obligated me to a certain standard of behavior. People knew who my family was, and I knew they knew. Although I dropped names when appropriate, I knew I could not repeat something said by someone else that would get that person in trouble with neighbors or the church elders. As a result, the community gained control, as I needed to behave in accordance with certain standards because I owed it to Aunt Ethel and, now, to everyone else I had interviewed and mentioned in the project; their reputations were involved, too. All this gave me context and legitimacy, but obligated me as well.

With the German Baptists I knew I had to avoid "publicity," and soon I realized that I had an additional problem. Because they avoid participation in the "world"—meaning among other things that they do not vote or speak at public gatherings or even write letters to the editors of newspapers—I knew that I had to avoid projecting a political stance onto them by implication, regardless of how I felt about an issue. Also, because of my sensitivity to their beliefs in world rejection, I found it increasingly hard to imagine conveying in my project anything critical or prophetic, because such a stance might seem as though I was projecting my critiques onto the German Baptists.

To give back to the community a token of my appreciation before going on to write a manuscript for a book, I compiled a 16-page booklet of quotations and photographs that communicates through the words of community members (without my own editorial commentary) the plight of Franklin County farmers and the challenges they will face in the future, leaving the possibilities for their survival open-ended. I wrote the booklet's introduction in my own voice, linking myself to the community through my family. I printed 2,000 copies of my booklet— entitled "They Go Quietly: Agricultural Change in Franklin County, Virginia"—and gave them away at a community forum in the county seat of Rocky Mount. Many people took multiple copies, including a local educator who took hundreds of copies for distribution to elementary school students. The focus for that booklet was on farming in general rather than on German Baptists in particular. I decided to present the work in this way because, within their own community, German Baptists do not want to stand out individually—they want to be part of a community experiencing change together. The German Baptists did not mind being represented in the latter manner.

The booklet makes clear that I lament the loss of community-based farms—a way of life that, like the best local documentary projects, is accountable to its neighbors. In the booklet, I quoted one of my own relatives by marriage, a former farmer who makes his living selling real estate. We did not agree on many issues, but that fact does not appear in the booklet. I went quietly in my approach, but for the insiders the subtle language was loud enough. Those people got the message.

Seventy people, including a number of German Baptists, came to my public presentation of photos and quotes from the booklet. After I presented the work I had completed to date, I asked for guidance from the audience, telling them I intended to go further with the project by turning the lengthy study into a book. The consensus from the meeting, spoken and written, was that the project had something important to say and that I should continue. So it seems that I had successfully raised an important social issue without making enemies, at least among the participants. Most importantly, my family members liked the booklet and asked for multiple copies. I could go home again—even if I was, at least in part, an outsider.

The Contents of the Booklet "They Go Quietly: Agricultural Change in Franklin County, Virginia"

Everyday

It was one of the three oldest dairy farms in the county, when people had to take their milk by horse and wagon to Boone's Mill and put it on the train to send it to Roanoke. Of course we started out very, very small. We probably had fifteen cows. My daddy said you needed to have some money coming in every day and dairy was something that was making money every day.

—Mary Layman, retired dairy farmer

When we went from milk cans to bulk tanks, the controversy was the large investment in tanks and trucks, transporting milk longer distances, and not having a local market. A lot of the small ones did go out of business, but I think it's fair to say that they were not forced out because of regulation, or anything other than job opportunity as people could go to Roanoke and Martinsville.

Photograph by Rob Amberg

Ethel Jamison Naff, b. 1904

Then as the dairies have become larger, they produce more milk than all of them produced back in the past. So there's still a lot of milk produced in the area, it's just produced by fewer farmers.

—Galen Brubaker, retired dairy farmer

When you get a conglomerate of maybe five corporate farms that are milking 20,000 cows each, that's 100,000 cows. That's a lot more cows than we have in Franklin County. If we don't watch out they're going to set the prices is what's going to happen. It won't be a monopoly as such, but they'll set their price.

—Terry Austin, dairy farmer

The government has got some good things that have helped the farmer, but when the government does something, it's for the big and small. There's nothing really that the small farmer can get that the big one can't get. It becomes a lot of chaos. Sometimes I wonder if it wouldn't be better to just to take out the government and let it drop.

—David Bower, dairy farmer and co-owner of Homestead Creamery

If somebody had told me in 1992 when I had 126 dairies that I'd be in the upper 70's in the year 2001, I don't know if I would've bought the business or not. The cow numbers per dairy grew, but we haven't kept all the cows here. We don't have as many cows in Franklin with 77 dairies as we did back in 1992 with 126, 128 farms.

—Richard Jamison, milking machine distributor

Raising Citizens

The Old German Baptist Brethren tend to settle in groups, though there's no rule to that. In Virginia, we have four church districts, central places where we worship and go back and forth to regularly, three being in Franklin County, one being in Roanoke County.

I think you would see in traditional religious circles lives based on family morals, with the climate of training our children to be good, honest citizens. That, we would all agree, makes rural environments prosper. We're not really in the business of raising milk, though we lose sight of that many times. We're in the business of raising citizens. We're trying to raise men and women that will make the world better instead of worse.

I'd like to preserve it as long as I can, the rural dairy, family life; but at the same time it's probably a vanishing breed. We know that. Just prolong it as long as we can.

—Billy Boone, Old German Baptist Brethren minister and farm equipment dealer

You see a lot of marriages as a team working together in the business and you see a lot that don't. But I think if the women are out there working with the cows and the calves, that really take interest in those animals, you'll see a lot of tender care that helps.

—David Bower

[Non-farm kids] can just sleep to eleven o'clock and they're ready to go. Most likely on a farm you have chores to do before you can go somewhere. And it's few households that require the children to do something before they go do leisure activities.

—David Matthews, dairy farmer

Work

It doesn't make economic sense to try to buy land for six, seven, eight thousand dollars an acre and plant corn and make a hundred dollars an acre.

—Bruce Layman, feed mill operator and former dairy farmer

We had $220 left over on a forty-eight-cow dairy. I paid my loan, and I paid my feed bill, paid my electric bill and my phone bill, vet bill, all my bills, and I had $220 left. That's not much of a cushion. I mean, a ton of feed at that time was $350. So, I didn't even have enough to buy one extra ton of feed at the end of the month. But all my bills were paid.

—Bruce Layman

We have fun on Sundays too, but Sunday we pretty much keep as a sacred day, and milk. You milk, but you don't go worrying about getting up hay or something. You do what you have to do and feed. Feeding and milking, that's it.

—David Bower

Restored 1800 Franklin County German homestead
at the Blue Ridge Institute at Ferrum College, Ferrum, Virginia.

Allen Layman guides his cattle into the milking barn at sunrise in Wirtz.

Photograph by Charles D. Thompson Jr.

Trevor Fox sits patiently during an afternoon milking at the Bowman dairy farm in Boones Mill.

It's definitely a way of life, but you do get burned out sometimes. And when you get burned out you start dwelling on the negative. But I think there are a lot of jobs you make a lot more money at and have a lot less investment and have things just as nice at home. I think the older I get the less I like milking on weekends, too.

—Terry Austin

We don't have any hired help. It's full-time for my husband and his partner. It's interesting, people's ideas of what farming is like. Some people find out that my husband and I have a farm, and they say, "Oh, that is so much work." But my husband has had somebody say to him one time, "What else do you do? That's not a full-time job." I think he probably wanted to punch him. People's ideas of how farming is—they're pretty mixed up sometimes.

—Rebecca Austin, dairy farmer

Neighbors

The family farm used to represent more of a community structure even among people who are not German Baptists. Fifty years ago it wasn't anything for all the farmers in this area to get together and thrash wheat, and then they'd go in and sit down and somebody would say the blessing.

—Bruce Layman

I think the people from Franklin County have a deep respect for farming because at one point in time in their family tree, they came from a farm. So when they see "fresh from our family farms," it means a whole lot more to them than somebody who doesn't really know.

—Brandon Montgomery, dairy farmer and co-owner of Homestead Creamery

This is the only nation I'm aware of that has never had a food shortage, so we don't put much strength in being our own food producers. But you go to Europe, and almost all of those countries at some point have had a food shortage. They value their food. They put a value on maintaining it locally. I hope, and I guess I pray, that we'll never face a time that we have a food shortage. But I have felt for quite a few years that we will approach that time and basically because of a lack of interest and concern of the consuming public.

—Galen Brubaker

This is an ideal area because it's got a pretty view of the mountains, it's got a good climate, good people. Of course you can tell I'm prejudiced. So people are going to continue to come down here from New Jersey, Connecticut, and Washington, D.C. All those people want a better place, a better quality living standard.

—Galen Brubaker

I know a lot of people complain about the way it smells out here. I think a lot of people want the country life, but they don't want what goes with it.

—Terry Austin

People in Transit

Never seems to fail, wherever the best farmland is, that's where they want to grow the most industry and houses. It's a lot easier to build houses on good land.

—Allen Layman

They can make a lot more money subdividing it than they can selling it as a farm, and they can't sell it for a farm anymore hardly. If they do, the person that's buying it is a hobby farmer. They're coming in, they've made their money elsewhere and they need a tax break. So they come in, buy a farm, and buy a tractor. That's everyman's dream in the world. They'll piddle around for a few years and then they say, maybe, this is not what I thought it would be.

—Billy Kingery, real estate agent and former dairyman

Interstate 73 will hasten what Smith Mountain Lake started many years ago, a long time before I-73 was ever dreamed of. This will be the hastening of it. Is it good or bad? If we're going to make automobiles and people, we've got to have somewhere to put them. We're a transit people. We've got to have roads to travel on. The roads are going to take up farmland.

—Billy Boone

Dina Laymon feeds young heifers being raised as future milk cows.

A dairy farmer bales hay in this field near Wirtz, Virginia, for the last time. At the time of this photograph (Fall 2001), lots for "countryside homes" had been surveyed, and houses were already under construction.

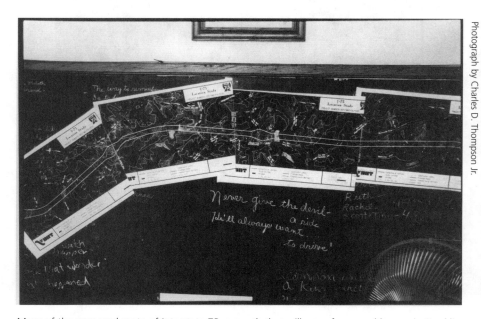

Maps of the proposed route of Interstate 73, a swath that will cross farms and homes in Franklin County, displayed on a chalkboard in a dairy farmer's kitchen.

As we get more urbanized, the cost of land gets higher. It's very hard for a young man to come up with assets to purchase property to farm, and he has to rent. He's just building up equity for the landowners. It's really why a lot of people are getting out.

—David Matthews, dairy farmer

'Heirs

My father and his three brothers started this business. At that time there were probably five equipment businesses in Rocky Mount, and each community around us had the same thing. Gretna had a couple of farm equipment businesses. Moneta had one. Floyd had three or four. And now they're all gone, except there's two in Franklin County. People have tried to get into business, and it's just not profitable enough or there's not enough business to keep them. It's gone.

—Billy Boone

If you take a farm family that's got four heirs and one of those chooses to be a farmer, and the other three decide they want the high dollars, there's no way he can live long enough to pay for it. There are farm programs that will guarantee a farm will be in agriculture from now on. That helps, but whether that's the solution I don't know. These decisions we make that are going to last forever, I'm a little skeptical of them, too.

—Billy Boone

He's an old retired farmer, and he was selling some of his land to farmers at two-thousand dollars an acre. That's a high price, but one that you can farm and do all right. Well, the children found out about it, and they had it fixed where he couldn't sell it. Power of Attorney, I guess. They sold it all for subdivisions, and they got ten and twelve thousand dollars for it.

—Franklin County dairy farmer

Pretty good farmer, but his sons lost interest. And he said, I can sell out now. Keep my farm, [but] my sons are never going to come back here and farm. And if my sons don't take it, the growth around here is going to take it. I can't sell to anyone else and them make it. So he said, I'm just going to go work a forty-hour week. I don't have to do any management, and it'll take the weight off me, have a richer life.

—David Bower

Some farms have been handed down from generation to generation. I've had plenty of opportunity, but none's been given me. We bought a farm about four years ago that was 70 acres. And I'm heavily indebted, I mean heavily indebted. I'm not ashamed to tell you how much.

—Irwin Ward, the county's sole African American dairyman

Hope

Farmers won't unite, and they can't come together, and the reason is they're too hard headed to work together. And the reason they're hard headed is that they've been taken advantage of so long in the marketplace. They got numb to people telling them they've got these theories about how they're going to help them make more money, but it usually ends up costing them. So that one's a dead end. That's when we decided to try to build our own milk facility and just do it small.

It was really kind of ironic that everybody you talked to said, "Naw, ain't no way." Ain't no way for a small farm to make it unless you do a little something different, subsidize it with something.

—David Bower

I think maybe September 11th brought everybody back to reality, back down to support local.

—David Bower

We've already lost one, two, three [dairies] this year that I can think of. Might be more than that. So, from what I'm seeing, in the next ten years we'll be down in the thirties. As far as holding what we got, important to who?

—Allen Layman

In Europe, farm vacations are subsidized by the government. They send someone to do your work while you go on vacation. I think that's a pretty big thing. Our government doesn't consider the long-term effects of all the farmers selling out or the end of small farming.

—Rebecca Austin

Irwin Ward, dairy farmer, drives by a house under construction
on former farmland near the dairy he rents.

"As far as holding what we got, important to who?" Scene from the Jamison farm near Ferrum.

I feel that there is always going to be a need for the family farm. Whether I'm hoping just for the sake of hoping, I don't know. But what I'm saying is, we're as practical and efficient as the big operations are. If we can find a way to pass it on to our posterity, if we do a few things to keep the farm in the family, I feel there are possibilities.

—Henry Jamison, dairy farmer

Acknowledgments

The publication of my booklet "They Go Quietly: Agricultural Change in Franklin County, Virginia" was made possible by grants from the Virginia Foundation for the Humanities and Public Policy and The American Academy of Religion. Special thanks for this booklet go to Bonnie Campbell and Jacky Woolsey, who designed it; Rob Amberg, who took some of the photographs; Lissa Gotwals, who developed my photographs; Roddy Moore and Tom Rankin, who served as project advisors; and to the Center for Documentary Studies at Duke University.

This work would not have been possible without the Franklin County, Virginia, people who contributed their time and their thoughts. I am deeply grateful for all their support, open conversations, and, most of all, their friendship. I hope that our work will yield positive results in the life of the Franklin County agricultural community. I welcome questions and suggestions, particularly any advice for correcting problems in this publication. For any mistakes, I take full responsibility.

Charles D. Thompson, Jr.
Curriculum and Education Director
Center for Documentary Studies at Duke University
cdthomps@duke.edu
919-660-3657

Dedication

I dedicate this work to my great, great grandparents Samuel and Mary Ellen Ikenberry, Brethren dairy farmers, as well as to their granddaughter, my Great Aunt

Ethel Naff. Aunt Ethel, a retired dairy farmer in Boones Mill, Virginia, made contacts with her neighbors to help start this project and has supported me throughout my work.

※

As both an insider and an outsider in the community portrayed in the booklet, I gave up the role of primary spokesperson and instead acted as a catalyst to community discussion. Communication ensued that otherwise might not have happened. Newspapers covered the topic of agricultural change, and farmers were quoted. School children began reading the words, and one school group used the booklet during their study of rural land use. And even the board of trustees of a local college used the words of farmers from my booklet in that college's considerations of campus land-use.

The truth is, it is very hard to be a prophet anywhere, at home or in another community, county, state, or country, even if one wanted to be. People do not take kindly to being told by other people that they should change. My goal was to encourage people to talk about issues so that change would emerge from the exchange of their own words. Community organizers have long worked from the premise that change must come from within, from people listening to each other. Going quietly is the key to listening. From listening, a person realizes other ideas that other people should hear—not as from a prophet, but as from a concerned community member.

Statements from people like the ones I documented in Franklin County, Virginia, are not normally heard in public. In fact, those who participated in my project included people who usually refrain from speaking publicly for religious reasons. Yet, all of those people wanted to be heard, as part of a collection of voices concerned with agricultural change. Those people care strongly about the future of Franklin County—even if they do not generally engage in intentional change.

I learned anew from my project that documentarians do not give people voices when documenting them. People already have voices and opinions long before documentarians arrive. Yet by listening to people, and by recording and photographing them, I as a documentarian can give people the chance to talk about their deepest concerns and joys of living in a given community—I can give people opportunities to think about how and why that community should be preserved. When they entrust me with their words, it becomes my job to take these words to wider audiences. I help to transmit their community-based, shared feelings for history and place that are grounded in their individual and collective experiences.

I would not trade the obligations of insider-status for the freedom of being an outsider. Neither would I like to take on the role of prophet. Give me the hard predicament of having to prove myself in a community where I become known and where I learn from others, each of us finding inspiration and challenge in the words that come from our shared experiences of living, at least for awhile, in the same time and place.

Ashes to Ashes

BY JAMES A. PERKINS

1.

Bunny Ellington had her daddy's ashes in the trunk of her car.

Clifford Ellington had died in November, Thanksgiving afternoon in fact, watching the Alabama-Auburn football game, sitting in that Naugahyde Barcalounger he got for $5.00 at the firemen's auction fifteen years ago. Bunny called 911 when she found him, and the EMTs took him into the hospital in Limestone, but Dr. Tolliver said he had probably been dead a couple of hours by the time they brought him in.

Bunny wasn't sure. Clifford went in to watch the kickoff, and Bunny started washing up after the big dinner for two she had cooked to keep her daddy from thinking about the fact that this was their first Thanksgiving since her mother had died of lung cancer. Mayleene, Bunny's mother, had always insisted that they go out for Thanksgiving. Usually they had to go to Aberdeen over in Ohio, because everything on their side of the river pretty much shut down for Thanksgiving. Bunny figured if she cooked up a big meal at home it would be different and wouldn't remind her daddy of past Thanksgivings. She couldn't tell whether it worked or not. Her daddy ate as much as ever and he didn't say anything about Mayleene, but very little ever threw Clifford off his feed and he was not one to chatter about anything. Anyway, when

Bunny came in after setting the roasting pan to soak, the game was well into the second quarter, but Clifford wasn't watching any more.

2.

There was no funeral. Clifford had thought they were barbaric. He had refused to go to Mayleene's funeral, which was just fine with her people who thought that marrying him was the worst thing she had ever done in her life, anyway. Clifford's body was cremated down at the Benson & Webb Memorial Centre, Inc. and placed in a heavy walnut box like a cigar humidor, which was now wedged into Bunny's trunk next to the spare tire. There had been a hastily organized memorial service on the eighteenth green of the Limestone Country Club. It had to be on a Saturday because Bunny managed Limestone Drugs and had to close every weeknight at 8:30. Bunny poured about a teaspoon of her daddy's ashes into the cup on the eighteenth hole. Banner Doud, one of Clifford's long time cronies, said, "That's the only time Clifford was ever down in one."

Then John Smiley reminded Banner of that six iron Clifford shot on the fourth at Green Willow that caught the edge of the green and rolled a snaky thirty five feet before dropping in for an absolutely unbelievable hole in one.

"I think he had one down South once, too," said Billy Ray Norton.

Banner said, "The only holes in one that I believe in are ones I see for myself. Ones I didn't see and ones that Clifford told me he shot down South, I don't believe in."

"Well," said Bunny, "he's right where he'd want to be."

"No indeed he isn't," said Billy Ray. "We talked about this last year when Mayleene died, and Clifford said he wanted to be cremated and have his ashes put in the charcoal filtering system down at the Jack Daniels Distillery in Lynchburg, Tennessee."

"Why on earth?" said Bunny.

"Clifford said that he had devoted much of his life preparing his body for this task of eternal purification."

"Well," said Banner, "no one can argue that one."

3.

"I'm sure you can appreciate our position on this, Miss Ellington." Bunny was on the phone to one Clyde Furth, the Community Relations Director for the Jack Daniels Distillery in Lynchburg, Tennessee. "Quite aside for the precedent which would be set by allowing you to mix your late father's remains into our charcoal filtering system, and quite aside from your assertion that your father was a lifelong user of our product, we have to consider the possible negative image that such an action might generate."

"It's a fairly small box, and the gentleman at Benson & Webb assured me that the ashes are very clean."

"I don't think the issue is size, Miss Ellington. This is an image thing. Funereal ashes have a connotation that is not consistent with the image we at Jack Daniels try to promote. Have you considered Phillip Morris? They use charcoal filters on some of their products, and, well, perhaps you can see where I am headed here."

"Daddy didn't smoke."

No, Clifford never smoked. Mayleene smoked two packs a day. If anyone in the family had earned the right to have her ashes molded into a filter tip for a cigarette, that person was Mayleene Crenshaw Ellington. But Mayleene's remains were not ashes. Her tiny body (she was down to under 90 pounds when the cancer finally let go of her) was buried in a coffin out in the Limestone Cemetery. That bothered Clifford. They had talked, never seriously, about having their ashes mingled, but those mean kin of hers had swooped in down at the hospital and taken over. They chased Clifford out and buried Mayleene out there at the Limestone Cemetery following what Clifford was convinced was a pagan ritual they held down at the Methodist Church.

4

"Well, like my Uncle Julius always said, 'There is more than one way to peel a tomato.'"

"What the hell does that mean, Banner?"

"Simple, Bunny. If that guy at Jack Daniels won't play along, we'll just find us another way of carrying out Clifford's request."

"Like what?"

"I don't know yet, but I have an old law-school buddy lives in Knoxville. Let me give him a call and see what I can do."

Every time Bunny put her groceries into the trunk of her car she saw that walnut box. It was gnawing on her. It was several weeks later, about the middle of December, before she heard from Banner. They were all together, Bunny and her daddy's cronies, in the Nineteenth Tee Lounge at the Limestone Country Club.

"Bunny, you ought to consider joining us," John Smiley said. "You know, make us a foursome again."

"I don't really like golf. That was Daddy's thing."

"Speaking of Clifford," said Banner, "I heard from my friend in Knoxville. He knows a guy who knows a guy who works at the distillery. Says he could pour maybe a salt shaker full of Clifford's ashes in the charcoal system."

"That's not much," said Bunny. "We put like a teaspoonful in the 18th hole. There's a lot of Daddy left."

"Well, hell," said Billy Ray, "a little here, a little there. That's pretty much how Clifford's life was anyway."

"There's something else," said Banner.

"What now?"

"My friend says this guy wants money, Bunny. Says doing this is dangerous. Says he could lose his job. Says he wants five hundred dollars."

"That's crazy. Five hundred dollars to drop a package the size of lipstick into—what do you think it looks like?" asked Bunny.

"How would I know? All I know is my friend says this guy wants five hundred dollars to do it."

"Why don't we all pitch in?" asked Billy Ray. "Like we used to in 'best ball.'"

"Jesus Christ," said John. "Clifford always took my money in 'best ball,' and now he's going to go right on taking it."

"You in, Bunny?"

"Sure, Banner."

"All right, that will be $125 apiece," said Billy Ray.

"Nope," said Banner. "My friend said he would pitch in a hundred just to be able to tell the story later on."

"Well, that's settled," said John. "Bunny, would you like to spend Christmas with us? You know, the three of us. We would always spend Christmas afternoon together at a bar somewhere."

"We were known far and wide as the Four Wise Men," added Billy Ray.

"I thought there were only three wise men," said Bunny.

Christmas. Bunny hadn't even thought about Christmas. Without her mother and daddy Christmas would be terrible. She had to do something. She couldn't spend Christmas afternoon in a bar somewhere with her daddy's old golf buddies.

5.

"Who is this one for?" little Amy Tolliver asked, on Christmas morning, holding the walnut box. "It's heavy, but there's no card on it."

Bunny was in the living room of Lucas and Carlotta Tolliver in Lexington. Bunny had called Carlotta and explained how she felt about Christmas. Carlotta, who had married Dr. Tolliver's son from Limestone, said for her to come down to Lexington and spend Christmas with them. Carlotta and Bunny had been best friends in high school and had been into everything together. They were cheerleaders, sang in the chorus, carved their names in the fresh cement when the high school sidewalk was repaired, swore they'd be best friends for life, then sort of drifted apart. Carlotta had gone to college at Transylvania in Lexington and started dating Lucas Tolliver, who was at the university in Lexington in medical school. Bunny had taken some business courses at the local junior college and had started keeping the books for the drug store. When the drug store was bought out by a chain out of Atlanta, Bunny was moved to a management position. But it was still the drug store, and it was still Limestone. How far apart they had grown was apparent to Bunny when Carlotta met her in the driveway holding a baby, with two girls maybe seven and five standing there beside her.

"This is Amy," said Carlotta, "and this is Beth."

"And, don't tell me," said Bunny, looking into the blanket in Carlotta's arms. "This must be Jo."

"Well, if he were a girl, he would be. Actually he is Lucas Joseph, but we do call him Joe. Girls, you get the presents from the trunk and put them under the tree, and I'll show Bunny her room. Golly, we have so much to talk about." They did have a lot to talk about, and it was fun. For two days they scurried around taking care of children, pulling the last-minute things together for Christmas, sharing Lucas's enthusiasm for his newly established practice in family medicine. Carlotta told Bunny about the social swirl in which she lived as a young married in Lexington. Bunny told Carlotta that because of taking care of her mother, and because of the fact that most of the eligible young men had left Limestone in search of jobs somewhere, she couldn't remember the last time she had been out with anyone. The two of them plotted and set Bunny up with one of Lucas's friends for a party that was to be held the day after Christmas. It was all fun, and Bunny had forgotten all about her daddy's ashes, the drug store, and the emptiness she was feeling, until Amy asked her question. Bunny glanced up and saw the little girl standing there struggling with the heavy walnut box in her arms.

"Oh My God," she screamed, "it's Daddy."

6.

Banner had sent the money to his friend, and about a week after Christmas, they got word that the deed was done.

"Well," said Banner, lifting a double shot of Jack in the black, "I guess that takes care of old Clifford's dreams and desires."

"It doesn't take care of Daddy, though. I still have that box in my trunk. You account for what we put out at the golf course and what we sent to Tennessee, and I still have damn near a box full of Daddy."

"Does this taste different to you?" asked Billy Ray.

"Different? How do you mean different?"

"I don't know, John. Just different."

"If you mean does it taste like it has Clifford's ashes in it, you can forget it," Banner said. "It will be a good eight to ten years before any whiskey Clifford has had a hand in purifying gets to the shelves. After it's distilled, it's put into big wooden kegs and aged in bonded ware-houses."

"How do you know so much about this?"

"Think, Billy Ray, you've been up against him in court," said John. "You know what Banner knows about the law. What do you think he was studying those two and a half years in Knoxville?"

"Well," said Banner, "I think Billy Ray is right. This tastes better to me just knowing our friend is on the job. How do you like it Bunny?"

"Never has been a favorite of mine, but I must admit this is smooth."

"That's Clifford's touch," said John. "Clifford ever was a smooth one."

"What are you going to do with the rest of the ashes, Bunny?"

"Hell, I don't know, Billy Ray. Daddy didn't have anything written down about anything. I'm just lucky you remembered him talking about Jack Daniels. Too bad we couldn't have put all of him there."

"I don't know about that," said Banner. "Clifford was a guy that a little went a long way."

"Once I did hear Mama and Daddy talking about if they died. Mama said she hoped they died together, like in a car crash or something. Then she wanted them to be cremated and have their ashes mixed together and scattered somewhere *romantic*."

"Well, that sure didn't happen," said John.

"You remember those relatives of hers?" asked Banner. "They went nuts when Clifford said he wanted to have Mayleene cremated. They…"

"That's it," said Bunny. "Don't you see? That's what he wanted. What he really wanted. I know he didn't talk much. But he wanted his ashes to be mingled with Mama's, just like she said. That's why he wanted her cremated."

"Well," said John. "Those Crenshaws put the fix on that when they had her buried."

"Not necessarily, John. We could always get a court order and dig her up," said Billy Ray.

"Billy Ray, where did you get your law degree?" laughed Banner. "Absent a will or power of attorney, how do you think we could get a court order to dig up Mayleene? We can't go into court and say, 'Bunny sort of remembers once Mayleene said she should like to have her ashes mixed with Clifford's and scattered some place *romantic*.' Judge Wilson would never stop laughing."

'Well," said Bunny. "I guess that puts an end to it."

"Not necessarily." Banner paused and looked at each of them one at a time. "You know, with all the crazy shit we've done together—I mean the three of us and Clifford, not you, Bunny—there's one thing we've never done. We've never robbed a grave together."

"Jesus Christ, Banner. We've never robbed a bank or burned down the court house either, but…"

"Billy Ray, are you chicken?"

"Chicken has nothing to do with it. You and I are both officers of the court. We are sworn to uphold the law. We can't go around robbing graves."

"I would hate," said John, "for Clifford to hear this. He would do anything for one of us. He would. And now you are worried about some oath. What do you think, Bunny?"

"Well, I just want to get those ashes out of my trunk. And do what Daddy wanted."

"Alright you people," said Billy Ray, "we'll dig up Mayleene and we'll cremate her remains and we'll mix the ashes up with Clifford's and scatter them around in the most *God Damn Romantic* place you can think of, but it's the middle of February. At least let's wait till the ground's not frozen solid."

"You got to hand it to him," said John, "the man can think."

7.

Grave robbing. It never came to that. By the time the ground was soft enough to make a midnight raid on the Limestone Cemetery worthwhile, Clifford's ashes were long gone. Bunny told it this way at the Limestone Country Club back in March.

"I was going down Tanner's Hill toward the old factory when I must have hit a patch of ice. Anyway, my back wheels cut loose, and I slid into the ditch."

"Were you hurt?" John asked.

"No, but I was pissed. If you were looking for a more desolate spot in this county to do something like that, you couldn't have found it. Cold. And I got out of the car and looked around for a farmhouse. I couldn't even see a light."

"What time was it?" John asked.

"Late. Real late. Probably one or two in the morning. I really didn't pay attention. I was in the office trying to get the tax shit ready. The last time I looked at the clock, it was just after twelve, and I worked a while longer."

"Girl like you shouldn't be out by herself late like that," said Billy Ray.

"Billy Ray, you're going to be buying new teeth, if…"

"He didn't mean anything by it, Bunny. We just worry about you; that's all. We feel like we sort of have to look out for you, what with Clifford…"

"John, you all act just like he used to. You…oh never mind. Just let me finish my damn story. Like I said, I looked around and there weren't even any lights. I tried rocking the car, but it was in there pretty good. I figured I had to get it out. There was a good chance no one would come along that way till morning, and I sure wasn't ready to walk out."

"Did you have a blanket, extra clothes, stuff like that?"

"Sure, Banner. I know how to drive in the winter around here. I have all that stuff. Even carry a short-handle shovel. I dug away the snow under the car. Then I put the floor mats from the back seat under the rear wheels. They still spun a little from the snow caked in the treads. Then it hit me that I had ashes, a whole box of ashes, right there in the trunk."

"You didn't!"

"Of course I did, Billy Ray. It was cold out there. What would you want me to do, sit there and freeze?"

"What exactly did you do?" asked Banner.

"I poured what was left of Daddy under those two back tires. Then I eased it into drive and came up out of that ditch as slick as the whistle."

"Did you shovel him back up?"

"No, John, I didn't shovel him back up. He was flung all over anyway, and I wasn't about to stop again till I got inside my own garage."

"Well," said Banner, "I think it is just perfect. Clifford, anyway, was a fool for helping everybody he could. If he gets his earthly remains flung to the four winds helping his daughter out of a snow bank, I say there's a good place for him."

"Can I have that box?" asked John. "Looks like it would be just about right for my pipe tobacco."

Funeral Trail

by Ron Rash

Never the most-traveled way
to the churchyard, not that path
walked Sunday mornings or when
couples married, but one used
only for death, and never
crossing where the living passed
but winding deeper through coves,
farther around rise and creek
because some feared the dead might
linger between home and grave.
I walked one once as a child,
traced through broom sedge and briar
a trail untrod three decades
my older kin claimed, though I
wasn't so sure when sun slipped
beneath a cloud, and the world
grew dark and colder as I
walked faster, did not dare
look back over my shoulder.

George Cooke, *Interior of St. Peter's,* Rome (1847),
University of Georgia Chapel, Athens, Georgia.

The Artist in the Garden:
George Cooke and the Ideology of Fine Arts Painting in Antebellum Georgia

BY KEVIN E. O'DONNELL

George Cooke, an itinerant fine arts painter, visited north Georgia in 1840, soliciting well-to-do patrons at their new vacation homes in the Appalachian foothills. Cooke was in the area only a year after Cherokee inhabitants had been forced out at gunpoint. What does his work tell us about art and ideology in the antebellum South?

⚜

During much of the 1830s and 1840s, itinerant painter George Cooke (1793–1849) traveled throughout the South, painting portraits, landscapes, and townscapes. Although generally considered a minor figure in the history of American art, he produced more than 1,000 paintings. While much of his work has been dispersed or destroyed, some of his paintings—mainly townscapes and Indian portraits—were lithographed and widely circulated. In 1991, curators affiliated with the Georgia Museum of Art organized the first show devoted to Cooke's work in more than 150 years. The resulting exhibition catalog shows how even a small portion of his work provides a remarkable record of antebellum Southern culture.[1]

---

[1] Donald D. Keyes, ed., *George Cooke (1793-1849)* [Exhibition Catalogue] (Athens: Georgia Museum of Art, 1991).

Although Cooke's name is largely unknown today, generations of University of Georgia students are intimately familiar with one of his paintings. *Interior of St. Peter's, Rome* (1847) has hung prominently in the University of Georgia Chapel in Athens, Georgia, since shortly after the Civil War. As its title indicates, this painting depicts the interior of the cathedral in Rome. The view, as seen from the great portal, looks out along the length of the high nave. The painting was an exercise in perspective, with all lines converging on a central point—the cross on the distant high altar. At 17-by-23 feet, the painting ranks among the world's largest works in oil. Although the painting's aesthetics are out of fashion now, at least one recent art historian, Estill Curtis Pennington, considers it to be "one of [Cooke's] greatest triumphs." As Pennington writes, in praise of the piece,

> Geometric solidity of the architectural form of St. Peter's basilica is not diminished by an overly florid presentation of architectural detail. In true baroque form, light and shadow are evenly balanced, left and right, with a diminution of detail enhanced by transparent light in the procession of angelic attendants perched atop each receding vault.[2]

During the nineteenth century, the people of Athens held the painting *Interior of St. Peter's, Rome* in special regard. University of Georgia trustees acquired the painting from Alabama industrialist Daniel Pratt immediately after the Civil War, and, in 1868, they voted that the chapel be renovated to accommodate the nearly 400-square-foot painting. At the same time, the chapel was designated as the university's commence-

---

[2] Estill Curtis Pennington, "Time in Travelling: Intimations of the Itinerancy of George Cooke," in *George Cooke (1793-1849)* [Exhibition Catalogue], ed. Donald D. Keyes (Athens: Georgia Museum of Art, 1991) 29-30.

ment hall.[3] The painting has hung in the chapel ever since, and has become part of Athens tradition.

Although decades have passed since the Chapel has been used for commencement ceremonies, the venue continues to serve for lectures, meetings, and even weddings. Imagine the procession of activity that has passed before the painting, over the past 130-some years. How many people have contemplated the painting for hours, in states ranging from sheer delight to—often enough, no doubt—boredom or utter indifference? While the painting today is in many respects seen as being a relic from a bygone era, the university has continued to take good care of it, renovating it a number of times in the twentieth century, most recently in 1995 at a cost to the State of Georgia of approximately $90,000. An image of the painting is featured online at the "University Chapel Home Page," under a web link entitled "Painting."

What are modern viewers to make of Cooke's painting that has been so long prized by one of the South's great universities? On the face of it, *Interior of St. Peter's, Rome* seems to emphasize the enormity and stability of the church—though not necessarily of the Roman Catholic Church in particular. Cooke himself was baptized Episcopalian and converted to Methodism, and Pratt, the patron who commissioned the work, was a devout Methodist. But religious denomination is beside the point. In the mid-nineteenth century, St. Peter's Basilica in Rome held a special fascination for an American ruling class still enthralled, if only nostalgically, by all things Classical and Roman. The painting was not about a particular religious institution, but rather it attempted to assert the stability of institutions in general—of social and cultural institutions, of those things nowadays lumped together under the term "the patriarchy."

---

[3] Beth Abney, "George Cooke and the Chapel Painting," *Papers of the Athens Historical Society* 2 (December 1979): 64.

But it would be too simplistic to dismiss Cooke's painting as another neoclassical prop for the patriarchy; the painting is part of a dramatic story that remains largely untold, a story involving not only the painter and his relationship with his patrons but also the history of the rolling countryside surrounding the town of Athens. Some art historians have written marvelously about George Cooke, but his ideological role in antebellum American culture has gone largely unexamined. More generally, as Pennington writes, "Study of the itinerancy of portrait artists in the antebellum South is one of the great missing chapters in the cultural and intellectual history of the region."[4]

Cooke himself wrote a travel article about north Georgia in late Summer of 1840, not long after his arrival there. In November of that year, the piece, entitled "Sketches of Georgia," appeared in the *Southern Literary Messenger*, an important pre-Civil War periodical.[5] When he wrote the article, Cooke was visiting Habersham County and the area around Dahlonega, soliciting well-to-do patrons at their new vacation homes there in the foothills. He was traveling in the area only a year after its former Cherokee inhabitants had been removed at gunpoint. Considered alongside his article, Cooke's work as a painter reveals the interplay between art and ideology in the antebellum South.

※

Born in Maryland in 1793, the son of an attorney, George Cooke was interested in art from an early age. His family, however, did not have sufficient money to pay for formal training. As a young man, Cooke tried his hand at mercantile ventures and land speculation, but abandoned such business for good in his late twenties, in order to work full time on his art. Meanwhile, at the age of twenty-three, he married Maria Heath,

---

[4] Pennington, 24.

[5] [George Cooke], "Sketches of Georgia," *The Southern Literary Messenger* 6 (November 1840): 775–77. The article is anthologized in *Seekers of Scenery: American Travel Writing from Southern Appalachia, c.1840-1900*, ed. Kevin E. O'Donnell and Helen Hollingsworth (Knoxville: University of Tennessee Press, 2004).

daughter of John Heath, of Richmond, Virginia. (Maria's brother, James, would later edit most of the first volume of the *Southern Literary Messenger*.[6]) Although lacking substantial family wealth, Cooke apparently had social and personal connections, which enabled him to live the vagabond existence he would share with Maria for the rest of his life.

The 1820s and 1830s were difficult times for painters in the U.S. Cooke struggled continually for money, yet he became known for being hardworking and prolific. Evidence suggests that he was also an especially charming man—charm being an important quality for a portraitist, who must spend hours alone with his sitters. Portraiture was Cooke's bread and butter, yet he aspired to paint histories and landscapes, "in the grand manner of two of his best known American predecessors, Benjamin West and Washington Allston."[7] Nevertheless, that aspiration seems to have been foiled by the press of everyday necessity. Mid-twentieth century art historian Virgil Barker judges Cooke in retrospect—and perhaps too harshly—when he speculates that "Possibly [Cooke's] busyness, perhaps something else, kept him from painting very well."[8]

In any event, Cooke did well enough by his patrons to fund a five-year "Grand Tour" of Europe for himself and Maria, from 1826–1831. The Grand Tour, involving a nineteenth-century travel itinerary through Europe, was pioneered by painters and was popular with other travelers. Not a hard-and-fast travel route so much as a set of popular destinations, the Grand Tour focused on Italy, where painters could encounter and copy the great works of the Renaissance and of the classical world. During the first half of the nineteenth century, the Grand Tour was considered an indispensible part of an education for a young American artist.

Among the Americans that the Cookes met in Europe was Henry Wadsworth Longfellow, who would become George Cooke's lifelong

---

[6] Frank Luther Mott, "Southern Literary Messenger," in *A History of American Magazines 1:1741-1850* (Cambridge MA: Harvard University Press, 1930) 631-34.

[7] Pennington, 27.

[8] Virgil Barker, *American Painting: History and Interpretation* (New York: Macmillan, 1950) 404.

friend. In an 1833 travel book, *Outre Mer* (the title means, loosely, "across the sea"), Longfellow mentions meeting the Cookes in the village of Ariccia, near Alban Lake, outside Rome. Longfellow passed a full month, August or September of 1828, "in company with two much-esteemed friends from the Old Dominion, — a fair daughter of that generous clime, and her husband, an artist, an enthusiast, and a man of 'infinite jest'."[9]

George Cooke and Longfellow appear to have taken to each other instantly. Letters from Cooke—preserved in the Longfellow Collection at the Houghton Library, Harvard University—reveal a chatty and empathetic friendship. Both the painter and the poet responded intensely to landscapes. And, as scholar William Nathaniel Banks observes, "both men had a keen, if always decorous, appreciation for feminine beauty."[10] Apparently, Maria's charm, like her husband's, was considerable, and she was one reason the couple found it so it easy to make friends in Europe.

Longfellow's description of artists in La Riccia revealed something of the life Cooke led in Europe:

> During the summer months, La Riccia is a favorite resort of foreign artists who are pursuing their studies in the churches and galleries of Rome. Tired of copying the works of art, they go forth to copy the works of nature; and you will find them perched on their campstools at every picturesque point of view, with white umbrellas to shield them from the sun, and paint-boxes upon their knees, sketching with busy hands the smiling features of the landscape.[11]

---

[9] Henry Wadsworth Longfellow, *Outre-Mer: A Pilgrimage Beyond the Sea* (1833; reprint, New York: Houghton, Mifflin, 1893) 335.

[10] William Nathaniel Banks, "George Cooke, Painter of the American Scene," *Antiques* CII, 3 (September 1972): 449.

[11] Longfellow, 346-47.

As Longfellow's remarks suggested, Cooke spent much of his time in Europe copying—that is, painting direct copies of other paintings. The common practice at the time, before the age of mechanical reproduction, was for American painters to copy master works, working from the originals. This was not only part of a painter's training, but it was also for the purpose of sending copies of great European paintings to the U.S. for sale. The role of these paintings was to transmit the power and authority of European culture back to monied Americans.

The Cooke that Longfellow met in the Italian countryside was light-hearted and affable. Yet Cooke worked very hard while he was in Rome. As scholar Marilou Rudulph writes, Cooke, when in that city, "spent every daylight hour painting, with the exception of Sunday and an afternoon each week for his receptions."[12] Cooke kept this schedule for more than a year and a half, producing at least thirty paintings, many of them copies, plus an early version of the interior of St. Peter's, while also filling sketchbooks with copies and studies.[13]

During his time in Europe, Cooke continued to send his works back to America, for show and for sale. In 1830, two of his paintings—including the early version of the *Interior*—appeared in a Washington DC gallery, eliciting the following comments, from a reviewer in the *National Intelligencer*. "It is hoped that Mr. Cook's [*sic*] paintings may prove a happy exception to the general fate of American productions, and that he may receive that generous patronage which his talents so richly merit."[14]

Due to the continuing difficulty that American painters experienced in selling their work, Cooke was chronically short of funds during his travels. To make matters worse, his health was generally poor. Signs are that, by 1830, he began to tire from working constantly. With the

---

[12] Marilou A. Rudulph, "George Cooke and His Paintings," *Georgia Historical Society Quarterly* XLIV, 2 (June 1960): 128.

[13] Banks, 448.

[14] Linda Crocker Simmons, "Chronological Survey: The Life of George Cooke," in *George Cooke (1793-1849)* [Exhibition Catalogue], ed. Donald D. Keyes (Athens: Georgia Museum of Art, 1991) 12.

humanist achievements of Europe losing their luster for the artist, Cooke began to long for home, as he revealed in a letter home: "Every object announces that it has long been the theatre of Man's restless passions. [Europe's] moral and intellectual grandeur like that of her architectural monuments, is mutilated and faded. I often sicken at the depravity of man, and languish for my native land."[15]

After leaving Italy to spend time in England and France, the weary Cooke returned to the U.S., landing in New York City in August 1831. His industrious spirit revived, and by November of that year, he had organized an exhibition of his paintings in New York.[16]

The Cookes spent the next few years traveling between New York City, Washington City (as the nation's capital was then called), and Richmond, Virginia, with occasional forays to Pittsburgh and to various places in the countryside. By the middle of the 1830s, Cooke was roaming farther south, developing contacts in rural Virginia, in Raleigh, North Carolina, and in Charleston, South Carolina. All the while, he continued painting portraits and the occasional landscape.

Evidence suggests that, towards the end of the 1830s, Cooke was tiring of the peripatetic lifestyle. He longed to settle down. In addition, Cooke's health continued to be unstable, and he often found himself fleeing disease epidemics and trying climates during these years. In 1832, for example, he fled from New York City to the Catskills, due to a cholera epidemic.[17] In 1835, he painted portraits in Raleigh, North Carolina, "until May or June, when the climate became disagreeable."[18] In 1837, Cooke and his wife returned to Georgetown (which was then outside the boundaries of Washington City). There, he wrote to his brother James, "Who would have supposed after twenty years of wan-

---

[15] Rudulph, 129.
[16] Simmons, 13.
[17] Rudulph, 135.
[18] Simmons, 15.

dering I should return to this my starting point and pitch my tent under the same shade that sheltered me in 1817."[19]

As it turned out, there was plenty of work for Cooke in Washington City that year, as his skill as a portraitist had developed dramatically in Europe.[20] At first, he found commissions in the city through an old friend, Charles Bird King, with whom he had studied for a time during the 1820s. King had a standing contract in Washington with the Bureau of Indian Affairs, under the War Department, to provide portraits of Indians who visited the city. King had more work than he could handle, and he farmed some of the commissions out to Cooke.

During the 1830s, whites were pushing rapidly west across the continent, warring continuously with natives. Whites, of course, had the superior arms. Thus, in an all-too-familiar cycle, treaties were made and then broken, followed by new treaties that were in turn broken. These activities drew a continuous, dispirited procession of Indian delegations to the nation's capitol. Visits to the city were known to be brutal for Indian delegates. The treaty work itself was grim—during this period, most of the tribes were in the process of ceding their best lands. Travel to Washington City was hard, and diseases there typically took their toll on Indians. It was rare for delegations to return to their homes without at least a few deaths.

The Indian portraiture policy that employed Thomas Bird King was established in the 1820s under Thomas L. McKenney, the Superintendent of Indian Affairs. McKenney's Bureau used portraits as a means of flattery, to smooth the delicate and often heart-rending negotiations with Indian chiefs. Oftentimes, copies of the portraits were given to Indians, and some Indians were known to treasure those copies for years.[21] In addition to using portraits as a diplomatic tool,

[19] Ibid., 16.
[20] Keyes, 60.
[21] Herman J. Viola, *The Indian Legacy of Charles Bird King* (Washington DC: Smithsonian Institution Press, 1976) 51.

McKenney valued them for preserving what he and others regarded as a doomed race. As McKenney's supervisor, Secretary of War James Barbour, wrote to him in 1832, the portraits were valuable because "this race was about to become extinct, and…a faithful resemblance of the most remarkable among them would be full of interest in after-times."[22]

There is no written record of what Cooke thought of the doomed "savages" who sat for him, hours on end, in King's Twelfth Street studio and gallery, that early Winter of 1837. Of Cooke's nine Indian sitters, probably less than half of them spoke English. Perhaps they sat in silence. Almost certainly, Cooke regarded them with something akin to pity.

The Bureau's Indian portraits from this period were destroyed by a fire at the Smithsonian Institution in 1865. However, six of Cooke's nine portraits were reproduced as lithographs in the three-volume work by McKenney and James Hall, *History of the Indian Tribes of North America*, published between 1837 and 1844. Of one of these lithographs, William Nathaniel Banks writes, "When he sat for Cooke, the Fox brave Kish-ke-kosh donned a buffalo skull he had taken in battle from an enemy Sioux and daubed his face with paint; but the expression portrayed by the artist is more woebegone than ferocious."[23]

Cooke also found plenty of other portrait work in Washington. The list of statesmen who sat for him in 1837–38 included the Superintendent of Indian Affairs himself—McKenney—as well as U.S. Senators from Alabama, Virginia, and New York, and Congressmen from Maine and Virginia. Cooke stayed in Washington City through much of 1839, planning and working on other paintings, including a portrait of Henry Clay.

By the Spring of 1840, Cooke had returned to the South. He took some portrait work in Augusta, Georgia. By the summer of that year, he was in the north Georgia mountains, the former Cherokee territory.

---

[22] Ibid., 13.

[23] Banks, 451. See Keyes, 100, for an account of Cooke's Indian Portraits. Also see Rudulph, 139–40. See Viola for an account of King's work and relationship with McKenney.

Shortly thereafter, he arrived with Maria in Athens, where the couple decided to remain for a time.

The cultured, well-traveled, and pious couple found themselves embraced by Athens' gentry—"a truly Athenian people," Cooke writes. Especially gracious was Mrs. Augustin Smith (Julia Carnes) Clayton, the widow of A. S. Clayton (1783–1839). Clayton had been a state judge and one-time U.S. Senator from Georgia, who had died in June of the previous year. The widow was left with plenty of money, yet she felt the void of the judge's absence. Cooke writes of her, in a letter to his brother James: "She is…left in affluence with her children all married except the two youngest daughters, aged 7 and 14 [, and she] insists on our staying with her as company and protection—and being a devoted member of the Methodist church, she and Maria agree like two angels in all that is good."[24] So, without having planned it, the Cookes stayed in Athens, with Mrs. Clayton, into the following spring.

Cooke's writings and the couple's subsequent behavior reveal that George and Maria quickly developed a special attachment to north Georgia. The Cookes were captured not only by the hospitality of the Athenians, but also by the healthfulness and beauty of the north Georgia climate. As Cooke writes, "We find the climate very little warmer than that we left in the mountains, and the atmosphere much dryer and more elastic. There has not been a case of fever this year, and I am told that there never is any but such as may be traced to the grossest imprudence." Months later, while still in Athens, Cooke writes to his brother, with more praise for north Georgia:

> We have had another delightful winter in this soft climate, having never seen snow and but little ice. The last month has been rainy, but not boisterous or cold, and neither Maria or myself have had the least irritation of the lungs for many months—indeed there are invalids

[24] Keyes, 66.

now here from Savannah for their health, as to a dryer climate; and I assure you, next to Italy I have seen nothing like it.[25]

It was later recorded that the couple longed to settle in Athens. Cooke himself would never realize that dream, though his wife Maria would—without him. Yet for a time, in the fall, winter, and early spring of 1840–41, he and Maria found respite in the foothills of north Georgia.

※

As noted earlier, Cooke was in north Georgia only a year after Cherokee residents were forcibly removed, in the notorious episode now known as "The Trail of Tears." Background about the Cherokees is crucial to understanding Cooke's work in the region.

During the American Revolution, most Cherokees aligned with the British. American armies then invaded Cherokee villages and towns, burning fields and causing severe famine and dislocation. After the war, surviving Cherokees abandoned the older towns and found a haven in the sparsely populated, mountainous areas of north Georgia, northeast Alabama, and lower east Tennessee.

Encouraged by a U.S. government program designed to "civilize" Indians, a number of Cherokees began to adopt white culture. By the first decades of the nineteenth century, Cherokees had established single-family homesteads in place of the old multi-generational villages. Some Cherokee took up European-style agriculture and stock-raising, while others maintained blacksmith shops and mills, and used looms and spinning wheels.

According to historian Theda Perdue, most Cherokees during this era were "traditionalists" who resisted cultural assimilation.[26] However,

---

[25]Keyes, 66.

[26] Theda Perdue, ed., introduction to *Cherokee Editor: The Writings of Elias Boudinot*, (Knoxville: University of Tennessee Press, 1983) 32.

those who adopted white ways became, by and large, the tribe's wealthy and prominent leaders. By 1820, some wealthy Cherokees lived in mansions, raised thoroughbred racehorses, owned fine silver and large libraries. Although most Cherokees did not own slaves, prominent tribal officials did: John Ross, the principal Chief of the Cherokee nation for almost forty years, held nineteen black slaves; his brother held forty-one. Others held 100 or more.[27] Tribal leaders, it should be stated, tended to be of mixed blood. Ross was said to be three-fourths white, for example. Almost all the prominent supporters of cultural assimilation, excepting John Ridge, were thought to be at least half white.

Twenty-first-century Americans are sometimes disturbed by the idea that the Cherokee leadership promoted white culture. People today often imagine that Native Americans were untainted by, or at least resistant to, European traditions. However, antebellum whites felt quite differently. Many whites then felt that "savage," unlettered, and un-Christianized Indians were not fully human and therefore could be exterminated without serious ethical or spiritual consequences.

Cherokee leaders in the early nineteenth century fought back against this way of thinking by trying to prove that Cherokees could indeed "civilize" and adapt white culture. This strategy was tricky, however, because it supported the idea that Cherokee culture was somehow inferior in the first place.

Elias Boudinot emerged as a key figure in promoting white culture among the Cherokees. Boudinot (*aka* Buck Watie), a mixed-blood born around 1804 in north Georgia, was educated in a Moravian missionary school. As a young man, he traveled to the northeast, where he adopted the name of a white benefactor and continued his education in Connecticut.

In 1825, the Cherokee Council appointed Boudinot to raise money for a printing press that could hold two sets of type—one Cherokee, one

---

[27] Theda Perdue, *Slavery and the Evolution of Cherokee Society, 1540-1866* (Knoxville: University of Tennessee Press, 1979) 58-59.

English. The plan was to establish a Cherokee newspaper. Four years earlier, Sequoyah, *aka* George Guess, had announced his invention of the Cherokee system of writing, or syllabary. Boudinot and others proposed to adapt this syllabary to mechanical print. These efforts would lead to the publication of the bilingual *Cherokee Phoenix*, the first issue of which came off the new press in February 1828, under Boudinot's editorship. Beginning in the Spring of 1826, Boudinot, as an emissary of the Cherokee Council, traveled to east coast cities such as Charleston, Philadelphia, and Boston, to raise money for the bilingual press. His billing as a "civilized Indian" drew crowds, to whom he delivered his "Address to the Whites," a speech that also circulated in pamphlet form. (This speech has been anthologized in recent decades, notably in the *Heath Anthology of American Literature*, a popular college textbook.)

In his address, Boudinot struggled to refute the common view that Cherokees were unlettered, pagan savages who deserved to be extirpated. Boudinot emphasized the steps the Cherokee were taking towards civilization. "The shrill sound of the Savage yell shall die away as the roaring of far distant thunder," he wrote.[28] He phrased his argument in the circumlocutory prose style of the early-nineteenth-century whites:

> It needs not the power of argument on the nature of man to silence forever the remark that "it is the purpose of the Almighty that the Indians should be exterminated." It needs only that the world should know what we have done in the few last years, to foresee what yet we may do with the assistance of our white brethren, and that of the common Parent of us all.[29]

---

[28] Elias Boudinot [Buck Watie], "An Address to the Whites, Delivered in the First Presbyterian Church [Philadelphia], on the 26th of May, 1826, by Elias Boudinott [*sic*], A Cherokee Indian," in *Cherokee Editor: The Writings of Elias Boudinot*, ed. Theda Perdue (Knoxville: University of Tennessee Press, 1983) 74.
[29] Ibid., 70.

Boudinot concluded with a peroration: "[S]hall red men live, or shall they be swept from the earth?…Will you push them from you, or will you save them?"[30]

In these efforts to promote Cherokee "civilization," the stakes were high, and Boudinot knew it. By promoting Cherokee writing, Boudinot tried to send whites a basic message: "Look, we can read and write. Please don't kill us."

In the course of arguing for the humanness of Cherokee people, Boudinot told his audience about the Cherokee land. During most of the 1820s, in those years before the discovery of gold in the region, the mountainous area of the southeastern U.S. was regarded by residents of the east coast as a nonproductive wasteland. At best, it was *terra incognita*. In his address, Boudinot touted the advantages of the mountains: "Those lofty and barren mountains, defying the labour and ingenuity of man, and supposed by some as placed there only to exhibit omnipotence, contribute to the healthiness and beauty of the surrounding plains, and give to us that free air and pure water which distinguish our country."[31] Boudinot's emphasis on clear air and water was more than just aesthetic. American cities in the early nineteenth century were regularly beset by disease epidemics, including cholera and yellow fever—the same diseases Cooke often fled during his itinerancy.

Boudinot went on to stress the natural beauty of the region, and also the healthiness of the climate: "These advantages, calculated to make the inhabitants healthy, vigorous, and intelligent, cannot fail to cause this country to become interesting. And there can be no doubt that the Cherokee Nation, however obscure and trifling it may now appear, will finally become, if not under its present occupants, one of the Garden spots of America."[32] Boudinot's reference to the region as a future "Garden spot" was almost prophetic. In the early nineteenth century, the term "garden spot" implied not only arable land but also a place of

---

[30] Ibid., 71.
[31] Ibid., 71.
[32] Ibid., 71.

respite, a vacation land. Today, many of the ten million people who yearly visit the Great Smoky Mountains National Park might understand what Boudinot meant by the term.

Modern readers might also hear a prophetic ring in Boudinot's heartrending, rueful aside—"*if not under its present occupants.*" Surely Boudinot intuited that the Cherokee territory would end up in white hands. Nevertheless, even he must have been surprised by how quickly white vacation homebuilders would overtake the region, in the handful of years after his address.

The Cherokee Territory remained independent until gold was discovered there in 1828. Then, the state of Georgia confiscated the land. Prospectors rushed in to seize Cherokee fields and homesteads, often at gunpoint. Opportunistic whites were protected by hurriedly enacted Georgia laws prohibiting Indians from filing lawsuits or testifying against a white man.

Meanwhile, Andrew Jackson was elected U.S. President in 1828, and in his inaugural address Jackson pushed for an Indian Removal Bill. After much debate and controversy, the Indian Removal Bill narrowly passed through Congress in 1830. By 1832, the federal government was signing removal treaties with many of the tribes that remained in the eastern U.S. (Charles Bird King did a booming business at his 12th Street studio during 1832.) At that time, the Cherokees, under principal chief John Ross, refused to sign a removal treaty.

Violence and turmoil continued in the Cherokee territory. By 1835, officials of the Jackson administration, in collusion with Georgia politicians, had persuaded a minority Cherokee faction to sign a removal treaty. Signers of the Treaty of New Echota included Boudinot—though he had previously argued long and passionately against removal—and Major John Ridge. This treaty was rejected by the vast majority of Cherokees, however, and the American public soon came to understand that it was a fraud. Considerable political and civil opposition arose, especially in the northeastern U.S. In the Spring of 1838, Ralph Waldo

Emerson wrote a famous letter to President Martin Van Buren protesting the removal.[33]

Nevertheless, that same spring, General Winfield Scott assumed command of all U.S. forces in the Cherokee territory, together with reinforcements. Scott marched under orders to move Cherokees out of that territory by force. By Summer 1838, nearly 17,000 Cherokees had been forcibly herded into stockades. By October of that year, the "Trail of Tears" was well under way. By the following spring, more than 4,000 Cherokees had died, either in the stockades, in transit, or in the Oklahoma territory shortly after arrival. Ethnologist James Mooney quoted a Georgia volunteer with the Federal Army, who later was a Confederate colonel: "I fought through the Civil War and have seen men shot to pieces and slaughtered by the thousands, but the Cherokee removal was the cruelest work I ever knew."[34]

Although the Cherokee removal would not take place until more than a decade after Boudinot's 1826 speech, Cherokee land was, in the interim, taken over bit by bit by well-to-do Southern whites. This land encroachment occurred under circumstances that were questionable even under Georgia laws. Here is how encroachment worked: In 1832, the state took control of the Cherokee territory that remained in north Georgia. The state then divided the area into land lots of 160 acres, and gold lots of 40 acres (reserved for gold mining). The lots were supposed to be raffled off to homesteaders. Yet, according to historian Wilma Dunaway, irregularities and corruption were rampant. "Despite state requirements that grantees live on the awarded parcels for at least five years," writes Dunaway, "nearly half the land was held by absentees, two years after the lottery. In spite of Georgia's 'free' acreage policy, 16 per-

[33] On opposition to removal in the northeast, see Robert D. Richardson, Jr., *Emerson: The Mind on Fire* (Berkeley: University of California Press, 1995) 275-79.

[34] James D. Mooney, "Myths of the Cherokee," in *Nineteenth Annual Report of the Bureau of American Ethnology to the Secretary of the Smithsonian Institution, 1897-98; in Two Parts—Part I*, ed. J. W. Powell (Washington, DC: GPO, 1900) p. 130.

cent of the households held all the land, while the majority of Habersham County families remained landless."[35]

The beneficiaries of the irregularities and corruption were members of Georgia's land-owning classes—a combination of the "old-money" families, the plantation owners, and the "new-money" industrialists. In short, these were the same people George Cooke sought as patrons.

If Dunaway's analysis is correct, then these people constituted, in effect, a kind of criminal class. People today might be tempted to affix culpability on Cooke's patrons, yet in antebellum Georgia the land encroachers were respectable society, the aristocracy of the South.

Consider the career of Augustin Smith Clayton, the deceased husband of Mrs. Clayton, the woman who so graciously opened her heart and Athens home to George and Maria Cooke. Born in Virginia, Judge Clayton, as he came to be known, was raised in Augusta and became a prominent Georgia statesman and industrialist. He entered the Georgia House of Representatives in 1810. Later, he became, in turn, a state court judge, a member of Georgia Senate and, finally—succeeding Wilson Lumpkin, who was elected Georgia's governor—a member of the United States Senate. He was also one of the founders of the Athens Factory, an early and profitable north Georgia cotton mill.

Judge Clayton was not only a successful politician and businessman; he was also a man of letters. In 1835, he ghost-wrote a campaign biography for Martin Van Buren, the Democrat who would succeed Andrew Jackson as U.S. President and who would implement Jackson's final Indian Removal policy. Clayton's *Life of Martin Van Buren*, appeared in print under Davy Crockett's name, though it was an open secret that Clayton was the author. Clayton also wrote a series of articles for the Boston-based *Columbian Centinel*. Using "Atticus" as his *nom de plume*,

---

[35] Wilma Dunaway, *The First Frontier: Transition to Capitalism in Southern Appalachia, 1700-1860* (Chapel Hill: University of North Carolina Press, 1995) 64.

Clayton wrote a feisty and spirited defense of the policies of the state of Georgia regarding the Cherokees.[36]

None of this is to point the finger at Clayton and say that he himself committed any actual violation of Georgia or U.S. law. By all accounts, Clayton was an honorable and respectable man in his time. It is not known whether Clayton owned "vacation" property in the former Cherokee Territory. Nonetheless, Clayton represents the values and ethos of the society that Cooke served with his art. Cooke's patrons—the antebellum Southerners who paid him money, who enjoyed and displayed his art—were involved in a land grab and were the direct beneficiaries of one of America's violent episodes of ethnic cleansing. It seems reasonable to expect that these circumstances were reflected in Cooke's art.

When Cooke traveled to north Georgia, he was there to sell his services. One service he provided was cultural legitimization. In his essay for the *Southern Literary Messenger*, Cooke delicately referred to the area's having been "recovered from the Cherokees but a few years since." He sprinkled his descriptions of the landscape with quotes and allusions from Euripides, Milton, Austen, and Byron. He drew comparisons between north Georgia sites and European "Grand Tour" sites that genteel readers would have known. Cooke thus inserted the newly confiscated landscape into the grand sweep of European tradition. He meanwhile referred to native occupants of north Georgia only in terms of a romanticized "ancient" myth. Cooke thus helped to secure the Georgia aristocracy's cultural possession of the land, by writing the area's recent inhabitants into the past.

Instead of portraying the former domain of the Cherokee as a contested terrain, then, Cooke in 1840 wrote of Habersham County as a "summer resort": "Habersham has become the summer resort of families from Augusta, Savannah and Charleston; and several gentlemen have

---

[36] The articles were republished in Athens as *A Vindication of the Recent and Prevailing Policy of the State of Georgia, both in Reference to Its Internal Affairs, and Its Relation with the General Government, in Two Series of Essays...* (Athens GA: O.P. Shaw [published at the Office of "The Athenian"], 1827).

purchased and are improving beautiful residences in these salubrious hills." Cooke went on to portray the area's new occupants in flattering, soothing terms: "To the artist, and the admirer of the picturesque, these lofty hills and verdant vales, these yawning chasms and foaming cataracts, throw wide their varied beauties, and invite his wandering steps." Thus, through the lens of Cooke's artistic sensibility, the north Georgia land encroacher is refigured as an aesthete, a lover of the picturesque. The recent brutal history is dismissed with a discreet nod to the reader. "This country, you know, was recovered from the Cherokees but a few years since."

One of Cooke's most distinctive landscape paintings to survive from this period is *Tallulah Falls*.[37] The painting portrays Tallulah Falls in Habersham County. (The site is now called Tallulah Gorge, since the falls were diverted in 1913 by Georgia Power Company, to provide hydroelectric power to the city of Atlanta.) The provenance of the painting is not entirely clear, but by the end of the nineteenth century it was owned—along with a companion painting (of Toccoa Falls), which no longer exists—by R. L. Moss, developer of the hotel that at one time overlooked the Falls.[38] *Tallulah Falls* is now owned by the Georgia Museum of Art and was on display in 2002 at the Tallulah Gorge State Park Visitor's Center, though it is now back in Athens.

The painting owes much to Claude Lorrain (commonly known simply as Claude), the seventeenth-century Frenchman who pioneered modern landscape painting in Italy. Estill Curtis Pennington summarizes some of the elements of Claude's work that influenced Cooke: "Claude perfected the art of the poetic landscape enhanced through subtle naturalistic touches by the use of a strong foreground, peopled with detailed characters or foliage, a midground which often pulses with commercial or narrative action, and a remote, atmospheric background."[39] In *Tallulah Falls*, viewers can see that Cooke had developed all three

---

[37] *Tallulah Falls*, 1841; oil on canvas, 35-3/4 x 28-3/4 inches. The painting is reproduced in Keyes' exhibition catalog, page 89, and also on the cover of *CrossRoads: A Southern Culture Annual* 2004.

[38] Keyes, 88.

[39] Pennington, 28.

grounds. The foreground in this case is peopled with politely dressed tourists, appreciators of the picturesque. The background recedes into the mist beyond the far rim of the gorge, its atmosphere enhanced by a Claudian golden backlighting. The middle ground, meanwhile, embodies the power of nature; rather than pulsing with commercial or narrative action, it pulses with the action of the falls themselves, the rushing water.

The painting is beautiful and accomplished, if in some ways conventional. Yet it also sent the same message that Cooke's travel essay delivers. The painting told its viewers that the north Georgia landscape was there to be possessed and enjoyed, by the aesthete and the tourist, the purchaser of paintings and the lover of the picturesque. By showing the middle ground of the painting as being unpeopled, the painting cleanses the landscape of its recent history by suppressing that history in the minds of its viewers.

⚜

After his brief respite in north Georgia, commercial circumstances forced Cooke to resume his wandering ways. He spent much of 1841 and 1842 as busy as ever, working in Georgia's population centers. "Numerous small paintings fill up my odd moments, so that no time runs to waste," he wrote in July 1841.[40] Yet he was able to maintain his residence in Athens for a while. Maria seems to have spent time there, probably with the Claytons, while her husband traveled. In the following few years, Cooke roamed beyond Georgia again, as far as Memphis, Pittsburgh, and New Orleans.

In New Orleans, early in 1844, Cooke met the man who would become his devoted patron, the man who would commission the painting that hangs today in the University of Georgia Chapel: Daniel Pratt (1799–1873), who has been called Alabama's first millionaire industrialist. Born in New Hampshire, Pratt moved to the South as a young man, and at first made his living as a builder of neoclassical homes. Early in

[40] Simmons, 18.

his career, he made the transition from homebuilder to industrialist. The book jacket of Curtis J. Evans' 2001 Pratt biography summarizes the trajectory of the industrialist's career: "After moving to Alabama in 1833, Pratt started a cotton gin factory near Montgomery that by the eve of the Civil War had become the largest in the world. Pratt became a household name in cotton-growing states, and Prattville—the site of his operations—one of the antebellum South's most celebrated manufacturing towns."

The relationship between Pratt and Cooke quickly became close. As William Nathaniel Banks writes, "At the age of fifty, sometimes discouraged, often ill, and tired of his peripatetic life, Cooke met the man destined to pay the highest tribute to his art."[41] In New Orleans, Pratt took Cooke in and gave him two upper floors of a warehouse on St. Charles Street (today, Avenue) for Cooke to use as a gallery and studio.

Within a few years, Pratt had determined to build a wing of his luxurious house in Prattville, Alabama, to be dedicated almost exclusively as a gallery for Cooke's paintings. It was common at this time for industrialists to patronize the fine arts. Yet, as Banks observes, "it was certainly unusual for a collector to create an art gallery primarily to display the work of a single artist."[42] Around this time, Pratt commissioned the enlarged version of *Interior of St. Peter's, Rome* to fill one end of the gallery—the same painting now hanging in the Chapel in Athens. Cooke spent most of two summers—1846 and 1847—completing this one enormous painting. Of its effect after it was installed in the gallery, Cooke wrote that "when you enter the [gallery] door the whole church with its arches and colonnades in perspective will appear as in nature."[43]

Gratified as he was by Pratt's patronage and friendship, Cooke found that his life continued to be as difficult and as vagabond as ever. His health during this period continued to decline. He traveled widely dur-

---

[41] William Nathaniel Banks, "George Cooke and Daniel Pratt: An Improbable Friendship," in *George Cooke (1793-1849)* [Exhibition Catalogue], ed. Donald D. Keyes (Athens: Georgia Museum of Art, 1991) 41.

[42] Banks, "George Cooke and Daniel Pratt," 39.

[43] Banks, "George Cooke and Daniel Pratt," 43.

ing what would turn out to be the last year of his life, dividing his time between New Orleans, Prattville, and Washington City, where he painted portraits, commissioned by Pratt, of powerful politicians. He also managed at least one trip to Athens in 1848, apparently still with the hope of establishing a more permanent residence there.

It was not to be. In March 1849, Cooke contracted cholera in New Orleans and died within forty hours. Thus, Cooke succumbed to the very disease he had hoped to escape in Athens. Marilou Rudulph, in her account of Cooke's death, comments that "It is like a doleful poem that Cooke knew so many cities and countrysides, but never a permanent home."[44]

Cooke conveyed in his will that he wished to be buried where he died. Nevertheless, Maria thought it better to have his body interred at Prattville, where it would be near his paintings. The body lies there still, marked by a nine-foot monument, in the Pratt cemetery, on a hillside overlooking the town.

In the meantime, Maria Cooke found a home for herself in Athens. It is not recorded where she lived in the dozen years after her husband's death. But in July 1861, she married lawyer Asbury Hull (1797–1866), a prominent Athenian. Her new husband, during his lifetime, had served in the Georgia State Legislature and as cashier of the State Bank; he was president of the Southern Mutual Life Insurance Company, and also the treasurer of the University of Georgia for forty-seven years. Such a distinguished husband offered Maria some stability despite the Civil War. Shortly thereafter, in January 1866, Hull died at the age of seventy.

Around the time of Hull's death, the gallery at Pratt's house in Prattville was discovered to have dry rot. Since it was attached to the house, the gallery was torn down, to prevent the rot from spreading.[45] George Cooke's paintings were dispersed. At this time, Pratt offered to donate *Interior of St. Peter's, Rome* to the University of Georgia.

---

[44] Rudulph, 149.
[45] Rudulph, 151.

According to the minutes from the Trustees meeting, the painting would be offered only under the condition that the University provided a suitable place for it. The minutes quote Chancellor Lipscomb: "I recommend that the College Chapel be so enlarged and refitted as to answer the twofold purpose of a Commencement Hall and an Art Building. I suggest that this provision be made for the acceptance of this magnificent donation." According to Rudulph, the decision to place the painting under the protection of the university was influenced by the now rewidowed Maria. "She was eager to have the painting in her adopted city," writes Rudulph.[46] To Maria, the painting, in a sense, was coming home to rest.

And there it continues to rest, more than 130 years later. Visitors to Athens can witness Cooke's *Interior of St. Peter's, Rome* today, if they make their way over to the University Chapel on the Old North campus. Between about 11:00 A.M. and noon, when the sun's rays in the chapel align with the sun's rays in the painting, the *trompe l'oeil* effect is most convincing, and viewers can perhaps imagine how the painting looked in the Pratt gallery for which it was commissioned. Or, better yet, people can imagine the view as it appears "in nature," as if they are seeing the actual interior of Christendom's greatest cathedral.

In the empty chapel, to an attentive viewer, the painting projects an aura of stability and order. Yet the painting is also a bit insistent, in its excessive size. Underneath its enormity lies the hint of an anxiety—perhaps an anxiety about its northern-born patron's place in the swirling, emerging economic order of a rapidly industrializing South; or perhaps an anxiety about the legitimacy of property rights, for an aristocracy whose dominance on the mid-South was built on a handily repressed historical injustice? In view of Cooke's rootlessness, the painting at least suggests the opposite of what it portrays. From the painter consigned to wandering comes this representation of a fixed, ordered place.

---

[46] Rudulph, 151.

Summer Art Colonies in the South, 1920-1940[1]

BY MARIEA CAUDILL DENNISON

Art colonies in the United States historically provided training to artists, encouraged a sense of community, and served as cultural incubators. By the early twentieth century, writers had already documented dozens of art colonies in the Northern U.S., where small groups of individuals gathered to learn artistic techniques from well-known painters as well as to make contact with fellow artists, and to create art in beautiful open-air settings. In 1917, newspaper columnist H. L. Mencken characterized the American South as a cultural desert. In 1920, Mencken repeated and expanded his comments. However, Southern art was not dormant during this era. A self-conscious Southern regionalism in art pre-dated a similar Midwestern development, which gained national attention around 1930. Several colonies that sprang up in the South during the 1920s and 1930s contributed to the growth of regionalist art while offering artistic instruction in a section of the U.S. where few reputable art schools existed.[2] Although an examination of people and events associated with these Southern gatherings provides insight into

[1] North Caroliniana Society provided partial support for this project. My thanks to Martha Severens for her careful reading of the manuscript.

[2] H. L. Mencken's "The Sahara of the Bozart" was first published in the *New York Evening Mail* on 13 November 1917. In 1920, it appeared in *Prejudices: Second Series*.

the South's cultural climate and suggests the region's artistic direction, little has been published about art colonies based in the South.

My survey of art colonies in the South before World War II revealed many similarities in terms of colony goals, locations, and operations.[3] Communities often supported artistic endeavors that called attention to regional subjects, and women played important roles in Southern art gatherings, financing and/or operating three of the South's most important colonies: the Texas Art Colony, the Natchitoches Art Colony, and the Dixie Art Colony. Surviving records show that women often served as colony directors or teachers, and that female students were in the majority at several Southern colonies.

The Texas Art Colony was one of the first Southern art colonies to be established after World War I. In 1921, a group of artists and their families camped on Dove Creek, about twenty-five miles from San Antonio. Their vacation included painting and sketching, and ultimately prompted Mollie Crowther, a painter and community leader from San Angelo, to envision a more structured gathering of Texas artists.[4]

In 1922, about a dozen artists attended the first session of Crowther's colony near Christoval, a town on the Concho River. Crowther—who had studied at the Art Institute of Chicago and with noted Texas landscape painter Frank Reaugh—was attracted to the beautiful hilly terrain.[5] A 1926 newspaper article described the setting of Crowther's art colony: "There are foothills that take on mauve and blues and green with a change of light, prairie with its inevitable cactus and

---

[3] There is no fixed definition of the term "art colony." Summer art classes that offered college credit to students are outside the realm of this study, as are fixed clusters of Southern artists like those found in Savannah, New Orleans, and Charleston. For more on the early development of regionalist art in the South, see the author's "Art of the American South, 1915-1945: Picturing the Past, Portending Regionalism" (diss., University of Illinois, 2000) 18–23, 88–97.

[4] The Texas Art Colony did not have a firmly established name. For example, it has been called the Texas Artists Camp, The Texas Artists Colony, and the Christoval Colony. Bernice M. Strawn, "Art Colony on Concho River Enters Fifth Summer Term with Plans for Simple Life," unidentified newspaper clipping, 20 June 1926, n.p. Southern States Art League Papers (hereafter cited as SSAL), collection 11, box 20, Tulane University.

[5] Frances Battaile Fisk, *A History of Texas Artists and Sculptors* (Abilene: privately published, 1928) 177–79.

mesquite…and a deep wood of pecan, elm and oak forming so thick a canopy overhead that the sun rarely breaks through…. Around the bend, the Concho ripples over rocks, and in its deeper pools it is still with the reflected glory of trees in its blue depths." The colony occupied cabins and rustic buildings owned by a Baptist camp, and Crowther oversaw activities for two or three weeks each summer until her death in 1927. Ella Mewhinney, who became Crowther's friend when they were fellow students in St. Louis, served as the first secretary of the colony, which eventually hosted over sixty students each session.[6]

Each year the Texas Art Colony recruited reputable teachers, including Olin and Kathryne Travis, the founders of the Dallas Art Institute; Jose Arpa, a Spanish-trained painter and later the director of the San Antonio School of Art; Xavier Gonzalez, an artist who later taught at Newcomb College (Tulane University); Will Henry Stevens, a professor at Newcomb College; and Sol H. V. Russo who studied at Columbia University and the Art Students League before becoming a professor at the University of Oklahoma.[7]

In the South, support for indigenous art grew. Vivian Aunspaugh, an influential Dallas artist and teacher, observed: "The South is so wonderfully picturesque, both in life of the people and natural beauty of the country." In a 1922 letter, she stressed the importance of Southern artists "developing in their own environment," and she concluded that "every effort which tends to keep the artist and art student in the South is a tremendous step toward creating a distinctive Southern art."[8]

[6] "Artists Camp at Christoval," unlabeled newspaper clipping, curator's file, Panhandle Plains History Museum, Canyon, TX. Strawn, "Art Colony on Concho River." Fisk 140–41, 177–79. John and Deborah Powers, *Texas Painters, Sculptors and Graphic Artists* (Austin: Woodmont Books, 1999) 356.

[7] Powers 520–22, 196–97. Fisk 29–30, 66–9. Strawn, "Art Colony on Concho River." Other colonies soon opened in Texas. Alexandre Hogue was associated with the Texas Art Camp on Paluxi Creek near Glen Rose and served as its director in 1927. By 1931 the Leon Springs Colony, which Rolla Taylor helped organize, was in operation near San Antonio. *Southern States Art League Bulletin*, March 1931. Fisk 23–24, 88–90. Powers 231–32, 506–07. A number of Texas colonies were launched later in the 1930s. Powers 579–80.

[8] Powers 18–9. Fisk 58–9. Vivian Aunspaugh, letter to Irma Sompayrac, 9 May 1922, Irma Sompayrac Scrapbook, Northwestern State University of Louisiana (hereafter NSU).

Ellsworth Woodward, Director of Newcomb College in New Orleans, held similar views, and his comments spurred the formation of the Natchitoches Art Colony in Louisiana. In 1920, Woodward visited Natchitoches, a river town about 250 miles north of New Orleans, and was struck by the potential of the historic village to become an art colony. He spoke with two young Natchitoches women, Irma Sompayrac and Gladys Breazeale, who had studied art at Newcomb, and a plan for a colony was soon formulated. As the first session opened in 1921, Woodward asserted that Natchitoches "is an ideal location for an art colony. Not only is the scenery unsurpassable, but there is the background of a social order two centuries old. The customs instituted by those old planters still live with the spacious old homes they built." Woodward agreed to teach for two weeks that first summer, and "the little Louisiana town…worked itself into its most enthusiastic pitch over the project." Sompayrac and Breazeale coordinated the planning and publicity for the art colony in Natchitoches. Townspeople made "offers to throw the old homes wide to the art students," and businessmen provided a steam launch to ferry painters to scenic sites up and down the Cane River.[9]

In a New Orleans newspaper story that marked the opening of the first session at Natchitoches, Earl Sparling wrote about the lack of colonies in the South; he quoted the man who was "in closer touch with the trend of Southern art than anyone in America today," Ellsworth Woodward. "Because we did not offer our young people the proper advantages," Woodward explained, "they have grown into the opinion that art is not here at home, but out yonder somewhere. They have gone away and forgotten even the ideals of their homeland…. It is the duty of the Southern artist to depict on his canvas that indefinable something which makes the South a distinctive country."[10]

Only about ten people enrolled at the Natchitoches Art Colony in 1921, but a local club provided space for an exhibition of students'

[9] Earl Sparling, "Southern Artists Camp at Natchitoches," *Item Magazine,* 12 June 1921, 2–3.
[10] Sparling, 2–3.

work. Members of the community also offered prizes and funds for scholarships to help ensure that the colony would continue.[11]

In 1922, Will Henry Stevens—then a new teacher at Newcomb College in New Orleans, became the Natchitoches Art Colony's primary instructor, a position he would retain through the tenth anniversary celebration of the endeavor. Sompayrac and Breazeale worked tirelessly as directors, and the colony attracted students primarily from Mississippi, Arkansas, and Alabama, but also from as far away as California. Summer sessions were lengthened to a month or more, and short spring and fall gatherings were also held. The colony in Natchitoches began to offer formal memberships, and in the late Summer of 1925 a cabin studio was built featuring a screened porch and a shower. Citizens of Natchitoches supplied many of the essentials (land, logs, bricks, and labor) and monetary donations to finance the structure came from all quarters.[12]

Attendance at the Natchitoches Art Colony reached thirty-four students in 1927, and it gained more national publicity than any other Southern colony of its type. In 1928, Stevens, Woodward, and a group of professional artists associated with the colony exhibited at the National Arts Club in New York City under the heading "Painters from the Natchitoches Group." The colony and its members were depicted in the April 1930 issue of *National Geographic*, discussed in R. L. Duffus' *American Renaissance* (1928), and represented in a photo published in the *New York Times*.[13] The years of the Great Depression, however, brought a slow decline to the Natchitoches Art Colony.

Will Henry Stevens, a native of south Indiana who studied at the Cincinnati Art Academy, was also instrumental in the development of several colonies in the mountains of the Southeastern U.S. During the

---

[11] Sarah Bailey Luster, "The Natchitoches Art Colony: A Southern en plein air art colony" (master's thesis, Tulane University, 1992) 60, 121.

[12] "Art Colonists Build Studio," *Shreveport Times*, 23 August 1923, n.p., details the contributions to the cabin. For a exhaustive story of the colony, see Luster or Irma Sompayrac's papers at NSU. In 1938 Charles H. Reinike had a colony at Bains, Louisiana. *Southern States Art League Bulletin*, May 1938.

[13] Luster 124, 76.

A 1917 "Land of the Sky" ad aimed at tourists.

World War I era, Stevens was one of a growing number of visitors attracted to the cool climate and beautiful vistas of the Southern Appalachians. In 1913, 1914, and 1917, for example, the Southern Railway advertised nationally to encourage travelers to visit North Carolina's "Land of the Sky" where they would find eighty peaks over five thousand feet high as well as "golf, tennis, riding, driving and motoring." The railroad offered service to Asheville, Black Mountain, Brevard, Lake Toxaway, Hot Springs, and other Carolina tourist destinations. In 1919 the Southern Railway transported 100,000 summer tourists to the "Land of the Waterfalls."[14] As the flood of visitors continued, Stevens found opportunities to teach and operate summer art colonies in the mountains of North Carolina and Tennessee.

Late in 1917, Stevens and his wife Grace wintered in Brevard, North Carolina, and they returned to the community the next summer. By August 1919, the town boasted that all three hotels and fifty-four boarding houses were full, and scores of travelers were being turned away. It is not clear if Stevens taught in Brevard, but around 1920, he painted nearby. The artist took advantage of both mountain subjects and the opportunity for sales to tourists. In 1921, Grace opened a Brevard tea room that catered to summer visitors and displayed her husband's paintings of local scenery.[15]

Stevens was known for trekking through the countryside in search of subjects, and by 1920 he had discovered Valley Town (the present-day town of Andrews), North Carolina. Early in 1921, he exhibited three works that depicted the township, including one of an historic inn called

---

[14] Southern Railway advertised in serials such as *American Magazine and Travel*. "Summer Tourists Swarm to 'Land of the Waterfalls'," *Brevard* (NC) *News*, 2 July 1920, n.p.

[15] The Stevens went to Daphine, AL, early in 1918. "Personal Mentions," *Brevard News*, 8 February 1918, n.p. "Brevard Popular Summer Resort," *Brevard News*, 29 August 1919, n.p. Around 1920 Stevens was painting Lake Sapphire, near Brevard. Jessie Poesch, "Will Henry Stevens, Modern Mystic: Beginnings to 1921" *Southern Quarterly* 25 (Fall 1986): 67–70. "New Tea Room in Town," *Brevard News*, 24 June 1921, n.p. "Pink Possum Opens," *Brevard News*, 8 July 1921, n.p. Later, Brevard would become the site of a colony that was held from August 1 to September 1, 1935, at Eagle's Nest Camp, one of the many youth camps in the area. Mary Hope Cabaniss and Walter Thompson, Savannah artists, offered instruction and arranged for artists to use camp facilities. "Art Colony Opens at Camp in Transylvania," *Transylvania Times*, 1 August 1935, n.p.

Tranquilla. The inn, which was owned by Fanny Wilson, a supporter of the arts, attracted cultured visitors and was probably the headquarters of Stevens' art colony.[16] On January 13, 1922, Stevens explained: "For the past two years I have had a class of outdoor painting in the North Carolina mountains." Seven days later he noted that he had his "own summer colony at Valley Town, Cherokee County." Stevens described the structure of his summer classes, the colors he recommended for students to use for landscape painting, and the difficulty caused by painters who came to the colony believing that they could buy art supplies in the mountains. He added that each Saturday it was his habit to give a general criticism and discussion of all the previous week's work. "This," he noted, "is really a class in composition and I have found it a very valuable part of instruction."[17]

In June 1922, Stevens taught for the first time at the Natchitoches Art Colony in Louisiana, but by mid-July he was back in his "old haunts" in Valley Town, "the loveliest of all mountain valleys." It is not clear if he operated a North Carolina colony in 1922, but he reported, "My studio is most satisfactory and is good looking both inside and out. It is covered with weathered shingles and lichen.... It is almost lost in the trees and looks like it has been there always." Stevens wrote from Tranquilla and may have been describing a cabin built on the premises.[18] The small North Carolina community demonstrated

[16] *Closson Art Gallery: Exhibition Catalogue, April 4 to 18, 1921*, Will Henry Stevens Papers, Archives of American Art, 4704 (hereafter cited as Stevens Papers, AAA). Tranquilla is now the historic Walker Inn, Valley Town (Andrews), NC. Gertrude Smith, a professor of art at Newcomb College, retired to Valley Town and had a long association with Wilson. For facts about Smith, see Melrose Scrapbook, Melrose Collection and Irma Sompayrac Scrapbook, NSU. Lillian Cover, Eleanor Ennis' mother, was Wilson's long-time friend, and Ennis' father described those who gathered at the inn as the "brain trust." Patti Cook and Eleanor Ennis, personal interviews, September 2001.

[17] Will Henry Stevens, letter to Gladys Breazeale and Irma Sompayrac, 13 January 1922, Irma Sompayray Scrapbook, NSU. Will Henry Stevens, letter to Gladys Breazeale and Irma Sompayrac, 20 January 1922, Melrose Collection, NSU.

[18] Will Henry Stevens, letter to Miss Cammie [Henry], 17 July 1922, Melrose Scrapbook, NSU. A mention of the cabin appears in Bernard Lemann, "Will Henry's Nature, The Pictorial Ideals of W. H. Stevens" ts., 53, copy in Stevens Artists File, Morris Museum of Art, Augusta, GA. Ennis and Cook confirm that two cabins once stood on the Tranquilla property and oral history suggests that they were used by artists. Patti Cook and Eleanor Ennis, personal interviews, September 2001.

#890, Untitled. Will Henry Stevens. Pastel on paper. 17" x 14 1/4"
Signed "Stevens" LL. Photo courtesy of Blue Spiral 1.

#2.93.22, *Woods Road* by Will Henry Stevens. Oil on canvas. 29 1/4" x 25 1/2"
Signed "Stevens '35" LR. Photo courtesy of Blue Spiral 1.

substantial support for art. In 1922, Fanny Wilson probably supplied Stevens with his studio, and businesses and ordinary citizens in Valley Town contributed five dollars each toward the community's purchase of one of Stevens' paintings. The $100 work depicted a view from Tranquilla.[19]

Stevens painted in the Great Smoky Mountains in the 1920s, and by the early 1930s he had moved his summer base of operations to Tennessee. "Gatlinburg Finds Favor of Artists...Permanent Art Colony May be Established in Smokies," read a newspaper headline that announced the successful completion of Stevens' first summer colony in the Tennessee mountains. The artist cited his reasons for establishing an art colony in Gatlinburg: "I feel that the environment is most conducive to creative work.... The climate is stimulating...so many arts and crafts are already established...and [it] is in the midst of a great section easily reached." The wealth of visual material in the area was noted, and Stevens added, "The South is comparatively unknown to artists."[20]

The summer gathering, according to Stevens, would "be an adventure in art for every student who enters my class." In the mid-1930s, the colony was called the Stevens Summer School of Painting and attracted students from as far away as Texas and Oklahoma. Landscape and figure painting were taught, and Stevens' weekly critiques included "a discussion of the modern trend in art...and talks on the philosophy of art." The Gatlinburg colony operated at least through 1939.[21]

[19] The painting is now in the Andrews Public Library, and an associated note on file explains the circumstances around its purchase. Stevens is reported to have planned a colony in Hot Springs, NC, for the summer of 1924. Luster (80) cites a 10 October 1923 letter from Stevens to Sompayrac in which he announces his 1924 plans. Stevens apparently visited the state only briefly in the summer of 1925. Will Henry Stevens, letter to Irma Sompayrac, 5 September 1925, Irma Sompayrac Scrapbook, NSU.
[20] Works with titles that indicate that Stevens was painting in the Smokies are listed in "Oil Paintings and Pastels by Will Henry Stevens," Brooks Memorial Gallery, July 1929, Stevens Papers, AAA 4704. "Gatlinburg Finds Favor...," unlabeled newspaper clipping, Stevens Papers AAA 4704.
[21] Untitled newspaper clipping, hand labeled *New Orleans Times Picayune—States*, 3 September 1939, Louisiana Collection, Tulane University.

There are indications that Stevens taught at several other mountain locations. He was still spending summers near Gatlinburg in 1941 when he rented space for a colony in a Baptist school near Sevierville. Smoky, Tennessee, was the site of another of his summer gatherings. He seems to have been involved in a colony in Dillard, Georgia, and he taught in Lebanon, Virginia, in 1943.[22]

In the mid-1930s, Catharine C. Critcher rented rustic buildings in the mountains near Saltville, Virginia, and operated the Red Rock Cove Art Camp. Like other mountain colonies, Red Rock Cove offered cool temperatures and panoramic views. In planning her Virginia endeavor, Critcher must have drawn upon her extensive experience as a teacher and a participant in colonies. She was a former instructor at the Corcoran School of Art and ran her own art school in Washington, D.C. from 1923 to 1940. During summers she often painted at the Provincetown Art Colony in Massachusetts and in Taos, New Mexico, where she was a member of the Taos Society of Artists.[23]

The mountains of Arkansas offered another scenic location for an art colony. The Travis Ozark Summer School of Painting was founded in 1927 and operated for about three years. Olin Travis and Kathryne Hail met when he was an instructor and she was a student at the Art Institute of Chicago. They married, moved to Dallas, and taught at Crowther's Texas Art Colony before they opened their own near Kathryne's hometown of Ozark, Arkansas. Each July, both artists taught at the colony in Cass, a nearly abandoned sawmill town at the edge of a forest preserve. The couple leased cabins which were "put in excellent condition," and one structure served as a clubhouse and gallery. A yearly art exhibition

---

[22] The Louise Trimble Kepper Papers, Archives of American Art, 4314. The reference is probably to one of several towns in Scott County, TN: Smoky, Smokey, or Smoky Junction. Lemann 36, 53. Stevens is linked to Dillard by a note on the back of a photograph at the Blue Spiral Gallery, Asheville, NC. "Black Mountain College Showing Works by Stevens," newspaper clipping, hand labeled Asheville, 30 January 1944, Stevens Papers, AAA 4704.

[23] Marguerite C. Munn also taught at Red Rock Cove. "Red Rock Cove Art Camp," SSAL, collection 11, box 51, Tulane University. *Southern States Art League Bulletin*, April 1934. Powers 115.

was well received by Ozark residents, and a colony-sponsored square dance attracted citizens from miles around.[24]

In the 1920s and 1930s, many summer art colonies thrived along the shores of New England, but relatively few coastal colonies existed in the South. Mississippi's Ocean Springs Summer Art Colony opened in June 1926 along the Gulf of Mexico. Mrs. Walter Anderson, an artist and the mother of a potter, provided the use of her house and grounds, Fairhaven, as a meeting place for the venture. The founder of the colony was Daniel Whitney, a popular New Orleans artist and teacher who was said to have offered instruction to "develop individuals and discourage imitation." Many New Orleans artists attended, and in the Fall of 1926, over forty works produced at the colony were exhibited at the city's Arts and Crafts Club. Nonetheless, the Ocean Springs colony seems to have lasted for only one season.[25] Similarly, a 1935 seaside colony that was housed at the Golden Eagle Tavern in the historic island town of Beaufort, South Carolina, may have been short lived. "Intense training in outdoor painting" was offered from June 15 to July 13 under the direction of Mary Hope Cabaniss and Walter Thompson, Savannah artists.[26]

For most of its long history, the Dixie Art Colony was associated with Lake Jordan, near Montgomery, Alabama. In 1933, however, the colony held its first session (and acquired its name) at Camp Dixie on Alabama's Lake Martin. The following summer a two-week session was held on the Gulf Coast at Sea Grove, Florida, before the colony moved to Spring Lake, Alabama, for a second session.[27]

[24] Powers 520–22. Travis claimed that a thousand people viewed the exhibition each year. "Travis Ozark Summer School of Painting in the Ozark Mountains," SSAL, collection 11, boxes 24, 27 and 28, Tulane University.

[25] Catherine B. Dillon, "Art Colony in Coast Mansion," unidentified newspaper clipping, hand dated 23 May 1926, SSAL, collection 11, box 20, Tulane University. Vera Morel, "Modern Painting Conservatively Done," *New Orleans Morning Tribune*, 22 September 1926, n.p. Artists also seemed to have regularly gathered at Biloxi in the 1930s. "Artists Making Vacation Plans," *Times Picayune* 19 May 1935, n.p.

[26] "Beaufort-Brevard Art Colonies: Outdoor Schools of Painting," SSAL, collection 11, box 51, Tulane University.

[27] Lynn Barstis Williams, "The Dixie Art Colony," *Alabama Heritage*, Summer 1996, 8–15.

J. Kelly Fitzpatrick, director of the school at the Montgomery Museum of Fine Arts and a well-known Alabama artist, founded the Dixie Art Colony and became its primary instructor. The venture, which became one of the South's best-known colonies, operated under the auspices of the museum and received significant support from Sallie B. Carmichael and her daughter Warree, who was an artist. After being held at several locations around Lake Jordan in 1935 and 1936, the colony moved to a permanent home, called Poka Hutchi. On wooded acreage overlooking the lake, Carmichael built a rustic lodge with a studio, sleeping quarters, and a kitchen. A cottage was also provided; the permanent buildings facilitated spring and fall sessions. For many years, Carmichael arranged for the feeding and housing of students and covered the colony's deficits.[28]

In 1937, the first year that the Dixie Art Colony occupied its new home, a month-long session was held in June. Fitzpatrick, a charismatic teacher, was instrumental in setting the tone of the colony and providing continuity as various teachers offered artistic criticism. Instructors in 1937 included Frank W. Applebee, later head of the art department at Auburn University; Richard B. Coe, a Boston-trained etcher from Alabama; and Lamar Dodd, later the head of the art department at the University of Georgia. During her summer visits to the South from New York City, Anne Goldthwaite, a nationally known artist and native of Montgomery, often visited the gathering on Lake Jordan and offered criticism. Over the years, Karl Wolfe, Mildred Nungester, and other well-known Southern artists were associated with the summer school.[29]

Just two years after the first meeting of the Dixie Art Colony, Fitzpatrick expressed his ardent belief that Southern artists should paint Southern subjects, and a 1940 article lists points of interest near Poka

[28] Williams 8–15. Montgomery Museum of Fine Arts, *A Symphony of Color: The World of Kelly Fitzpatrick* (Montgomery AL: Montgomery Museum of Fine Arts, 1991) 10–19.

[29] One surviving copy of the flyer "Dixie Art Colony, Season 1937" has an addendum which states that for two weekends Lamar Dodd would be a visiting critic at the colony. H. Maxon Holloway Papers, State of Alabama Department of Archives and History. Williams 8–15. Patricia Phagan, ed., *The American Scene and the South: Paintings and Works on Paper, 1930–46* (Athens, GA: Georgia Museum of Art, 1996) 36–50.

#867, Untitled by Will Henry Stevens. Pastel on paper. 13 7/8" x 16 7/8"
Signed "Stevens '34" LR. Photo courtesy of Blue Spiral 1.

Hutchi: "Besides the hills, brooks, and lake, farms only a few miles away afford an opportunity for painting cotton culture in all its phases; also negro cabins, cotton gins, [and] country churches." Most members of the colony were from Alabama, but students also came from Mississippi, Louisiana, Georgia, Tennessee, North Carolina, Virginia, New York, Ohio, and Pennsylvania. Each year from 1933 to 1945, the Montgomery Museum of Fine Arts hosted an exhibition of works produced at the Dixie Art Colony, and prizes were offered. Sallie B. Carmichael suffered a stroke in 1946, and the colony's summer session was canceled. In 1947, a decade after the colony moved to its headquarters, the last gathering of artists was held at the lodge.[30]

In archival papers associated with Southern art colonies of 1920s and 1930s, the South is often described as a particularly beautiful region and one that has been overlooked by native artists. Such materials also document considerable grassroots support for art in the South during that era, especially from women. Collectively, Southern art colonies not only provided instruction in scenic locations but also fueled interest in visual art, built a sense of community, encouraged the development of a distinctively Southern approach to painting and contributed to a regional pride that buttressed separate efforts to establish museums and permanent schools of art in the South.

---

[30] J. Kelly Fitzpatrick, letter to Ethel Hutson 28 July 1935, SSAL collection 11, box 51, Tulane University. Carla Robison, "Dixie Art Colony Ends Eighth Successful Season," *Montgomery* (AL) *Advertiser*, 25 August 1940. Until the 1960s, Warree LaBron, Carmichael's daughter, sponsored colonies at other locations. Williams 8–15.

A Letter from Mississippi

—TEXT AND ARTWORK BY BART GALLOWAY

September 2003

Dear Mom and Dad,

I wanted to drop you a line and let you know how I am. My move from Tupelo to Utica this past August went smoothly, thanks to the help of Sylvain and Julie. One of my new neighbors, who restores antique furniture, showed up midway through unloading the truck and was soon carrying one of the big couches by himself without breaking a sweat. He quietly received our thanks, then went back to his store when the truck was empty.

Utica is a quiet town near Vicksburg that is surrounded by rolling hills and a few cattle ranches. A local told me that Utica was once known as the "Tomato Capital of the World." The downtown is about as long as my arm, yet they are keeping it alive with a fierceness that is great to see. As I write this, they have just finished replacing and enhancing the cement sidewalk, and they have created spaces at both ends of the downtown walk for large flowerbeds, with street lamps in the center.

I have set up my studio in the front room of the large old house in which I am living. It has been over ten years since I have lived where I paint. Behind the house is an old school with a large gymnasium that is not in use. However, next to the school is a football field with field goals, a track, and some playground equipment. They keep all of this in working condition. I have been spending some of my time out on the field kicking field goals. From about forty yards out I am a lock, but I can't seem to crack the forty-five-yard range with any consistency.

My health is good, and I am employed teaching art again. Several of my drawing students hold real promise. With any luck they'll fight off the pressure of immediate success and allow themselves to age slowly into adept, expressive artists. I have hope for them. And as for me, I am painting and drawing on a regular basis—some good and some bad. I have a few challenging portrait commissions that I should be working on. But of course I am spending more time doing what I want to do. Making art seems to be as much about shifting around guilt to make space for my selfishness as about anything else.

These four images that I have sent you were begun while I was in Tupelo. They are dry point prints. I worked on the plates within the last year, but I was never able to print them up until now.

I found that barn on a road north of Tupelo near the Natchez Trace. My friend Dan and I used to walk the road a lot. There always seemed to be strange things to see on this road. (Once I saw a white kitten hanging upside down, caught in the vine of a roadside tree. When I went to untangle it, the kitten bit into the meat of the middle finger of my left hand like a snapping turtle. After I finally pried its mouth open, the kitten quickly ran under a car across the road, where there was a man sitting on a bucket fixing one of the car's tires. The man made no sign that he was aware of us, the kitten, or what had just happened.) There was nothing particularly strange about the barn, though. The way it sat wide and round on the crest of this hill attracted me, as well as the crack and flow of the fence and weeds. I had hoped to finish the trees around the back of it. This old barn had a sound and color to it much like other old barns. No one uses that barn now; it is just bugs and vines. There was something very soothing about drawing this barn.

Terry was a co-worker of mine at the newspaper in Tupelo. He is an advertising designer and computer consultant, and I think he still works there. Terry is a happy guy, and we laughed a lot together. Working in those cubicles at the computer all day long can really wear one down. I used to sneak into Terry's space at the newspaper office, and we'd tell stories and laugh about some of the other workers and about ourselves.

I think I found these cows in Plantersville. I used to explore dirt roads outside Tupelo, and I'd watch the cows. You know I am more interested in painting people, but I love to look at the Mississippi landscape. I drew these cows from a photograph I took. I like this image, and I may now work with more subjects from the landscape.

The "dancing bottle" is basically a still-life. The inspiration happened while I was listening to the music of John Coltrane, who is such an enormous inspiration to me. It's also the first dry point I have done on a copper plate. All these others were done on plexiglass.

I wrote this letter not just to let you know how I am doing, but also to let you in on something. When you moved the family to Jackson from Montgomery, it was a shock. As much of a shock as our earlier move from Dahlonega to Demopolis. Coming to Mississippi at the age of ten seemed frightening—I only knew what I had heard about Mississippi. For the last twenty-three years, in the back of my mind, I have believed that my stay in Mississippi was only temporary. I am changing my mind.

The subject matter in these prints is what I like to think about and work with. And it is all from Mississippi. So, if I am going to keep drawing and painting this subject matter, I will have to stay here. So there.

Julie and I are looking forward to seeing you both there in October and watching Dad's football team play in the championship. I will check to see what is showing art-wise around Atlanta. Well, take care of yourselves. See you soon.

Love,
Bart

"Barn" by Bart Galloway

"Terry" by Bart Galloway

"Cows" by Bart Galloway

"Dancing Bottle" by Bart Galloway

Postscript

BY JAMES E. CHERRY

Dear Mama,
The last time I said I love you
was six years ago on the seventh floor
in a semi-private room at the county
hospital where you lay shackled by tubes
and machines whose cold indifference mocked
my weary sighs and unrequited moans.
Moments later, you slipped just beyond.
And in the pursuing days, I wrestled with the
meaning of lymphoma, cultivated a growing anger
towards a God omniscient with His or Her
precepts of sin, suffering and death. And since
that time I have filled this space with the compass
of your smile, whispers of words encouraging, and
the thought that eternity exists within the speaking
of your name, as I seal this letter within
the folds of my heart, stamped with a kiss
and the letting go.

Love,
Your youngest son

Wisteria

BY KIMBERLY GREENE ANGLE

"Damn you!" Raymon yelled at the lavender blooms billowing up into the oak and sprawling in a shady expanse over his yard. *"Damn that wisteria!"*

Beads of sweat glistened on Raymon's iron gray hair as he removed his black-framed glasses. His nose, temporarily relieved of its burden, felt light. For over six decades, the bifocals had molded two caverns on each side of his nose that were so deep they now seemed to join under the thin bone.

Wincing at the mid-afternoon sun, Raymon replaced the glasses, wiped his hands on his soiled work pants, and surveyed the vined yard again in a look of disgust. It had been twenty-five years since his petite wife had sailed into the living room in her white cotton dress and exclaimed, "Wisteria, that's what we'll have in our yard when we retire in Macon." Twenty-five years later, he could still picture how Clytie's bony frame stuck out at sharp angles under the thin cotton while her mouth and eyes curved in excitement.

Raymon and Clytie bought the green-shuttered brick house after their children had grown and scattered. In their early sixties, they wanted a home and yard with low maintenance. They were ready to sit back on Brumby rockers and enjoy retirement from work and parenthood. But Clytie wanted the place to look more like a home: a few plants here, a birdbath there. That's when the idea of wisteria had been conceived.

Raymon had always felt oppressed under the reign of Clytie's enthusiasm because he knew she would get her way with it. That day he'd let her brightness bounce lifelessly off his face, as he always had, so his somberness could counteract her energy. Raymon reasoned that he and his wife balanced each other out: his tall stoutness leveled her unusual smallness; his steadiness anchored her flightiness.

But, unwavering in her display of jubilance, Clytie insisted that the vine was the most romantic and most Southern plant she had ever seen. She had to have one in the yard of her new house, along with a live oak and a magnolia.

Now, a small cynical grin eased the wrinkles on Raymon's upper lip as he mused how Clytie had passed on, but the oak, the magnolia, and the wisteria had survived her. Especially the wisteria.

Due partly to his own neglect, the wisteria had grown even more fiercely in the three years since Clytie's death. The innocent-looking vine curled its way around the oak, across the telephone wires, and up the gutters of the house—then strangled all in its grasp. It draped from branches over to the roof, creating an arbor of purple blooms, but no fruit. That was what irked Raymon most about the wisteria—it served no purpose. It bore no fruit. All it did was sprawl and twist and squeeze.

With his glasses readjusted, the old man picked up his hatchet and began chopping at the vine again while snippets of his life replayed in his mind.

"Raymon, look at that beautiful wisteria in the pines," Clytie had drawled as the sky blue LTD soared down I-75 toward Macon. "You know, we may as well pull off here and get some. We can have the wisteria in hand when we arrive at our new home."

"No," Raymon said in a low but firm tone, his eyes unwavering from the horizon ahead.

"Look now," Clytie whined. "We passed some more. Well, if we don't get it now, just *when* and *where* are we gonna get it?"

Raymon made no response but started imagining the alternatives. Sneaking into the yard of a white-pillared house and clipping some. Making a special trip to scout the woods near Macon.

At the fourth sighting, Raymon abruptly pulled the car off the interstate and braked with a sudden jerk. He may have to stop, he thought to himself, but it wasn't going to be pleasant for her. But the jolt did not faze Clytie. A look of silent satisfaction settled over her face as she neatly clutched the looped handles of the white purse in her lap. Now she was the one who looked to the horizon.

Raymon sighed and slid out of the car. Muttering, he braced himself against the searing heat that rose in blurring waves from the black asphalt.

"Risking my life for a stupid plant," he mumbled to the impervious stream of cars.

Raymon had pulled over as quickly as Clytie had given the signal, but now it seemed like he had to walk a mile or more back up the road to find the purple blooms. He thought how insignificant his steps felt next to the black highway that stretched for mile upon mile, how slow his body was as he faced the cars speeding though the hot, still air. By the time he reached the wisteria, he was breathing hard and his clothes were soaked with sweat.

Raymon pulled out his pocketknife, but the dull blade was almost useless against the hard vine. Finally, Raymon used his bare hand to tear off a cutting—it drew blood.

The vine appeared harmless enough as Clytie placed the cutting in a small glass jar in the kitchen window of their new home. The water caught the sunshine and glowed an incandescent green around the white, fine strands that would become roots.

By the time Clytie felt the roots were big enough to plant in the yard, the vine had already curled itself around the cold water faucet and crawled into the toaster. The toaster had to be replaced.

"I'm inviting Sam and Gertie over for the planting tomorrow," Clytie had called to Raymon over the sizzle of breaded steak in grease and the six o'clock news.

Raymon shifted his eyes from the TV and glanced out the window at their neighbor's house. It was an exact replica of theirs and every other house on the street, excepting the color of shutters. Raymon recalled how Sam and Gertie Mason had first arrived on their doorstep with a pecan pie. Gertie's brown eyes shone under her black-dyed beehive as she stood at the door. Sam, standing behind his plump, smiling wife, looked at the ground and picked at the green flannel shirt he insisted on wearing despite the season.

After that day, the two couples became fast friends. Clytie was overjoyed to have someone to play spades with so close by. Sam and Raymon both liked to sit and watch TV and utter monosyllabic grunts of criticism while their wives endlessly chattered and cackled in the kitchen.

The day of the wisteria planting began with a drizzle that later settled into a hot haze. After supper, Sam and Gertie stood by the shoveling Raymon and tried to catch some of Clytie's excitement for the project. Clytie's enthusiasm, however, was so overpowering that everyone else either stood in quiet awe of it or held themselves quietly aloof. Not even Gertie felt adequate to participate in Clytie's delirium.

Clytie insisted that the wisteria be placed in the exact center of the backyard. "It'll grow into a nice blooming bush when we prune it. Oh, I can't wait. It's gonna be my baby!" Clytie clapped her hands and gave a little hop as Raymon mechanically shoveled red clay.

"Now, I promised Gertie I wadn't gonna say nothin, but really Raymon … ," Sam began. Gertie interrupted him with a hiss.

"No, Sam … ," she said, glaring at her husband.

Sam took the glare head on and slowly turned his head towards Raymon in emphatic defiance and continued. "I don't think you should plant this old weed in your yard. I had an uncle, and the stuff took over his whole place. It was horrible. It only blooms part of the year, ya know."

Raymon looked back at Sam and then swung his eyes down and over to Clytie. The look meant both, "I know" and "It's no use because Clytie has her heart set on it."

Sam gave an almost imperceptible nod, curled one corner of his mouth, and shifted his eyes to the tip of his black shoe.

"Nonsense," Clytie said in a defensive, pouty tone. "It'll be beautiful."

"I agree," Gertie responded in an attempt to atone for her husband. "I'll have a view of it from my kitchen window, and I'll feast my eyes on it every day. As my grandmama always said, *'Something mysterious about Wisteria.'*"

"W-*hysteria*, you mean," Sam mumbled, now nosing his black wing-tip into the red clay.

Clytie fumed at such a blasphemy.

"Sam," Gertie reprimanded before turning to Clytie with her sweetest knowing smile. "Oh, don't you mind him, Clytie. Sam's just lived in Macon too long. He pretends to be cynical about everything Southern, but he's really not. Likens to his father that way. You're lucky Raymon is just retiring here, maybe he won't catch the disease."

Clytie heaved a little sigh. "I'm afraid the same disease was rampant in Cornelia," she said.

Sam silently shrugged while Raymon patted down the dirt around the vine.

"Well," Clytie finally said. "Ya'll come on in. I made some pound cake for the occasion."

The three spectators started toward the house, but Raymon stayed transfixed in his spot.

Clytie looked back. "Raymon?"

"Ya'll go on in. I'll be in in a minute," he said.

Raymon wanted to stay outside to catch his breath and clean up. "A job is never finished," he could remember telling his kids, "until everything is put away."

As he carried the shovel and rake back to the shed under a pinkening sky, Raymon wondered again about what he had just planted in his yard. He could understand the oak and the magnolia. After all, they'd had oaks and magnolias at the old home place in Cornelia. But wisteria! Why wisteria? Clytie had only said that when she thought of Macon she thought of Southern mansions and wisteria; they had to have wisteria to live in Macon.

Raymon was surprised to find that though he disliked the reason, he was enjoying having something to do, the simple satisfaction that comes from completing a job, working with his hands. The project had eased for a moment the slight discontentment that had settled over him at retirement. He would often sit and watch TV while his body yearned to stretch and move, and his hands itched to use the tools they had spent their life using. At the old place in Cornelia, he had tinkered with the radio, the TV, and the lawnmower, which managed to keep him somewhat busy, but Clytie had bought all new appliances when they moved to Macon—now nothing ever broke. There was nothing to fix.

Lost in his thoughts, Raymon felt a little disoriented as he approached his shed. For a moment the old place in Cornelia and the new place in Macon mixed together in his mind, and the very ground beneath him seemed to sway in confusion. His work shed often had that effect on him. It was a portable tin shed that had been moved intact from Cornelia. Raymon had long thought of his shed as an old friend. It had endured through the years with him. It was his one corner of the earth, and it never changed—unless he wanted it to. He was especially proud that the shed retained the same patch of coolness that always lingered within its doors even on the hottest days in Cornelia. He felt that familiar quality of air now as he opened the door and stepped inside.

A naked bulb with a beaded string hung from the ceiling, but Raymon waited in the silent blackness until objects started to take shape in the shadows. It had been a while since he'd been in his work shed, and he breathed in the scent of stale grass that mingled with the dank, slightly greased odor peculiar to such places. It smelled almost as if some strange mechanical plant grew there. Finally, he moved by memory around the lawnmower and boxes to put away his tools.

After bolting the shed door, Raymon turned back to the house and caught sight of the ragged vine rising up out of the scarred earth in his yard.

"That wisteria will be the death of me," he groaned.

After the pound cake had been eaten and the Masons had left, Raymon found himself alone again with the wisteria. Even though it was dark, he decided that he'd better let the hose run on it awhile to irrigate the roots. After all, Raymon sighed as he thought to himself, if it doesn't take root now, I'll be back on the side of I-75 chopping weeds.

He turned on the hose and let it run for a minute in the moonlight and then took a sip from the sparkling arc of water. It had a bitter metallic taste that brought back all the years of summer gardening and children playing in sprinklers.

Those children: he could still hear their laughter and screams of delight in his mind. They were in his domain then, his yard, but they seemed so distant now. He realized that he never really knew them, never really knew what they were thinking, what they were feeling.

The family had gone through the motions flawlessly, with all the right smiles and hugs in all the right places—school plays, college graduations, weddings. But now that they were grown and scattered, he felt even more detached from the three little strangers who had lived under his roof. He had even forgotten exactly how old each was.

Raymon lay the hose down at the root of the wisteria and watched the water rush out of the small metal ring. Every time he saw a free-flowing hose he was reminded of how he had hemorrhaged after a gall stone operation. The doctor had described the cut artery as a garden hose gushing water. A chill came over him as the night finally subdued the heat of the day, and he realized that the trail of muddied red water had found his feet.

Raymon turned off the hose. The wisteria was now on its own.

For almost fifteen years the vine grew. A few years later the mammoth task of taming the wisteria began. Then Clytie died and, despite all the past battles, Raymon let the vine go as a type of memorial to her. But, by the next summer, Raymon was back into full-fledged war. He realized that the wisteria was sucking up all the nutrients in his lawn. His grass had turned to a lifeless beige. The vine even seemed bent on killing the oak and magnolia.

Last spring Raymon decided that he would simply saw the huge vine off at the base.

"Damn you," he muttered as he cut the last of the thick trunk.

He took the wisteria behind the shed with plans to burn it.

Raymon was a little ashamed at how much he was looking forward to nightfall when he would burn the wisteria. He jokingly invited Sam over for the bonfire, but Sam wouldn't give up his nightly *Jeopardy!* session. Raymon was kind of glad it would be just him and the vine. Cutting and burning the wisteria was something he had threatened to do for years, and now, without Clytie's protests, he felt he could finally get it done once and for all.

Raymon ate his supper of grits swimming in butter. His meals had become simpler after Clytie's death, and he found that he could make grits, so they became a staple to him. He had tried eating out, but he preferred having something warm to eat in his own home.

Raymon missed Clytie most at mealtimes. Not because of the food, but just because mealtime was so regular, so stable, so secure. No matter if it was election night or if war had broken out in the Middle East or if an earthquake had rattled California, Clytie had still prepared their breakfast, lunch, and supper like clockwork.

It wasn't the conversation that Raymon really missed, either, as they had never said much at the table; they ate wordlessly and shared a kind of silent contentment. He just missed the surety of the meals, the rhythm of them. Now Raymon often lost track of the time and didn't eat supper 'til well after dark when his stomach reminded him of the missed meal.

Finally, night fell. Raymon walked out onto his black lawn to start the fire. The gasoline clumsily lurched and splattered out of the can as Raymon doused the wisteria. The flame sprang to life with a small shout as the match met the gasoline.

Raymon took off his glasses and stared at the flames licking yellow against the shadows. He watched the cloven tongues of light even after his eyes started to sting and his cheeks grew hot. He felt as if his eyes had become fastened onto the fire, and for a few moments he couldn't tear his eyes from the blaze. When he finally lowered his lids, his eyes felt dry and parched.

Raymon turned on the hose and wet the ground around the fire so that he could let the old stump smoulder through the night. He paused to watch the ashes fluttering like lazy moths into the night sky. Satisfied, he went back to the house.

The next morning Raymon put on his olive green shirt and pants that had been his work uniform for thirty years. He then slid his black-framed glasses onto the bone of his nose.

When he opened the back door, he stared in disbelief as he surveyed the yard. His efforts of the day before had not produced the result he expected. The sprawling vine hung like a witch's shawl across the trees and power line, its grip even tighter than before. The stump was charred but still stood stout in the smoldering fire, refusing to be burnt. Not only that, but Raymon soon realized for the first time that the wisteria had seeded smaller vines throughout the yard. Some of the green creeping vines were separate from the mother vine and had taken root on their own.

In the months that followed, the wisteria grew back with a vengeance. The problem intensified when Raymon's blood pressure soared and the doctor ordered him to stay out of the summer heat. The voices of his scattered children suddenly could be heard on the telephone, dutifully echoing these orders from afar. The children even managed to hire a gardener as a belated Father's Day gift.

But Raymon found the gardener rather shiftless. The hired man would only tend to the wisteria one day a week. Raymon knew that the other six days the plant was gaining ground. After a few weeks, he let the hired man go.

Macon was so hot, and Raymon couldn't remember why they had decided to retire here. He thought it had something to do with Clytie's first cousin twice removed who had once lived in Macon. All he knew was that he was now living the twilight of his life in the boiling basin known as Middle Georgia.

In the dog days of August, Raymon was forced to sit idly by and watch out of windows as the wisteria regained all the ground Raymon had attempted to clear the previous weeks. The plant seemed to grow so quickly that he often focused on one part for several minutes at a time, convinced that he might actually see it creep an inch or two.

Raymon poured gasoline, weed killer, vinegar—everything imaginable—on the wisteria in hopes to kill it, or at least hinder its growth. But it seemed that anything he put on it made it grow more relentlessly.

Sam often watched Raymon from the window. One day Sam said to Gertie, "He's trying to kill it again. Dudn't he know that once you plant that weed it's there forever?"

"Yes," Gertie said. "His health won't allow that anymore. You really should do something, Sam."

"You kiddin?" Sam replied. "A man's gotta have somethin' to live for, dudn't he?"

This spring, the third since Clytie's death, Raymon decided to ignore the plant for his health. If I don't look in the backyard, he thought, I can pretend that weed doesn't exist. He found this easier said than done, however. He would often find himself peeking out the window, and sometimes, at night, he would wake up in a sweat after dreaming that the vine had curled around him in his sleep. Despite all his efforts of denial, his bouts of high blood pressure grew worse.

Then this very morning, Raymon had discovered wisteria crawling under the screen of his bedroom window.

"Oh, no you don't," he yelled. He knew that he'd waited long enough. Raymon didn't care anymore about the doctor's orders. He was determined to cut the wisteria down to size.

But when he walked into the backyard, his breath stopped short. The spring growth was worse than he'd imagined. Sam and Gertie were even out clipping tendrils clamoring for new territory in their yard.

The wisteria and its purple clusters of blooms draped over the yard, almost blocking the sun in some places. The heavy, sweet scent of the purple flowers hung in the humid air and turned Raymon's stomach.

He went to the shed and had to tear some brown leeching shoots with his bare hand to get into the door. He grabbed his hatchet from a corner and started flinging it wildly and randomly at the plant.

"Damn you," he yelled. With every hack he felt as if he was reclaiming a piece of his land, a piece of himself.

At two o'clock in the afternoon, Raymon was still out working, his past flicking through his mind like a cheap slide show. Sam and Gertie had long since gone inside, their earlier calls of warning about the heat seeming distant and muffled. At times, the old man felt lightheaded and dizzy, but he didn't care, he kept fighting.

The sweat stained black rings around the armpits of his olive green shirt and poured in rivulets from his iron gray hair down his jaw line before dripping steadily from his chin. Hour after hour passed. Now, even his memories seemed alien, as if they belonged to someone else's life. Before long the images of the past melted away altogether into the steady white-hot rage that blazed inside him.

At twilight, a cool dampness finally settled over the yard, but Raymon was still pulling and chopping at vines. He was exhausted, and the last light was draining quickly from the sky, but he kept telling himself, *"One more hack, just one more hack."*

Finally, Raymon saw purple liquid gush from one vine.

"I've drawn my blood back," he gasped. *"I found your heart. I finally killed you."*

The blood splattered across his shirt and felt warm, as he stumbled over a pile of roots and fell to the earth. Then, clutching the vine like a child grasping his mother's hand in the dark, Raymon lay down on the cool orange clay.

Remnants of My Father's Childhood

Telephone Insulator Lamp

Lost Tribes: Indian Mormons
in the Blue Ridge Mountains of Virginia

By Ruth Knight Bailey

Indians in Virginia's Racial Records, 1670–1963

In the year 1670, the English Colony of Virginia decided to classify American Indians as free people of color.[1] Then a 1705 colonial law stated that descendants of any Indian "should be deemed, accounted, held, and taken to be mulatto."[2] By 1793, Virginia required all free colored people to register with the state unless they wanted to be sold into slavery or jailed. However, the remoteness of the Blue Ridge Mountains made it possible for some people to be unaware of the registration requirements or to avoid visits from the sheriff.[3] Nonetheless, in the 1830s, some Indians in Virginia's Amherst County voluntarily registered as "free issue negroes" to keep from being driven from their homes onto the Trail of Tears.[4]

---

[1] Sherrie S. McLeRoy and William R. McLeRoy, *Strangers in Their Midst: The Free Black Population of Amherst County, Virginia* (Bowie MD: Pointer Ridge Place, 1993) 4.

[2] Samuel R. Cook, *Monacans and Miners: Native American and Coal Mining Communities in Appalachia* (Lincoln NE: University of Nebraska Press, 2000) 58–59, quoting William Walter Henning, ed., *Statutes at Large: Being a Collection of all the Laws of Virginia* (Philadelphia: DeSilver, 1823). See also Louise M. Hix, "Indians of Oronoco, Amherst County, Virginia" (Bear Mountain VA: St. Paul's Episcopal Church files, 1941).

[3] McLeRoy and McLeRoy, 7, 18.

[4] *Indian Removal Act*, Ch. 148, 4 Stat. 411 (1830); McLeRoy and McLeRoy, 41–42.

Due to increased state concerns about runaway slaves and a law requiring local sheriffs to list all free colored people, involuntary registrations increased in the 1850s. Despite this, by the end of the War Between the States in 1865, only a third of Amherst County residents who were required to register had actually registered.[5]

Most Caucasians in the eastern United States had long preferred that Indians live somewhere else. Not surprisingly, Amherst Indians tended to keep their ancestry private by blending into the mountain cultures where they lived, whether or not they ever registered as free issues.[6]

Although Northern abolitionists had severely criticized Southern slavery before slaves were freed in 1863–1865, most Northern free states had also passed comprehensive segregation laws well before 1860.[7] In contrast, Southern slave owners had consistently used frequent contact and association so as to maintain control of their slaves. It was only after slavery and post-war reconstruction ended that Southern state governments followed the Northern example in using mandatory separation of white and colored races to maintain white control.[8] For a few decades prior to 1860, free people of color—blacks and Indians—had formed their own communities without much intrusion from government. However, with the onset of Southern segregation, government suddenly placed free people of color into the same category as former slaves.[9]

---

[5] McLeRoy and McLeRoy, 18–19.

[6] McLeRoy and McLeRoy, 9–10, 41–42.

[7] These northern segregation laws excluded northern blacks from rail cars, omnibuses, stagecoaches, and steamboats or sent them to separate compartments. Northern segregation applied to churches, schools, prisons, hospitals, and cemeteries. C. Van Woodward, *The Strange Career of Jim Crow, 3rd Ed.* (Oxford: Oxford University Press, 1974) 18–19. See also the Emancipation Proclamation and the Constitution of the United States, Amendment XIII.

[8] Woodward, 18–25, 65–83, 140. In 1896, the United States Supreme Court upheld a state statute segregating white and colored races in railway carriages, clearly setting the precedent for all states in the nation (*Plessy v. Ferguson*, 163 US 537 [1896]). Virginia enacted its own "separate-but-equal" statutes in 1902. These provisions added to the statutes that had been in place, since 1691, to banish or imprison whites who intermarried with "negroes, mulattoes, or Indians." *Code of Virginia*, Chapter 4, § 28 (1902); *Code of Virginia*, Offences Against Chastity, Morality and Decency (1847–8); Chapter 17.1 (1866); Title 54 (1873); Chapter CLXXXV, §§ 3786, 3788, 3789; McLeRoy and McLeRoy, 4; Kareen Wood and Diane Shields, *The Monacan Indians: Our Story* (Madison Heights VA: Monacan Indian Nation, circa 1997) 27.

[9] Cook, 65.

In 1883, Sir Francis Galton, a cousin of the British naturalist, Charles Darwin, introduced a new science he called "Eugenics."[10] Eugenicists applied Darwinism, based upon Darwin's theory of human evolution, to explain why suppressing "defectives" and "inferior races" was part of "natural selection" and the will of God.[11] Well-respected scientists that studied in this field stressed the need for increased reproduction among persons considered of superior human stock and the need for decreased reproduction or sterilization among "inferior strains of humanity."[12] The Eugenics Record Office, centered in Cold Springs Harbor, New York, solicited massive family-history records from physicians, individuals, and local eugenics societies throughout the nation. The office then encouraged and assisted local governments in locating regions where "defectives" might be "breeding."[13]

On the 1880 Virginia Census, all Amherst Indians, who had registered as "Free Issues" before 1865, were listed as "mulattoes" or

---

[10] Mary V. Rorty, "Mormons and Genetics" (proposed paper presented at the SanFrancisco Sunstone Symposium, 2003), citing Francis Galton, *Inquiries into Human Faculty* (London: MacMillan and Company, 1883) 24–25. See also Paul Popenoe and Roswell Hill Johnson, *Applied Eugenics* (New York: MacMillan Company, 1933) 217–227.

[11] J. David Smith, *The Eugenic Assault on America: Studies in Red, White, and Black* (Fairfax VA: George Mason University Press, 1993) 2; Charles Benedict Davenport, *Heredity in Relation to Eugenics* (New York: Henry Holt and Company, 1913) iv–vi; Edward M. East, *Heredity and Human Affairs* (New York: Charles Schribner's Sons, 1927) 235.

[12] See, e.g., Edwin Grant Conklin, *Heredity and Environment in the Development of Men*, 5th ed. (Princeton: Princeton University Press, 1922); East; Samuel J. Holmes, *The Trend of the Race: A Study of Present Tendencies in the Biological Development of Civilized Mankind* (New York: Harcourt, Brace and Company, 1921); Popenoe and Johnson; Lothrop Stoddard, *The Rising Tide of Color Against White Supremacy* (New York: Scribner, 1920). See also Paul Lombardo, "Eugenics Bibliography," The Center for Biomedical Ethics at the University of Virginia (2004), online at www.healthsystem.virginia.edu/internet/bioethics, accessed 7 April 2004.

[13] Davenport, iv–vi. In the initial years of the eugenic movement, "defectives" included people deemed to be actual or potential criminals," imbeciles," "insane," "feeble-minded," or paupers. Soon the eugenicists included "inferior races." See, e.g., East, 157–204, 235; Popenoe and Johnson, 281–297.For example, the National Eugenics Record Office hired a eugenicist from Carnegie Institute and a professor from Sweet Briar College in Amherst County to study the Bear Mountain people. The resulting book, *Mongrel Virginians*, unfairly characterized the people as mentally defective and backward because of tri-racial mixed blood. Cook, 94; Peter Houck and Mintcy D. Maxham, *Indian Island in Amherst County* (Lynchburg VA: Warwick House Publishing, 1993) 84–89; J. David Smith, *Eugenic Assault*, 83–88. See Arthur H. Estabrook and Ivan E. McDougle, *Mongrel Virginians: The Win Tribe* (Baltimore: The Williams and Wilkins Company, 1926).

"blacks,"[14] but in the 1900 Census, all of the Amherst "M" notations inexplicably turned into "B"s.[15] By the turn of the twentieth century, most Virginians thought Indians no longer existed in the Commonwealth.[16]

In 1912, Dr. Walter Plecker took over as Director of Virginia Vital Statistics. With Plecker's assistance and the advice of some prestigious eugenicists,[17] prominent Virginians[18] successfully lobbied the Virginia General Assembly to pass The Racial Integrity Act of 1924. The Act required all Virginians to register as to race: "Caucasian, Negro, Mongolian, American Indian, Asiatic Indian, Malay, or any mixture thereof, or any other non-Caucasian strain."[19] It strictly prohibited whites from marrying people with *any* mixture of blood other than Caucasian, with one small exception for less than 1/16th of pure American-Indian blood.[20] Influential First Families of Virginia (FFVs), who claimed Princess Pocahontas as a distant ancestor, had effectively

CROSSROADS

---

[14] Cook, 68.

[15] Cook, 59, 68, 85.

[16]Buffalo Bill's Wild West Show and western novels had popularized stereotypical Indian images, which looked nothing like Virginia Indians. Most Americans thought Indians lived only on reservations. Cook, 57–68. *See also*, J. David Smith, *Eugenic Assault*; Hix; Houck and Maxham.

[17] Madison Grant authored *The Passing of the Great Race* (New York: Arno Press, 1916) and *The Conquest of a Continent* (New York: Charles Scribner's Sons, 1933). Harry H. Laughlin authored *Eugenical Sterilization in the United States* (Chicago: Psychopathic Laboratory of the Municipal Court of Chicago, 1922). Paul Lombardo, "Eugenics Laws Against Race Mixing," Image Archives of the American Eugenics Movement, DNA Learning Center of the Cold Springs Harbor Laboratory (2004), online at http://www.eugenicsarchive.org/html/eugenics/essay7text.html, accessed 7 April 2004.

[18] Two particularly powerful lobbyists were John Powell and Earnest Cox. Powell, a well-known composer, served as president of the Anglo-Saxon Clubs of America. Cox assisted in founding the Anglo-Saxon Clubs of America and wrote the book, *White America* (Richmond VA: White American Society, 1925), 13–57.

[19] This meant descendants of white Anglo-Europeans, black Africans, yellow Asians, red Native Americans, brown East Indians, and brown Polynesians. Derryn E. Moten, "Racial Integrity or 'Race Suicide'—Virginia's Eugenic Movement, W.E.B. Du Bois and the Work of Walter A. Plecker," *Negro History Bulletin* (1 April 1999) 6.

[20]Acts of Assembly, Chapter 371, Senate Bill 219, approved 20 March 1924.

lobbied to include the exception.[21] Plecker determined that any Virginian claiming Indian blood was really a "mixed-blood Negro," unless a Pocahantas exception could be proven, which proof was practically impossible for anybody other than FFVs. Furthermore, Plecker deemed any "mixture of blood" as the genetic cause of "defective children." In fact, light-skinned people with a few drops of "colored blood" ranked at the very bottom of Plecker's caste system, because their existence indicated a violation of the anti-miscegenation laws.[22]

Of course, previous Virginia anti-miscegenation statutes had more flexibly defined "colored" as more than one-fourth Negro blood, and "Indian" as non-colored with more than one-fourth Indian blood.[23] The Racial Integrity Act raised the bar considerably by declaring that if a person had any "discernable trace" of any color other than white, the law deemed him a "colored" person who posed a danger to the purity of the white race.[24]

Richmond bureaucrats apparently used the antebellum Amherst register of free issues to trace individuals named in the register down through descendants who had dutifully obtained birth, marriage, and death certificates. They tagged whole generations of family members who "passed" for white. They traced people with white vital statistics who married descendants of people who had registered as free issues before 1865.[25]

Two thirds of the Amherst Indians never registered as free issues in the first place, so the Act segregated Indians from each other because the Department of Vital Statistics labeled some as white and some as

---

[21] In the year 1614, British colonizer, John Rolfe, married Chief Powatan's daughter Pocohantas, at least partially "for the good of the nation." Cook, 57, quoting Sidney Kaplan, "Historical Efforts to Encourage White-Indian Intermarriage in the United States and Canada," *International Science Review* 65:3 (1990) 126–32.

[22] Cook, 66,104; Wood and Shields, 26.

[23] *Code of Virginia*, Chapter 17.1 (1866); Title 5, §49 (1887).

[24] With the exception of the Pocahontas loophole. Acts of Assembly, Chapter 371, Senate Bill 219, approved 20 March 1924.

[25] McLeRoy and McLeRoy, 17–18; Moten, 2.

black.[26] When Indians from the Bear Mountain community in Amherst County[27] tried to straighten out the red tape, they ended up calling Plecker's attention to them. Plecker went on the warpath, publicly identifying Amherst County as a region where "so-called Indians" would try to sneak into the white gene pool.[28] He extended his attack to Rockbridge County, asserting that the ancestors of many Irish Creek people had moved there from Bear Mountain.[29]

Insisting upon the support of white health workers, school administrators, and county officials, Plecker and the bureaucrats reporting to him actually changed notations on existing birth, marriage, and death-certificates from White, Indian, or Mulatto to Black.[30] Plecker even wrote threatening letters to mothers of new babies and ordered bodies exhumed from white cemeteries. He threatened local officials with the penitentiary if they issued white certificates against his wishes, and a few local officials went to prison over it.[31] In 1943, after some intense genealogical work, Plecker distributed widely a list of surnames to be subsequently classified as "Negroes by all registrars in the state of Virginia." He warned courthouse officials, health workers, and school administrators throughout Virginia to watch for "mongrels" who

---

[26]Houck and Maxham, 81.

[27] In 1896, Edgar Whitehead described the Bear Mountain people as Cherokee. Whitehead recorded their family stories of the 1830s, when clergymen first told the Bear Mountain Indian people to either sit with the slaves in church or leave—and they left. The children were not allowed to attend white schools. Because of Whitehead's article, a few Methodist and Baptist home missionaries visited Bear Mountain for the first time in fifty years, but they never stayed. Finally, the Episcopalians came in 1908 and built a mission church for Bear Mountain and turned the log meeting house into a mission school that served the community until 1963. Cook, 85–93; Houck and Maxham, 93–94; Wood and Shields, 23–25.

[28] Cook, 108–111. Plecker widely distributed John Powell's brochure entitled, *The Breach in the Dike: An Analysis of the Sorrels Case Showing the Danger to Racial Integrity From the Intermarriage of Whites with So-called Indians* (Richmond, VA: Anglo-Saxon Clubs of America, circa 1925).

[29] *See* "Irish Creek Wedding Plans Rattled State's Race Law," *The Advocate* (March 2003) 44, J. David Smith, *Eugenic Assault*, 91.

[30] Cook, 109.

[31] Cook, 107; Wood and Shields, 27–28.

changed their surnames and/or moved from Amherst or Rockbridge into other Virginia Counties.[32]

In the early 1980s, Peter W. Houck, a medical doctor in Lynchburg, Virginia, noticed that some of his patients had "copper skin, high cheek bones, and straight backs." These patients came from Bear Mountain in Amherst County. Dr. Houck's scholarly research, and his conversations with the people themselves, revealed a tight-knit community whose Native American identity had been completely lost to the dominant culture around it. Older individuals from Bear Mountain told Dr. Houck about their grandparents speaking "fluent Indian." Many others maintained detailed knowledge of native medicines and other elements of their ancestry. These aboriginal people remembered their heritage, but had stayed quiet about it in public. Houck wrote a book about them.[33] In 1989, the Commonwealth of Virginia recognized the Bear Mountain people as remnants of the ancient Monacan Indian Nation.[34]

Now some obscure Mormon-missionary diaries, church documents, and oral histories indicate that another tight-knit community with a similar history survives in nearby Rockbridge County, Virginia.

Mormon Missionaries in the Blue Ridge Mountains, 1883–1898

On December 30, 1883, Elders[35] J. Golden Kimball and Charles Welch stepped off the Shenandoah Railway car at Riverside Station in Rockbridge County, Virginia. They represented the Church of Jesus

---

[32] "Surnames by Counties and Cities (illegible word) Virginia Families Striving to Pass as 'Indian' and/or White," with the cover letter from W. A. Plecker addressed to "Local Registrars, Physicians, Health Officers, Nurses, School Superintendents and Clerks of the Courts," January 1943 (photocopies in possession of the author).

[33] Cook, 57-68; Houck and Maxham. See also, Horace R. Rice, *The Buffalo Ridge Cherokee: The Colors and Culture of a Virginia Community* (Madison Heights VA: BRC Books, 1991).

[34] Houck and Maxham, iv–vii.

[35] Although a missionary might be young in years, the title "Elder" indicated priesthood rank and call to mission work. Leonard J. Arrington and David Bitton, *The Mormon Experience: A History of the Latter-day Saints* (Urbana: University of Illinois Press, 1992) 206–07.

Christ of Latter-day Saints. Members of their church called themselves "Saints" or "Latter-day Saints," according to the Bible. Almost everybody else called them "Mormons."[36]

On January 11, 1884, in a hard rain, the two repeatedly waded the icy Pedlar Creek[37] as it wound along the remote tops of the Blue Ridge Mountains in Amherst County, Virginia. Eventually they found the home of a referral named "Mr. Mason." Glad to have arrived safely, Kimball wrote, "I could not stand erect in the house. They had two beds and nine of us to stow away. It was accomplished but how I cannot tell."[38]

A few days later, the elders made their way to a nearby schoolhouse where they were supposed to preach. A "Dunkard exhorter" finished his prayer meeting and then served them with a notice from the school commissioner forbidding them to use the school. So they stood outside in the snow, singing hymns. Mr. Mason insisted that they spend another night with his family and urged them to come there "any time…night or day."[39]

On January 20, 1884, twenty people "who did not belong to any church" showed up to hear the elders preach. Appalachian uplanders

[36] Originally, in 1830, the name of the church was "The Church of Christ." In 1838, its leader and prophet, Joseph Smith, said he received a revelation changing the name to "The Church of Jesus Christ of Latter-day Saints." The change emphasized the restoration of the primitive gospel of Jesus Christ and the relationship of Jesus Christ to members in the Latter-days. It also reflected the Biblical injunction to avoid being called by the "name of a man." "Saints" was a more Biblically appropriate nickname than "Mormonite" or "Mormon." Rom 1:7; 1 Cor 1:2; Eph 1:1; Eph 4:12. See also *Doctrine and Covenants* 115:4; *Book of Mormon*, 3 Nephi 27:8; and B. H. Roberts, *A Comprehensive History of The Church of Jesus Christ of Latter-day Saints, Volume 1* (Salt Lake City UT: Deseret News Press, 1930) 392–93. However, Latter-day Saints good-naturedly tolerate use of the nickname "Mormon." This paper uses the terms interchangeably.

[37] Elders J. Golden Kimball and Charles Welch rode the Shenandoah Railway into Riverside Station in Rockbridge County, VA, where they struggled in the mud to get up and over the ridge of the mountains to Oronoco (J. Golden Kimball journal, 30 December 1883, University of Utah archives, Salt Lake City UT). A few months later, Elder Joseph Underwood Eldredge said that the missionary "diagram" he used to get up to Pedlar Creek was "about as comprehensive and useful as a map of the Valley of Jehosephat." He described Oronoco as "merely a post office," noting that people lived "in a scattered condition in the woods." Michael W. Eldredge, ed., *The Mission Journals of Joseph Underwood Eldredge, Virginia Conference of the Southern States Mission* (Salt Lake City UT: Mill Creek Press, 1992) 3–4 November 1884.

[38] J. Golden Kimball journal, 11 January 1884.

[39] J. Golden Kimball journal, 13 January 1884.

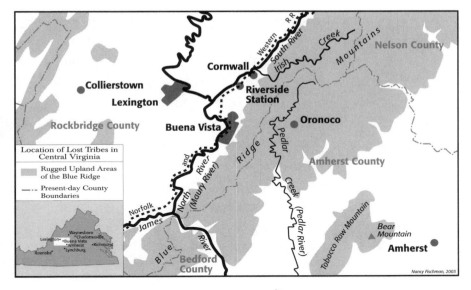

often worshiped with obvious emotion.[40] Yet, these upland listeners stood "without spirit" in the winter cold. After the elders preached for more than an hour, not one person said a word about the sermon. This discouraged Kimball. Then, surprisingly, most of the people quietly asked the missionaries to call on them at home.[41]

The elders discovered that tiny log houses dotted the craggy landscape. Many belonged to members of the Mason family. One day John Mason took Kimball and Welch up to the cabin belonging to his parents, Peter Mason and Diannah Sorrells Mason. Fifteen unusual family members gathered to meet them.[42] That night, Elder Kimball wrote in his journal:

---

[40] For example, Elder Joseph Underwood Eldredge described a woman at a revival "crying and rocking herself as [he had] seen a female Indian do when grieving for dead friends" (Joseph Underwood Eldredge journal, 23 August 1885). J. Golden Kimball described "incoherant prayers which were mixed up with groans and moans" (J. Golden Kimball journal, 13 January 1884, 5 March 1884). See also Newell Kimball journal, 11 May 1884 (Salt Lake City UT: Archives of the Church of Jesus Christ of Latter-day Saints, hereinafter "LDS Archives").

[41] J. Golden Kimball journal, 20 January 1884.

[42] J. Golden Kimball journal, 23 January 1884.

[A] stranger sight I never saw. He [Peter Mason] was seventy years old. [He] was born and raised at this same place (top of the Blue Ridge Mts). He was of Indian descent, his skin being almost as dark as an Indian's. His hair was long and black. Mrs. Mason—his wife—was very old. She said what she thought and was somewhat of a doctress. They had seventeen children—twelve boys and five girls. Children and grandchildren about forty-two. Indian blood was discernable in most of their faces. Look which way you might—poverty was everywhere to be seen. They were but little ahead of the Indian people in education. None of them had ever belonged to a church of any kind.[43]

If the elders had seen any indication that a group of Native Americans lived along Pedlar Creek at the top of the Blue Ridge, they would have sought them out as "chosen people" just as other elders had sought out the Catawba Indians in South Carolina[44] and the Cherokee Indians in North Carolina.[45] Yet, no Indian reservation existed in Amherst County, Virginia.[46] The area looked like a fairly typical Appalachian mountain community, except that the missionaries—who were very familiar with western Indians[47]—clearly recognized these par-

[43] J. Golden Kimball journal, 23 January 1884. In 1992, Alvin Woodrow Coleman and Garvis Wheeler mentioned several people who had remembered their great-grandfather, Peter H. Mason, when he was very old. All described Peter Mason as an "Indian" with long, straight, "coal black" hair that "hung down to his hips." Alvin Woodrow Coleman and Garvis Wheeler, interviews by author, 27 December 1992.

[44] Nearly all members of the Siouan-speaking Cawtawba Nation joined Mormonism in the 1880s. See Charles M. Hudson, *The Catawba Nation* (Athens GA: University of Georgia Press, 1970); Jerry D. Lee, "A Study of the Influence of the Mormon Church on the Catawba Indians of South Carolina" (master's thesis, Brigham Young University, 1976); *Columbia South Carolina Stake Fortieth Anniversary* (Columbia SC, 1987) 11–14, 199–204.

[45] Andrew Jensen, *Encyclopedic History of the Church of Jesus Christ of Latter-day Saints* (Salt Lake City UT, 1941) 821; *Columbia South Carolina Stake Fortieth Anniversary*, 13–14, 201, quoting the *Deseret* (UT) *News*, 31 July 1885. See also E. S. (initials only) "In the Hands of the Lawless: A Missionary's Experience in North Carolina," *Deseret News*, 20 April 1887.

[46] But see Hix; Houck and Maxham; Rice; Wood and Shields.

[47] See Arrington and Bitton, 145–158; David J. Whittaker, "Mormons and Native Americans: A Historical and Bibliographical Introduction," *Dialogue: A Journal of Mormon Thought*, 18/4 (Winter 1985) 33–64.

Mary Agnes Mason Duff, daughter of Peter and Diannah Mason. Photo courtesy of Garvis and Juanita Wheeler.

ticular uplanders as "Lamanites."[48] Elder Newell Kimball even described Peter Mason as a "full-blooded Lamanite";[49] Latter-day Saints often used the *Book of Mormon* term "Lamanite" to mean "American Indian."[50] In the *Book of Mormon*, the Israelite prophet Lehi brought his family from Jerusalem to the Americas during Old Testament times. To

---

[48] Newell Kimball journal, 11 May 1884. The fact that several missionaries who visited Pedlar Creek did not mention skin color, with regard to the Masons, indicates that they did not consider them black. The elders mentioned black skin so often in other communities that they surely would have mentioned it in this one had they seen it. See, e.g., Joseph Underwood Eldredge journal, 1884–1885; Newell Kimball journal, 1882–1884; Peter Peterson journal, 1888–1889 (LDS Archives).

[49] Newell Kimball journal, 4 June 1884.

[50] See Terryl L. Givens, *By the Hand of Mormon: The American Scripture that Launched a New World Religion* (New York: Oxford University Press, 2002), 99, 127.

Latter-day Saints, this made modern Indians a precious remnant of one of the Lost Tribes of Israel, who would gather in an American Zion to welcome the second coming of the Messiah. They believed that God especially favored Indians.[51]

The Masons and their upland neighbors often confused the missionaries by saying that they had never been baptized into any religion, but that they loved the Bible. In fact, Kimball said that Peter Mason "was deeply imbued with the doctrine of the Old Primitive Baptists." The old man asked the missionaries to come again and again, said he would like to be in their company all the time, and repeatedly "God blessed" them. Tears rose in Peter Mason's eyes when they read the Bible with him. But he felt no call to baptism. In the old upland way, he had to wait until God told him it was time, and not the other way around.[52]

"Mother Mason" healed the sick with herbal medicines.[53] The elders helped her by anointing ailing people with consecrated oil and by laying hands upon them.[54]

"Father Mason" warned the elders not to visit Old Man Vest and his family, because the Vests were "dangerous." In spite of the warning, the missionaries climbed Stight Cove Mountain in the snow to visit the Vests. Old Levi Vest "declared himself to be a great reasoner, reader of

---

[51] Latter-day Saints believed that people of Israelite lineage had special responsibility to gather together to welcome the second coming of the Messiah. They thought the Tribe of Judah would gather in Jerusalem to welcome the Messiah, who was of the lineage of Judah. However, the Messiah would also appear in the western hemisphere as he had done in *Book of Mormon* times. Native Americans, who had descended from the Tribe of Joseph through Manasseh, had special responsibility to welcome the Messiah. White gentiles with "believing blood" could be "adopted" into Israel, as part of the lineage of Joseph's son, Ephraim, and help with the American welcoming. See *Gen 9; Gal 3:7;* Givens, *By the Hand of Mormon,* 67–69; Armand Mauss, *All Abraham's Children: Changing Mormon Conceptions of Race and Lineage* (Urbana: University of Illinois Press, 2003) 2–4, 43.

[52] J. Golden Kimball journal, 23–24 January 1884; 3 March 1884. Peter H. Mason was finally baptized 21 May 1888. International Genealogical Index, LDS Ordinance Records, FamilySearch.org. It was commonplace for Appalachian uplanders to wait years for baptism or to never opt for baptism. Deborah Vansau McCauley, *Appalachian Mountain Religion: A History* (Urbana and Chicago: University of Illinois Press, 1995) 14–17, 21, 101.

[53] J. Golden Kimball journal, 24 January 1884; Newell Kimball journal, 2 June 1884.

[54] J. Golden Kimball journal, 24 January 1884; Peter Peterson journal, 1 December 1889, 20 March 1889.

the Bible and a Lover of the Word of God." Kimball wrote that Vest was an "Old Iron Side Baptist, Hard Shell." Kimball hadn't had much luck baptizing "Primitive Baptists" in the past; but he didn't think old Levi Vest or any of the Vest sons would hurt him, and they did not.[55]

However, all Mormon missionaries feared the mob violence that sometimes formed against them. Although the Ku Klux Klan and other mobs mainly targeted Negroes, they also terrorized people they considered "social deviants," including Mormons.[56]

In the early days of Mormonism, from 1830 to 1846, the Church had been unique in that it was somewhat color-blind. Joseph Smith's writings did indicate that lineage mattered to God, with Israelites receiving covenant promises first and the descendants of Cain receiving them last.[57] However, the early church also welcomed all converts, "black and white, bond and free."[58] All people sat together in meetings, including

---

[55] J. Golden Kimball journal, 5 March 1884. One should not confuse Appalachian Mountain Baptists with mainstream Baptist denominations. Historian J.H. Spencer wrote in 1885 that the various sects of Baptists in the Appalachian Mountains had "seceded" from the "real" Baptists even though they hung onto the name. McCauley, 23, citing J.H. Spencer, *A History of Kentucky Baptists from 1769 to 1885*, revised and corrected by Mrs. Burrilla B. Spencer (Cincinnati: J. R. Baumes, 1885) (reprint in Gallatin, TN: Church History Research and Archives, 1984).

[56] "Mormon Elders Reported Murdered by Masked Men in Tennessee," *Deseret* (UT) *Evening News*, 12 August 1884; "What a Man from Evansville Learned in Tennessee," *Deseret Evening News*, 2 September 1884. Heather M. Seferovich, *History of the Southern States Mission, 1875–1898* (master's thesis, Brigham Young University, 1996) 123–37: William Whitridge Hatch, *Mormons in the Southern States: A Century of Religious Bigotry, Murder, and Civil Mayhem*, 1831–1923 (self-published, 2003, 1-932203-20-6); *Columbia South Carolina*, 215, quoting an article from the *New York Sun*, 26 July 1887 (KKK raid on Mormon meeting near Augusta, GA); J.T. Heninger, Correspondence, *Deseret News*, 7 February 1884; Newell Kimball journal, 27 April 1884, 18 May 1884; Henry Charles Eddington journal, 26 February 1887 (LDS Archives); Peter Peterson journal, 29–30 November 1888, 28 July 1889; Thomas C. Romney journal, 24 February 1898 (LDS Archives). See also Milo A. Hendricks' letter to Josiah Burrows, 23 December 1887 (later published in the Deseret Evening News, 10 February 1888) and John W. Tate, letter to his wife Lizzie (23 December 1887, in possession of descendant Barbara Jo Lee Baldwin). These letters describe mobsters near Irish Creek, in Rockbridge County, VA seriously injuring Elders Tate and Hendricks by blasting them with double-barreled shotguns. They also threatened to cut the elders' hearts out with razors.

[57] Joseph Smith, *History of the Church of Jesus Christ of Latter-day Saints, Volume II, 2nd ed.* (Salt Lake City UT: Deseret News Press, 1948) 436–440. See Mauss, 2–3.

[58] *Book of Mormon*, 2 Nephi 26:33. In the 1830s, Missourians drove the Saints out of Missouri—a slave state—partly because potential immigration of free blacks Saints was perceived as "tampering with slaves." Joseph Smith, *History of the Church of Jesus Christ of Latter-day Saints, Volume I, 2nd ed.* (Salt Lake City UT: Deseret News Press, 1951) 377–379; Arrington and Bitton, 48–49.

the few free-black members. All faithful men held the lay priesthood, including at least two blacks.[59]

Then, in 1852, Utah governor and prophet, Brigham Young, asked the Territorial Legislature to pass "An Act in Relation to Service." The act legalized slavery in the Territory, though very few blacks lived there. Young's statement to the legislature also denied priesthood ordination to Negro Latter-day Saints.[60]

---

[59] Both Elijah Abel and Walker Lewis were ordained elders in the time of Joseph Smith. Abel was also ordained a seventy (the ordination higher than elder) and he served three full-time missions for the Church. Newell C. Bringhurst, *Saints, Slaves, and Blacks* (Westport CT: Greenwood Press, 1981) 35–53, 90; Lester Bush, Jr., "Mormonism's Negro Doctrine: An Historical Overview," *Dialogue: A Journal of Mormon Thought*, 8/1(1973) 17, 33.

[60] Brigham Young, statement to the Utah Territorial Legislature, 5 February 1852. See also, Bringhurst, 25. Mormon doctrine condemned "human bondage." *Book of Mormon,* Alma 27:9 and Mosiah 2:13; *Doctrine and Covenants* 98:5; 104:16–18, 83–84. Joseph Smith had once run for president on an anti-slavery platform, but the Saints deeply distrusted abolitionists. As a result, Latter-day Saints attempted to remain detached from both sides of the national controversy over slavery. By 1850, only twenty-four free blacks and sixty or seventy southern-immigrant slaves lived in the isolated Latter-day Saint communities. However, Mormons periodically bought Indian children out of the irrepressible Indian-Mexican slave trade, so as to free them and nurture them. The Act in Relation to Service obviously protected the adoption of Indian slave children. It protected the few slave owners in Utah. Certainly, Young and his advisors remembered Missouri violence in the 1830s, directed against Mormon policies that appeared to welcome free blacks to that slave state. Historians speculate that the Act might have been intended to maintain southern sympathy in a US Congress, which was becoming increasingly hostile to Mormon interests. They speculate that the Act may have made Utah look more attractive to southern converts. Possibly Governor Young wanted to defend Utahans against Republican writers from back east, who accused Mormons of miscegenation that produced "an inferior race of people." Most devout members of the Church avoided speculation, because they believed that Brigham Young spoke for God. In any event, the official priesthood ban stayed in place until a revelation removed it in 1978. Arrington and Bitton, 150–151; Bringhurst, 54–56, 66–68, 99–100; 110; 126–30; 225. See also O. Kendall White, Jr., "Boundary Maintenance, Blacks, and the Mormon Priesthood," *The Journal of Religious Thought*, 37:2 (Fall–Winter, 1980–81). Joseph Smith's early translations of some Egyptian papyri, canonized in 1880, were used to explain the priesthood denial. *Pearl of Great Price*, Abraham 1:1–27; Moses 7:8, 12, 22. See Mauss, 238–241. Smith's translation lined up with a large body of eighteenth and nineteenth-century European writing interpreting Genesis 4:15 to mean that the Lord marked Cain and his descendants with a black skin. By the mid-nineteenth century, these writers interpreted Genesis 9 to mean that Noah's son, Ham, married one of Cain's descendants and thereby perpetuated the black race and its curse. Stephen R. Haynes, *Noah's Curse: The Biblical Justification for Slavery* (London: Oxford University Press, 2003) 15-16, 99; Mauss, 238. The *Book of Mormon* told of a curse upon the Lamanites, as well. The *Book of Mormon* promised that repentance would lift the curse to offer full salvation to all people, "black and white, bond and free." *Book of Mormon.*, 2 Nephi 26:25, 33; 30:6.

As reconstruction ended and government-sponsored segregation began in the South,[61] former abolitionists in the Northeast turned their full attention toward Mormons. Political cartoons in Republican newspapers began showing polygamous Mormons allying themselves with other dangerous minorities by marrying them and giving birth to mixed breeds of every ethnic origin.[62] Federal government officials accused Mormons of stirring up western Indians by promising them a restoration of ancient greatness.[63] Mainstream Protestant ministers accused Mormons of barbarism and immorality.[64]

In some ways, it must have been a relief for the elders to journey into the Blue Ridge Mountains and find a different set of challenges. For instance, one day Hannah Mason announced that she was getting baptized "on Monday at eleven o'clock." This was news to the elders. First, they were not entirely sure that she had studied long enough to understand the doctrine.[65] Secondly, it didn't look like most of the Masons could prove they were married;[66] Latter-day Saint rules forbade the baptizing of people living in sin. They finally brought up the delicate subject. Hannah and John said they could prove they had been married

[61] Garth N. Jones, "James Thompson Lisonbee: San Luis Valley Gathering, 1876–78," *Journal of Mormon History*, 28/1 (Spring 2002) 228. See Woodward, 31–65.

[62] Davis Bitton, "Troublesome Bedfellows: Mormons and Other Minorities," in *The Mormon Graphic Image: Cartoons, Caricatures, and Illustrations, 1834–1914* (Salt Lake City UT: University of Utah Press, 1983) 75–94. Brigham Young encouraged Anglos and Indians to intermarry, and emphasized real marriages rather than concubine arrangements. Mauss, 64.

[63] Arrington and Bitton, 156–157; Garold D. Barney, *Mormons, Indians, and the Ghost Dance Religion* (Lanham MD: University Press of America, 1986) 69–228; Lawrence Coates, "The Mormons and the Ghost Dance," *Dialogue, A Journal of Mormon Thought*, 18/4 (Winter 1985) 89–111; Givens, *By the Hand of Mormon*, 96; Gregory E. Smoak, "The Mormons and the Ghost Dance of 1890," *South Dakota History*, 16/3 (Fall 1986) 269–294. See *Book of Mormon*, title page; 2 Nephi 6:13–18; 2 Nephi 9:1–3; 2 Nephi 30:3–6.

[64] Arrington and Bitton, 177–179. See also Horace Bushnell, *Barbarism: The First Danger: A Discourse for Home Missions* (New York: The American Home Mission Society, 1847) 5–27; Newel Kimball journal, 27 April 1884; Joseph Bourne Clark, *Leavening the Nation: the Story of American Home Missions* (New York: The Baker and Taylor Co., 1903) 238; Platt Ward, ed. *Methodism and the Republic: A View of the Home Field, Present Conditions, Needs and Possibilities* (Philadelphia: The Board of Home Missions and Church Extension of the Methodist Episcopal Church, 1912) 89.

[65] J. Golden Kimall journal, 24 January 1884; 3 February 1884; 4 February 1884.

[66] J. Golden Kimball journal, 29 January 1884.

seventeen years.[67] Then Peggy Sorrells told the missionaries that Marvel Mason had been living with her daughter without marrying her.[68]

Although many in the neighborhood avoided recorded documents, others willingly procured the proper marriage licenses and baptismal certificates.[69] It appeared to the missionaries that the white uplanders on Pedlar Creek assimilated with the Indians, rather than the other way around. Or perhaps they had had Indian ancestry all along. In any event, the "Mason Neighborhood" on Pedlar Creek served as the hub of the community. It also became a Mormon-mission headquarters for the Virginia Conference of the Southern States mission.[70] At the same time, as directed by the centralized priesthood hierarchy, the missionaries continually urged the Pedlar people to move to the American Zion in Utah and nearby territories. Households began to immigrate west,[71] including two Mason daughters and their families.[72]

As the months went by, a constant arrival of western elders moved from family to family along Pedlar Creek. One end of the Pedlar Creek community came near the Irish Creek community, in Rockbridge County, where the elders found more uplanders who opened their homes and their hearts to Mormonism.[73] On February 15, 1888, Elder John W. Tate wrote his wife, telling her that several members from Irish Creek prepared to immigrate in the spring provided they could raise the

---

[67] J.Golden Kimball journal, 3 February 1884.

[68] J. Golden Kimball journal, 18 February 1884. From the context of J. Golden Kimball's journal, it appears that Marvel Mason was the "Mr. Mason" who initially assisted Elders Kimball and Welch on Pedlar Creek.

[69] Index to Ward Record of Members and Children of the Virginia Conference of the Virginia Conference of the Southern States Mission, 1875–1930, hereinafter "Index of Members" (LDS Archives).

[70] J. Golden Kimball journal, 17 January 1884; Peter Peterson journal, 4 October 1888 to 27 September 1889. See also *Southern Star*, 1/234 (28 September 1884); "Virginia Conference," *Deseret News*, 20 October 1884; N. L. Nelson, "Conference in Virginia," *Deseret News*, 13 September 1886; "The Outlook in Virginia," *Deseret News*, 13 October 1886; Josiah Burrows, "Conference in Virginia," *Deseret News*, 20 October 1887.

[71] See immigration notes in the margins of the Index of Members. Many families gathered to Manassas, Colorado, although some went to Utah, Idaho, and Arizona.

[72] Sarah Mason Whitmore and Susan Mason Knowles. International Genealogical Index, Familysearch.com.; Peter Peterson journal, 21 May 1889.

[73] Irish Creek residents housed at least nine elders when they met for a conference on 15–16 October 1887. Josiah Borrows, "Conference in Virginia," *Deseret Evening News,* 20 October 1887.

money. He added, "It is in the mountains we are called to labor, among the timber, hills, holes, and rocks. It is only the poor that will receive the gospel. There are no Saints in the valleys, people are better off down there and will not listen."[74]

The Pedlar and Irish Creek communities touched a lofty tip of Nelson County, Virginia, where a group of "Campbellites"[75] asked for rebaptism as Latter-day Saints. Milton Fitzgerald, their minister of sixteen years, led them west to Zion.[76] Historic overlaps between some restorationist beliefs of the Campbellites and the Latter-day Saints may also explain why Mormon elders of the 1880s generally received a warmer welcome from religious people in the mountains of Appalachia than they received from mainstream Protestants in the valleys below.[77]

None of these Mormon elders of the 1880s predicted the dramatic political changes of the 1890s that would take them out of the mountains and into the towns down in the valleys. Change came for the missionaries when the Church ended its priesthood domination over

[74] John W. Tate, letter to his wife Lizzie (in possession of descendant Barbara Jo Lee Baldwin), 15 February 1888.

[75] Disciples of Christ, as well as members of the Churches of Christ and the Christian Churches (often called Campbellites by outsiders) believed in a restoration of the primitive church of the New Testament. They called themselves "Disciples" or "Christians," because they did not follow anyone but Christ and rejected all denominationalism. The practices of the non-centralized Churches of Christ and Christian Churches shared many practices with "Primitive Baptists" and other independent upland religious people. G. R. Hand, *Dr. Ray's Textbook on Campbellism, Exposed* (Washington, DC: Christian Publishing Co., 1880) vi; Terryl L. Givens, *The Viper on the Hearth: Mormons, Myths, and the Construction of Heresy* (Oxford: Oxford University Press, 1997) 68; McCauley, 65–68; Frank S. Mead and Samuel S. Hill, *Handbook of Denominations in the United States*, 11th ed. (Nashville: Abingdon Press, 2001) 103–113.

[76] Index of Members (immigrated to San Pete County, Utah in November 1890). See Peter Peterson journal, June–August, 1889.

[77] Sidney Rigdon, a sophisticated Campbellite minister and close associate of Alexander Campbell, helped bring forth the Stone-Campbell Restoration Movement on the Appalachian frontier in the 1820s. Rigdon later believed that Joseph Smith's latter-day visions provided miraculous proof of the restoration of primitive Christianity. He and his large congregation converted to Mormonism in Ohio in 1831. Rigdon then helped develop many of the religious practices inherent to Mormonism. Claudia Lauper Bushman and Richard Lyman Bushman, *Building the Kingdom: A History of Mormons in America* (Oxford: Oxford University Press, 2001) 12; Givens, *By the Hand of Mormon*, 67, 158–159; Henry E. Webb, *In Search of Christian Unity: A History of the Restoration Movement* (Cincinnati: Standard Publishing, 1990) 142–43. See also J. H. Milburn, *Origin of Campbellism* (Chicago: Regan Printing House, 1913) title page, 34–51.

Utah politics, its support of plural marriage, and its intense efforts to physically gather the Lost Tribes of Israel. The federal government recognized Utah as the forty-fifth state in 1896, and Latter-day Saints began to assimilate into a more middle-class mode of American life.[78] At the same time, both industrialization[79] and segregation[80] dramatically altered the lives of the Appalachian uplanders who had so kindly cared for the elders over the years.

Industrial Boom and Administrative Change, 1890–1918

With regard to the people on Pedlar and Irish Creeks, the first indication of change came in the form of a big boomtown named Buena Vista, in Rockbridge County, Virginia, at the foot of the Blue Ridge Mountains. On April 30, 1890, Elder Edward J. Eardley wrote home to describe developers grading streets and laying water pipes in what had been a "fertile plain devoted to agriculture." Two railroads brought guests to four spacious new hotels. The "splendid" Hotel Buena Vista sat high on a hill with a "charming view of the new town and the North River." The railway companies loaded their freight cars with goods from the newly built iron works and paper manufacturers along the river, as well as from the new tannery, saddle company, wagon firm, and fence supplier.[81]

While valley people welcomed the booming job market, they expressed concern about the "influx" of laborers "from Amherst on the

---

[78] For discussion of these changes, see Thomas G. Alexander, *Mormonism in Transition: A History of the Latter-day Saints, 1890–1930* (Urbana: University of Illinois Press, 1996).

[79] Royster Lyle, Jr., "Buena Vista and its Boon, 1889–1891," *Proceedings of the Rockbridge Historic Society*, Volume 8 (1971). See generally David E. Whisnant, *All that Is Native and Fine: The Politics of Culture in an American Region* (Chapel Hill: University of North Carolina Press, 1983).

[80] *Plessy v. Ferguson*, 163 US 537 (1896); *Code of Virginia*, Chapter 4, Section 28 (1902). For an excellent overview of segregation in the United States, see C. Van Woodward, *The Strange Career of Jim Crow, 3rd Ed.*, (Oxford: Oxford University Press, 1974).

[81] Edward J. Eardley letter, *Deseret Weekly*, 30 April 1890. See also Oren F. Morton, *A History of Rockbridge County* (Staunton VA: The McClure Co., 1920) 154; Royster Lyle, Jr., "Buena Vista and Its Boom, 1889–1891," *Proceedings of the Rockbridge Historic Society*, Volume 8 (1971).

other side of the Blue Ridge." Townspeople described the new workers as "a rough, disorderly element, partly white and partly colored."[82]

Beginning in 1895, Latter-day Saint elders moved most of their missionary efforts down from the Amherst County mountains into Buena Vista below.[83] Jobs brought some of the younger Masons down into town, where they continued to open their doors to the elders.

On December 22, 1895, Elder Thomas Romney and his companion visited the mayor of nearby Lexington at his "beautiful brick mansion" and had "a long friendly talk" with him. The mayor loved hearing Romney's stories about Mexico. He promised Romney that Mormons could preach on the streets anytime they wanted and that the laws of the city would always protect them.[84]

Later on the same day, Elder Romney wrote, "We find in the east end of the city two or three families of Saints by the name of Mason who were baptized in Amherst County…. They are reported to be part niggar." Romney spent that night with one of the Mason families, in spite of the "reports."[85]

A couple of years later, Elder David Call's diary added that "some of the members" in Rockbridge County "are part nigar" and that "some of the leaders years ago baptized them through a mistake." Call wrote, "They said they was Indian but I don't." Call stayed overnight with members near Collierstown, rather than with the Masons.[86]

[82] Morton, 154.

[83] In 1895 and 1896, the southern states mission president counseled all elders to discourage immigration, to organize local congregations, and to ordain lay priesthood leaders for those congregations. Elias Kimball letters to Southern States missionaries, 23 May 1895 and 25 March 1896 (LDS archives).

[84] Thomas Romney journal, 22 December 1895. Thomas Romney's father had moved his wives and families to Mexico when the federal government outlawed polygamy. Romney's mission journal does not say whether he told the mayor why his family lived in Mexico. See Catharine Cottam Romney and Jennifer Moulton Hansen, eds., *Letters of Catharine Cottam Romney, Plural Wife* (Urbana: University of Illinois Press, 1992).

[85] Thomas Romney journal, 22 December 1895. It may be worth noting here that the N-Word "did not originate as a slur, but took on a derogatory connotation over time." Randall Kennedy, "'Nigger': The Strange Career of a Troublesome Word," *Washington Post* (11 January 2001) 256.

[86] David Call journal, 3 September 1897 (LDS Archives).

No previous missionary to Pedlar or Irish Creek had mentioned anything about black people. Neither did any of the copious records that had been sent to Salt Lake. The people did not look African-American. Yet the rumors persisted.[87]

In 1895 and 1896, President Elias Kimball, of the Southern States Mission, directed all Southern-states missionaries to shift their emphasis from rural service to city service. He also told missionaries that members "should be restrained as much as possible from emigrating." He counseled missionaries to organize locally-led "branches and Sunday schools" wherever there were enough members to gather into a small group. He wrote, "Select good men and ordain them priests to preside over the branches, and efficient instructors to take charge of the Sunday schools."[88] Elders obeyed this counsel throughout the uplands of Appalachia, usually ordaining local men whose families had faithfully harbored the elders for years.[89]

The mission president's major shift of focus freed missionaries to spend the bulk of their time in more populated areas where prejudice against Mormons had lessened. Official church records show priesthood ordinations taking place for local men in various rural areas of Virginia during this time, so as to comply with the mission president's instructions. However, none of the ordinations took place in Amherst or Rockbridge Counties. Tiny Sunday Schools could be held without priesthood, but where enough members existed to form a "branch" or "ward," local priesthood became a necessity.[90]

The church records for Amherst and Rockbridge Counties between 1897 and 1918 show a distinct pattern of growth that clearly took them into the "branch" or "ward" range:

---

[87] Amherst's antebellum register of free blacks included the names of Peter and "Deannah" Mason, together with seven of their children. McLeRoy and McLeRoy, 177.

[88] Elias Kimball letters to Southern States missionaries, 23 May 1895 and 25 March 1896 (LDS archives).

[89] Index of Members, Ordinations, 40. See also F. W. Neve, "Some Mountain Missions in Virginia," *The Spirit of Missions: An Illustrated Monthly Review of Christian Missions.* 66/12 (December 1901) 806–807.

[90] "Ordinations," Index of Members, 40. For a discussion of Latter-day Saint congregational organization (branches, wards, and stakes), see Arrington and Bitton, 206–19, 292–93.

From 1897 to 1912, elders established locally-led Sunday Schools in Collierstown, Oronoco (Pedlar Creek), Buena Vista, and Cornwall (Irish Creek).[91]

June 15, 1918. Five hundred people attended the Latter-day Saint meeting in Buena Vista. Missionaries wrote, "It completely blocked the street; much literature was disposed of and several invitations to homes were received by elders."[92]

July 13, 1918. A missionary wrote, "The Saints in Buena Vista are anxious to have a church built of their own. They have subscribed over four hundred dollars for that purpose. The site chosen is in the Long Hollow near Brother Coleman's residence."[93]

August 24, 1918. The branch conference held in Buena Vista was so big that it filled the Star Theater for both meetings.[94]

---

[91] On 10 October 1897, missionaries organized a Sunday School in the mountains near Collierstown with Joseph Knick as superintendent. The Collierstown Sunday School was reorganized 5 May 1917 and local members built a church house at about the same time. Ethnicity was never an issue in Collierstown. See "Sunday Schools Organized," Index of Members, 290; Southern States Manuscript History (hereinafter MH) (Salt Lake City UT: Church of Jesus Christ of Latter-day Saints, LDS Archives) 16 August 1916; 4 June 1916; and 5 May 1916. On 17 October 1897. Missionaries organized a Sunday School in the mountains near Oronoco with James W. Stinnette as superintendent and Mary L. Mason as secretary. "Sunday Schools Organized," Index of Members, 290. On 24 February 1898, missionaries organized a Sunday School in Buena Vista with Elmer Crown as superintendent. After the organization of the Sunday School, an armed mob confronted Elders Thomas Romney and Joseph B. Kendall, threatening to whip them with hickory switches and shoot them. After keeping the elders up most of the night, the mobsters put both of them on the train to Basic City (now part of Waynesboro) in Augusta County, VA, warning that they would kill them if they ever came back. MH 24 February 1898; David M. Mayfield, Assistant Church Librarian Archivist, letter to Aubrey Coleman, 22 April 1976 (Buena Vista, VA: Church of Jesus Christ of Latter-day Saints, Buena Vista Stake Family History Library, hereinafter "BV Family History Library"). On 8 July 1911, Elder Isaac C. MacFarlane reorganized the Buena Vista Sunday School with Jacob Mason as superintendent and George Coleman as his assistant. MH 8 July 1911. On 17 August 1912, missionaries organized a Sunday School near Cornwall with R.M. Southers as superintendent. MH 17 August 1912.

[92] MH, 15 June 1918; *Liahona*, Chattanooga TN: Southern States Mission (1918) 16:895.

[93] MH 13 July 1918; *Liahona*, Chattanooga TN: Southern States Mission (1918) 16:942.

[94] A priesthood holder, named R. S. Gilley, helped with the conference. R .S. Gilley was not listed in the membership records for Rockbridge or Amherst Counties from 1884 through 1918. Even though this 24 August 1918 entry includes the word "branch," no other record of a local branch president exists for that year. Perhaps a traveling elder served as branch president or the word "branch" was used in error. *Liahona*, Chattanooga TN: Southern States Mission (24 August 1918) 18:1037.

Then, suddenly, in spite of the large numbers of people interested in Mormonism there, entries for Buena Vista, Cornwall (Irish Creek), and Oronoco (Pedlar Creek) totally disappeared from all official Latter-day Saint records.[95] Regular entries abruptly ended in the Sunday School Mission History. No entry appeared for any of the three in a 1921 list of all the Latter-day Saint branches and Sunday Schools in Virginia.[96] According to church records, church activity ended in and near Buena Vista, Virginia, in 1918.

Where did the missionaries go? Where did the members go?

Actually, the members did not go anywhere.

Recognizing Legally Non-Existent People. 1932....

Seventy-four years later, Will Southers told what happened there in Virginia. He said: "I remember the old men that started the Church at Pedlar Creek and Cornwall.... They were mostly Masons and Colemans.... My dad and mother were baptized in 1912. Elder Turley baptized me in 1913 when I was fifteen years old. It felt real good. When the elders came, they preached about every night on top of the Blue Ridge Mountains." Will added: "What schooling I got was when we moved everything out of a room and had to pay a teacher to come." After trying for more than a year to get a schoolhouse through regular channels, Will and his father, Robert Southers, finally built a school on family land for Will's younger siblings. They used streetcar ties and logs

---

[95] Missionaries stopped in Buena Vista in 1920 to preach a funeral for "Brother Staten," but then the record went blank for seventeen years. However, centralized church leadership continued to support the congregation near Collierstown, where ethnicity never became an issue, and to make routine Virginia entries in mission records. See MH 29 September 1929.

[96] MH 13 April 1921. The Virginia District became part of the East Central States Mission in 1928, but no entries were made for Buena Vista until 1937 when a new church was dedicated by William Tew, President of the East Central States Mission. Later Virginia joined the Central Atlantic States Mission. Buena Vista had one entry for 1944 and one for 1953. Then in 1957 continuous entries began once again. See David M. Mayfield, Assistant Church Librarian Archivist, letter to Aubrey Coleman, 22 April 1976 (Buena Vista, Virginia: BV Family History Library).

they cut in their own sawmill. "Seventy dollars built it," said Southers, "and we had church there sometimes…. Jacob Mason was one of the head members. He worked at a factory in Buena Vista. He preached to us when there were no elders. He knew the Bible pretty good."[97]

Years went by. And a remarkable thing happened, considering the highly centralized nature of the larger Church of Jesus Christ of Latter-day Saints. Although the existence of Latter-day Saint meetings in and near Buena Vista totally disappeared from official records before 1921, and local members say that infrequent visits by elders ended before 1923,[98] an Appalachian mode of Mormonism continued completely on its own.[99]

Myrtle Wilhelm Coleman[100] said that in 1932, when she was nine years old, her family had "always belonged" to the Church, but "at the time we didn't know anything about elders or anything."[101] Members met at each other's homes, or out under the trees, with Jacob Mason and others preaching. They read the *Bible* and the *Book of Mormon* to each other. They did not gather together every Sunday, but met often enough that they held together as a distinct religious community—even though

---

[97] Will Southers (1898–1994), interview by author, 26 December 1992. Garvis Wheeler said that Jacob Mason was "one of the greatest Biblical scholars around here." Garvis Wheeler, interview by author, 27 December 1992.

[98] When the missionaries first left, local members sometimes wrote to the mission home to ask to have elders sent to lay hands upon family members who were ill or to baptize them. If missionaries were passing through, they stopped. But even those visits ended in 1925. See Lizzie Wadsworth Clemmer (granddaughter of Esau Mason, baptized in 1923), handwritten manuscript, (BV Family History Library, 9 July 1992); Alvin Woodrow Coleman, interview by G. Douglas Larsen, 13 October 1997 (BV Family History Library); Thelma Lilley Conner, unpublished manuscript, (BV Family History Library, circa 1985); Lizzie Southers, unpublished manuscript edited by G. Douglas Larsen, (BV Family History Library, 1974).

[99] For insight into Appalachian mountain religion, and how it differs from mainstream Protestant denominations, see Loyal Jones, *Faith and Meaning in the Southern Uplands* (Urbana: University of Chicago Press, 1999); Deborah Vansau McCauley, *Appalachian Mountain Religion: A History* (Urbana and Chicago: University of Illinois Press, 1995); David E. Whisnant, *All that Is Native and Fine: The Politics of Culture in an American Region* (Chapel Hill: University of North Carolina Press, 1983).

[100] A great-granddaughter of Peter and Diannah Mason.

[101] Myrtle Wilhelm Coleman, interview by author, 27 December 1992.

families no longer lived along the same mountain creeks. Sometimes they visited other churches but seldom joined them.[102]

One day in 1932, nine-year-old Myrtle Wilhelm watched as her Aunt Eva Southers made biscuits with "a rolling pin full of moonshine." An automobile stopped at the bottom of the hill with two young men in it.[103] Will Southers said that the men made their way up through the field to the house he was building for his family. Southers stopped work on the floorboards. Recognizing the pair as Mormon missionaries,[104] Southers wondered where they had been for the last many years.

Elder Alvin Pocock asked Southers, "How about us helping? And then maybe we can have a meeting on your new floor?"

Southers nodded assent.

Pocock added, "Do you think we can get a crowd?"

In retelling the story nearly sixty years later, Will Southers laughed out loud as he tried to describe the elders' faces when people kept arriving. People sat all over the house, porch, and hillside. Cars stopped to listen. Excited people wanted to hear more, so the elders preached from home to home and even up at the "school house on Pedlar Creek way up in the mountains."[105]

---

[102] Thelma Lilley Conner, unpublished manuscript (BV Family History Library, circa 1985); Will Southers, interview by author, 26 December 1992; Garvis Wheeler, interview by author, 27 December 1992.

[103] Myrtle Wilhelm Coleman, interview by author, 27 December 1992.

[104] Elders Alvin Pocock and John E. Paget. Alvin Pocock handwritten manuscript, transcribed and edited by Steven A. Pocock on 4 September 2003 (LDS archives, circa 1960).

[105] Will Southers (1898—1994), interview by author, 26 December 1992; Alvin Pocock manuscript, circa 1960; Lizzie Southers, handwritten manuscript (BV Family History Library, 1974). Alvin Pocock wrote, "I met a fine man there [near Cornwall] by the name of William Southers. We baptized his wife into the Church. Will was already a member and a good one at that!" Pocock also recorded several stories about the multiple meetings he and Elder Pagett held there for audiences as large as 600. The first Sunday he was there he said that a female minister showed up for their meeting where people were already sitting on hayracks outside. She brought her whole congregation, with their Bibles, in the backs of five trucks. Pocock said, "I quoted scripture faster than the minister could find it, even as I gave her chapter and verse. Of course, the rest of their congregation was like a lot of Mormons, unlearned in the letter and word, and could not find the quotations I was giving them by the Bible." Years later Will Southers telegrammed Alvin Pocock to come to Cornwall. The minister's daughter had prophesied that she would die in a month and wanted Elder Alvin Pocock to preach her funeral. Pocock preached the funeral and the minister's congregation provided the music. Alvin Pocock manuscript, circa 1960.

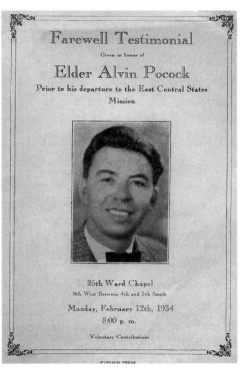

Mission Program covers courtesy of Steven Alvin Pocock.

Pocock baptized scores of people in the South River near Cornwall,[106] and just about anywhere else that he could do a full-body immersion. Will Southers said, "Elder Pocock baptized my wife, Lizzie, in the 'blue hole' from where they took the iron ore. They both like to drowned. I had told him not to step back. At first he didn't. He said what he had to say. Then he put his left foot back to baptize her. And they both went straight down out o' sight. I jumped in and grabbed her by one hand and him by the other."[107]

Brigham D. Madsen, another Elder in the East Central States Mission, knew Alvin Pocock when Pocock returned from Salt Lake City

---

[106] Elijah Clark, interview by Wilford Teerlink, 12 December 1990; Nellie Cash Clark Southers, interview by author, 26 December 1992.
[107] Will Southers (1898–1994), interview by author, 26 December 1992.

for a second mission in 1934. Madsen wrote, "He [Elder Pocock] began to proselyte in an African-American community and eventually converted and baptized an entire congregation of about 150.... This was at the same time, of course, when African-American males were not allowed to hold the Mormon priesthood, a practice which was reversed in June 1978.... I never learned what the church officials in Salt Lake City in 1935 did about their new members or Pocock."[108]

Indeed, church leaders in Salt Lake City faced an administrative challenge. After Latter-day Saints demonstrated obvious patriotism during World War I, they enjoyed increasing acceptance from the federal government and the Protestant mainstream. Many church members became rather Republican and middle class.[109]

Without a revelation from God through the current prophet, the earlier ban on priesthood for blacks could not be lifted. It appears that boom-time townspeople in Buena Vista had tipped off the missionaries as to what they might find if they read the vital statistics in the courthouse, namely that some of their members had been officially classified as black. Without local lay priesthood leadership, the centralized Church in Salt Lake City could not authorize the formation of a branch of that church in Buena Vista. Early missionaries and local church members had found the priesthood ban irrelevant to this community, given that these

---

[108] Brigham D. Madsen, *Against the Grain: Memoirs of a Western Historian* (Salt Lake: Signature Books, 1998) 85. Alvin Pocock knew that some other elders thought he had baptized African-Americans in and near Buena Vista in 1932 and again in the second mission he served from 1934–1936. Elder Maurice P. Monson, who held a leadership position at the mission home in Louisville, initially applauded the Buena Vista baptisms, but later insisted that Pocock had baptized blacks. Pocock wrote, "Little did he know." Then Pocock added, "There was a great deal of prejudice concerning the color and different class of people there. But who am I to pass judgment on people? It says in Acts 17:26, 'God had made all men of one blood.' So I labored among them...." He said that the people diligently did their own genealogy and the research showed that they were "Cherokee Indians." He noted that early missionaries, B. H. Roberts and J. Golden Kimball, also believed they were Indians. Alvin Pocock manuscripts, circa 1960 (includes a clipping from an unnamed mission publication, circa 1932); e-mail correspondence between Steven A. Pocock and author, 4–8 September 2003; "Farewell Testimonial [s] Given in Honor of Elder Alvin Pocock Who Will Leave Shortly for the East Central States Mission," (Salt Lake City UT: 25th Ward, 1930, 1934).

[109] Thomas G. Alexander, *Mormonism in Transition: A History of the Latter-day Saints, 1890–1930* (Urbana: University of Illinois Press, 1996) 48–49.

Latter-day Saints in front of the Long Hollow church house near Buena Vista, Virginia, c. 1944. Photo courtesy of Leroy Wheeler.

chosen people obviously descended directly from the Lost Tribe of Joseph.[110] But before elders ordained these remnants of the house of Israel, the mission president sent the elders down out of the mountains into a society that classified the Pedlar and Irish Creek people differently. Apparently, the courthouse classifications swayed the elders. Although local people continued with the church in the Appalachian tradition, they remained loyal to the Mormon model of lay priesthood authority, and waited for priesthood holders to come and perform baptisms.

---

[110] The twelve tribes of Israel are: Judah, Levi, Dan, Naphtali, Asher, Simeon, Zebulun, Benjamin, Gad, Joseph, Reuben, and Issachar. *Genesis* 35:22–26.

Then, in the midst of the Great Depression, along came Elder Alvin Pocock and a tidal wave of baptisms and religious enthusiasm.[111] Some of the older members argued against the building of a church house, because of the cost and the fact that they had gotten along fine without one for years. However, Robert Southers went ahead and donated the land in Long Hollow, next to the Coleman home. Families seriously sacrificed to donate money to the building fund. Richard Clark owned a sawmill and sold lumber at a discount. Salt Lake City sent two elders to help with construction. Will Southers said that Elder Burton knew what he was doing and worked hard, but the "other elder was off reading out in the shade." All the members worked on the new building. They lighted it with oil lamps and heated it with a coal stove. The building cost between $400 and $500.[112]

On May 30, 1937, Elder Reid Tippitts wrote that the members in Buena Vista "have succeeded in building a chapel." Sixty people attended Sunday School the next Sunday morning and 130 people showed up at Sacrament Meeting that evening. Tippitts added, "They were very attentive, too. I quite enjoyed the day. But these people do present quite a problem. They claim they are not Negro, but...."[113]

In 1937, Latter-day Saint elders ordained nineteen-year-old Hansford Cash as branch president for the Long Hollow congregation. Although Cash's sister married into the Mason line, Cash had a white pedigree at the courthouse. Will Southers served faithfully as his counselor, though unordained. Cash served thirteen years as the only priesthood-bearer in the whole congregation.[114]

---

[111] Elijah Clark, interview by Wilford Teerlink, 12 December 1990; Alvin Woodrow Coleman, interview by G. Douglas Larsen, (BV Family History Library, undated); Lizzie Southers, handwritten manuscript (BV Family History Library, 1974); Nellie Cash Clark Southers, interview by author, 26 December 1992; Will Southers (1898–1994), interview by author, 26 December 1992; Alvin Pocock, handwritten manuscript, transcribed and edited by Steven A. Pocock on 4 September 2003 (LDS Archives, circa 1960).

[112] Lizzie Southers handwritten manuscript, (BV Family History Library, 1974); Will Southers interview by author, 26 December 1992.

[113] Reid Tippitts journal, 30 May 1937 (LDS Archives). See also entries dated 25 April 1937 and 31 May 1937.

[114] Peggy Cash Goodsell, interview by author, 5 January 2003; "A Brief History of the Church of Jesus Christ of Latter-day Saints in the Area of Buena Vista, Virginia" (BV Family History Library, 1978).

Latter-day Saints in front of the American Legion Hall where members met for church in Waynesboro, Virginia in 1950. After racial issues came to a head that year, Claude Clark's elderly grandfather proved their family's American Indian ancestry. Wayne Larsen and Claude Clarke are the twelve-year-olds with large white collars on the far right of the photograph. Photo courtesy of G. Douglas Larsen.

Meanwhile, in 1934, William Eugene Larsen moved his young family to Waynesboro, Virginia. With his new Ph.D. from Purdue University, he worked for E. I. DuPont DeNenours and Company as a research chemist. After being officially called through the centralized priesthood hierarchy, Larsen led a Latter-day Saint Sunday School in his home and took services to members who lived in remote locations in the Blue Ridge. The Larsen-led Sunday School included blessing and administering the sacrament,[115] which required priesthood ordination.[116]

In the 1940s, two Irish Creek families named Clark moved into Waynesboro. They held Sunday school, too, on their own without sacrament. The Clarks knew about the Larsens, but the Larsens did not know about the Clarks. After some traveling elders stumbled onto the Clarks and reported their existence, Eugene Larsen rented the American Legion Hall so that everyone could meet together. The congregation grew large enough to form a "branch" with Larsen as branch president.[117]

Jim and Elijah Clark's father and mother had been baptized back in 1911, and other Irish Creek relatives had been baptized before the turn of the century. Many Clarks had participated in home Sunday Schools, though members partook of the sacrament only when priesthood-bearing elders visited from the Latter-day Saint communities in the western US. Now part of the new "branch," the Clarks saw local priesthood bearers administering the sacrament every Sunday. They saw local men using the priesthood to lay hands upon people for healing. Finally, Jim and Elijah Clark respectfully asked Eugene Larsen to ordain the worthy males in their family. Jim Clark was particularly concerned because his son Claude was nearly twelve years old, the age of first ordination.[118]

Eugene Larsen, having heard the rumors about "colored blood" in the Buena Vista congregation, asked the mission president what to do to "clear the Clark family." The mission president assigned a missionary to search Clark genealogy. The missionary responded:

---

[115] All worthy members could partake of this bread and water to remember Christ's broken flesh and the blood he shed to atone for their sins. By participating, members also promised to take upon themselves the name of Christ, to always remember him, and to keep his commandments. 1 *Corinthians* 11: 23–25; *Doctrine and Covenants* 27: 2.

[116] Tursell Larsen and Flora Larsen Patterson, interview by author, 5 June 1992; Program from the Waynesboro Branch Dedicatory Services (21 May 1978) 6–7.

[117] Elijah Clark, interview by Wilford Teerlink, 12 December 1990.

[118] Claude Edward Clark, interview by author, 26 December 1992.

May 1, 1951

Dear Brother Larsen,

I made a trip to Amherst and in the court house there I was shown the marriage record of Joseph Anderson Clark and Mary Susan Clark, the parents of Jim and Elijah Clark, and they were married in 1906 as colored. May the Lord bless you in your efforts to solve the problems in your branch. I know they are discouraging.

Sincerely,

Elder Wm. S. Tanner[119]

In 1992, Claude Edward Clark, by then an experienced attorney, reminisced about being twelve years old and Mormon in Virginia in 1950:

> [It was] the week of my twelfth birthday. I was all excited. When you are twelve you receive the priesthood. I told my cousin [in Buena Vista] I was going to be ordained a deacon.
>
> "No you're not," he said.
>
> "What do you mean I'm not?"
>
> "They don't give the priesthood to niggars."
>
> "What's that got to do with me?"
>
> And he wouldn't say any more. I guess he figured he'd said too much already. I found out later they refused him the priesthood. He was a couple years older. They refused him the priesthood! And sure enough, I didn't receive the priesthood when I was twelve.

---

[119] Letter from W. E. Larsen to William S. Tanner, 1 May 1951; letter from Elder Wm. S. Tanner to Brother Larsen, 3 May 1951 (in possession of descendant G. Douglas Larsen). The names of many Clarks appear on the Amherst's antebellum register of free blacks. McLeRoy and McLeRoy, 53–213.

Revealing Appalachian religious attitude, Claude added, "This is where I really criticize the [priesthood] officials in the Buena Vista area.... We have a way to find out anything we need to find out. [It is] a simple matter for a branch president [to go] in prayer to Heavenly Father. 'Should this person be allowed to hold the priesthood or not?' Where were their minds, their hearts, their spirits?"[120]

When Claude turned twelve in the Summer of 1950, Eugene Larsen served as the Waynesboro branch president. He also served as the district president over several other congregations in the mission, including the Long Hollow church in Buena Vista. In addition, he was the father of a boy a little younger than Claude. When Wayne Larsen was twelve, his father delayed Wayne's ordination because he did not want to embarrass Wayne's friend, Claude. Finally, Eugene Larsen and other priesthood-bearers called Wayne to the front of the congregation and laid their hands on his head. Claude Clark stood up, strode out the door, and did not look back. Claude's uncle Elijah Clark, the congregation's clerk, wrote the newest ordination in the record book and remained in his seat.[121]

In 1950, Joseph Anderson Clark, Claude's grandfather, still lived near Irish Creek at the edge of National Forest land where his ancestors once lived. He knew about his Native American lineage. In fact, he joined Mormonism in 1911 because he believed that people with the blood of Israel had special responsibilities to prepare for the second coming of the Messiah.[122] A couple of genealogical missionaries from Utah visited the Long Hollow church shortly after his twelve-year-old grandsons were denied the priesthood. Joseph Anderson Clark took them to

---

[120] By "officials," Claude must have meant full-time missionaries or regional priesthood leaders, because Hansford Cash was the lone priesthood holder in the Buena Vista congregation at the time. For a discussion of Appalachian Mountain beliefs with regard to going "straight to the throne" for divine guidance, see McCauley, 14–17, 21, 78, 95, 101, 406.

[121] Claude Edward Clark, interview by author, 26 December 1992; Wayne Larsen, interview by author, 15 October 1993.

[122] Claude Edward Clark, interviews by author, 26 December 1992 and 9 September 2002. See *Genesis 9*.

the Rockbridge County Court House in Lexington, Virginia. Clark had never attended school, but by the time he was an adult he could read sufficiently to search through the dusty document boxes. Together the missionaries and Brother Clark found many of the court documents for the 1925 Atha Sorrells case.[123] In that case, the County Clerk had denied Atha Sorrells a white marriage license, telling her that the Vital Statistics of the Commonwealth of Virginia listed her as "colored." Miss Sorrells sued the county clerk over the marriage-license denial, and she won by proving that she had a distant Indian ancestor but no black ones, therefore falling within the legal exception for 1/16 Indian blood.[124]

Atha Sorrells was Joseph Anderson Clark's double first cousin, so he knew they had the same ancestors.[125] In 1951, after the missionaries took pictures of the documents, Clark took the roll of microfilm to Eugene Larsen. Just like the lawyer for Atha Sorrells, Clark produced the evidence to prove that "colored" was not confined to "Negro." President Larsen read the evidence very carefully. Larsen then looked Clark in the eye and said, "Brother, I believe you're right."[126]

Claude's "cousin's husband," ordained in 1951, was immediately called to the Buena Vista Branch Presidency.[127] Alvin Coleman and Garvis Wheeler, both direct descendants of Peter and Diannah Mason,

---

[123] Claude Edward Clark, interview by author, 26 December 1992.

[124] *Sorrells v. Shields*, Circuit Court of Rockbridge County, court documents dated 1–15 November 1924, 9–10 January 1925. See also "Irish Creek Wedding Plans Rattled State's Race Law," *The Advocate* (March 2003) 41–46.

[125] People in Virginia who considered themselves Indians, and were barred from marriage to neighbors with white vital statistics, often chose intermarriage within their own small communities rather than searching for African-American mates in unknown communities. Claude Edward Clark, interview by author, 26 December 1992; Garvis Wheeler, interview by author, 27 December 1992; Wood and Shields, 27. See also Arthur H. Estabrook and Ivan E. McDougle, *Mongrel Virginians* (Baltimore: Williams and Wilkins Co., 1926); Morton, 139.

[126] Claude Edward Clark, interview by author, 26 December 1992. The author has in her possession 76 pages of the Atha Sorrells court documents that Claude Edward Clark printed from his grandfather's microfilm.

[127] Ernest Lilley married Fannie Clark in June 1933. Fannie Lilley Conner, unpublished manuscript, circa 1982. "History of the Latter-day Saints in Buena Vista," 1993 (BV Family History Library); Claude Edward Clark, interview by author, 26 December 1992.

were also ordained that same day. So was Hansford Vest, the great-grand-son of old iron-sided Levi Vest.[128]

Hansford Vest credited his "Lamonite [sic] brothers" with "comprising most of the membership of the Church in Rockbridge County as late as 1940," and he listed "a few of them" as Masons, Colemans, Southers, and Clarks.[129] Both Alvin Coleman and Garvis Wheeler later served as branch presidents, and Coleman as a bishop.[130]

In 1957, Elder Claude Edward Clark served as the first full-time missionary from Waynesboro, Virginia Branch.[131] From then on, the church record keepers in Salt Lake City kept detailed records of the Buena Vista congregation.

In 1996, Latter-day Saint businessmen from outside Buena Vista acquired the entire campus of Southern Virginia College, including the building that was once the splendid, boom-time Hotel Buena Vista.[132]

At about the same time, Garvis and Juanita Wheeler, from Buena Vista, participated in an unpaid Latter-day Saint mission, as retired couples often do. A distinguished member of their mission presidency told them that when he was nineteen years old, he had served on a proselytizing mission in Buena Vista, Virginia. Excited to meet people from Buena Vista, this prominent priesthood leader asked Garvis Wheeler, the great-grandson of Peter H. Mason, "Are there any white people in the Buena Vista ward now? It used to be an all black congregation."[133]

---

[128] History of the Latter-day Saints in Buena Vista, 1993 (BV Family History Library); International Genealogical Index, Familysearch.com.

[129] Hansford Vest, "The Gospel and Jacob Lee Hamilton," unpublished manuscript, circa 1980 (BV Family History Library).

[130] "History of the Latter-day Saints in Buena Vista," (BV Family History Library, 1993). A branch president presides over small congregations, called branches. A bishop presides over larger congregations, called wards.

[131] Claude Edward Clark, interview by author, 26 December 1992.

[132] Brochure for Southern Virginia University, 2003. Due to rapid growth of the university, by the year 2004 seven large congregations of Latter-day Saints attended church in Buena Vista every Sunday.

[133] Juanita Wheeler, interview by author, 25 July 2003.

The American Indian Mormons in Virginia's Blue Ridge originally dwelled alongside Pedlar and Irish Creeks. Today, their descendents remember their Native-American lineage. Through oral histories, they recount family stories of nineteenth-century missionaries who valued their ancestors as a remnant of a lost tribe of Israel.

These people never lost themselves.[134] The dominant culture lost them, rejecting their Indian heritage in what some scholars have called "documentary genocide."[135] For 300 years, well-respected lawmakers, scientists, and bureaucrats methodically rewrote reality through choosing the race and social value of the rural Indian people of Virginia's Blue Ridge. Powerful men of means in distant city offices virtually eliminated the legal existence of whole indigenous communities, including the Monacans[136] in Virginia's Amherst and Rockbridge Counties.

A few old diaries and other Latter-day Saint records still exist, which suggest that the early Mormons in Amherst and Rockbridge comprised another one of these Indian communities. As researchers study the historical documents, they may help the Commonwealth of Virginia and the federal government reconstruct the story of a lost tribe, and perhaps may lead these governments to recognize the historical and cultural significance of Virginia's Indian Mormons.

169

L O S T   T R I B E S

---

[134] Alvin Woodrow Coleman, interview by author, 27 December 1992; Garvis Wheeler, interview by author, 27 December 1992.

[135] J. David Smith, "Legal Racism and Documentary Genocide: Dr. Plecker's Assault on the Monacan Indians," *Lynches Ferry: A Journal of Local History* (Spring/Summer 1992); Houch and Maxham, 193.

[136] Houch and Maxham, 193. See also, Rice.

Sin in Memphis:
Organized Crime and Machine Politics
in a Southern City, 1935–1940

BY G. WAYNE DOWDY

One of the most important developments in the history of American politics was the creation of tightly-knit organizations, commonly referred to as "machines," which expanded city services to the poor and included them in the electoral process. Political machines were welded together in such urban centers as New York City, Boston, and Chicago, changing the makeup of the American electorate.[1] Although generally thought to have been confined to the largest cities of the Northeast and Midwest, political machines were also formed in the smaller cities of the American South.[2] Perhaps the most important Southern political machine was the party apparatus built in Memphis, Tennessee, in the first half of the twentieth century.

Scholars examining the South have concluded that Southern politics during that period tended to be hamstrung by the general disenfranchisement of African Americans and by the dominance of the Democratic Party.[3] Exploiting this situation with considerable political

---

[1] James Duane Bolin, *Bossism and Reform in a Southern City: Lexington, Kentucky, 1880–1940* (Lexington: University Press of Kentucky, 2000) 182–92.

[2] Ibid.

[3] Numan Bartley, "Politics and Ideology," in *Encyclopedia of Southern Culture*, ed. Charles Reagan Wilson and William Ferris (Chapel Hill: University of North Carolina Press, 1989): 1151–55.

acumen was Memphis's Mayor and Congressman Edward Hull Crump. He and his lieutenants carefully merged the government employees of the City of Memphis and Shelby County with the Democratic Party, unifying local government under one political faction. A series of alliances with every major ethnic, racial, and economic group in Shelby County augmented the strength of this organization, making it one of the most powerful political machines in the United States.[4] The creation of a multi-ethnic coalition in the midst of a region perceived to be politically backward suggests Southern political arrangements were more complex than once thought.

No one in Memphis was left out, not even the criminal class. According to a former police chief, gangsters contributed campaign funds in exchange for permission to operate their illegal gambling establishments.[5] This was also apparently true of prostitution and the liquor trade. The money was very important to the operation of the machine, but other factors were at work. An alliance with the underworld afforded the machine a certain amount of control over crime. Criminal behavior was contained within poverty-stricken sections of the city and thus was prevented from encroaching into middle-class neighborhoods.

Historically populated by a raucous and violent citizenry, Memphis had a culture of crime that was hard to uproot. For example, the notorious gangster George Barnes, alias "Machine Gun Kelly," hailed from Memphis and was captured there in 1933.[6] Not even the local correctional institution was free of vice; a moonshine still, several thousand gallons of mash, and fifteen gallons of whisky were discovered at the county penal farm in 1935.[7] According to the FBI, Memphis had a

---

[4] Kenneth D. Wald, "The Electoral Base of Political Machines: A Deviant Case Analysis," *Urban Affairs Quarterly* 16 (September 1980): 3–29.

[5] Lamar Whitlow Bridges, "Editor Mooney Versus Boss Crump," *West Tennessee Historical Society Papers,* 20 (1966): 96.

[6] Linda McGregor Scott, "Machine Gun Kelly—A Return to Paradise," *West Tennessee Historical Society Papers,* 50 (1996): 27.

[7] *Memphis Press-Scimitar,* 17 December 1935, 1.

higher crime rate than New York City.[8] The most damaging figures came from the statistician for the Prudential Insurance Company, Dr. Frederick L. Hoffman, who claimed that Memphis was the murder capital of the United States.[9]

City officials countered that Hoffman's figures were unfair because they did not take into account violent encounters in the surrounding countryside, which led to victims being taken to Memphis hospitals. "If a man gets shot at Blytheville [Arkansas] and dies in a Memphis hospital, we're charged up with another murder," said Police Chief Will Lee.[10] In its propensity towards violence and crime, Memphis reflected the angry culture of the southern United States.[11]

Accusations that Memphis was a hotbed for violence did little to influence the city's approach to law enforcement until 1935, at which time the national media focused attention on the city's crime rate. In January 1935, *Colliers* Magazine published an article entitled "Sinners in Dixie," which surveyed criminal activities in Tennessee, Mississippi, and Arkansas. As the biggest city in the Mid-South, Memphis received the most attention.[12]

The author, Owen P. White, traveled to Memphis in the Fall of 1934 under the guise of studying soil erosion,[13] but in reality White was studying the city's erosion of law and order. Witnessing a nightclub brawl and other illegal activities while investigating the growth of organized crime in Memphis, White concluded that vice flourished there because the city's residents wanted to participate in illegal activities and because local politicians received campaign contributions from criminal

---

8 *Memphis Commercial Appeal*, 22 June 1934, 7.

9 Roger Biles, *Memphis in the Great Depression* (Knoxville:University of Tennessee Press, 1986) 15; *Memphis Press Scimitar* 31 March 1933.

10 *Memphis Press Scimitar*, 22 June 1934, 7.

11 Raymond D. Gastil, "Violence, Crime, and Punishment," in *Encyclopedia of Southern Culture*, ed. Charles Reagan Wilson and William Ferris (Chapel Hill: University of North Carolina Press, 1989): 1473–77.

12 Owen White, "Sinners in Dixie," *Colliers*, 26 January 1935, 16, 43–44.

13 *Memphis Press-Scimitar*, 17 January 1935, 3.

leaders. As he explained in his *Colliers* article, "[I]t is upon commercialized vice that the burden of paying its overhead has been placed by Congressman Crump's political organization, which runs Shelby County."[14]

White also wrote, "Another popular method whereby the citizens of Memphis contribute to the pampered upkeep of their politicians and gamblers is for them to play policy." "Policy" was an illegal lottery where players purchased a number with which they might win a large sum of money. The *Colliers* article did mention other Southern cities, most notably Little Rock, but Memphians felt they had been singled out for extreme condemnation. The *Memphis Commercial Appeal* printed an editorial stating that *Colliers* should apologize for being "unfair,"[15] while a staff writer for the *Memphis Press-Scimitar* argued that the "big shots who came to Memphis found booze because they looked for it.… They found what they were looking for—just as they can find it anywhere in this country."[16]

White was essentially correct in his assessment of illegal activity in Memphis. Crump and his stalwarts always balanced the desires of the voters with the need to protect and expand the machine's power. Looking realistically at the situation, machine leaders in Memphis determined that city residents were anxious to engage in certain illegal activities. Therefore, Crump had to walk a fine line between maintaining law enforcement and permitting recreational sin if he wanted his political organization to stay in power. The acceptance of contributions from criminal operations was also necessary to finance political campaigns. For instance, instead of using taxpayer money to pay for free food provided at Democratic Party voter rallies, Crump used revenues collected from gambling and liquor.

---

[14] White, "Sinners in Dixie," 43.

[15] *Memphis Commercial Appeal,* 18 January 1935, 10.

[16] *Memphis Press-Scimitar,* 19 January 1935, 3.

The same week *Colliers* appeared on Memphis news-stands, police moved against several criminal enterprises. Arrests were made for possessing illegal liquor, gambling, and policy writing.[17] Because large amounts of cash were available for gangsters to post bond, procedures were changed to allow only property to be used for bail.[18] This made it harder for alleged criminals to flee and forfeit their bond. Although all vice activities were targeted, the policy racket received the lion's share of attention.

The police department was intimately familiar with the policy racket; one runner even sold numbers in the police station.[19] It was estimated that in Memphis, policy employed 2,000 people who handled 15,000 bets daily. Paying usually no more than fifteen cents, a player would select three numbers between one and seventy-eight. If one of their numbers were among twelve drawn, they won a certain amount of money.[20] In order to put a "lid" on the racket, police systematically raided policy establishments, confounding the underworld and press alike. The *Commercial Appeal* asked, "Why these 'lids' on vice and crime? Why are they opened now, then closed, then opened again?"[21] Echoing the newspaper, gangland leaders vowed they would be "back making our rounds again soon."[22]

Memphians were accustomed to frequent raids against organized crime that ended when enough publicity was garnered. It was expected by all concerned that policy games would reopen as soon as public interest waned. But city leaders became determined to eradicate gambling and to restore confidence in law enforcement. Racketeers—such as Nollo Grandi, owner of the Red Onion Club—pleaded with city officials for permission to begin again,[23] but the answer given was "You're

---

[17] *Memphis Commercial Appeal,* 21 January 1935, 11.
[18] Ibid.
[19] *Memphis Commercial Appeal,* 4 March 1935, 1.
[20] *Memphis Commercial Appeal,* 3 March 1935, 1.
[21] Ibid.
[22] Ibid.
[23] *Memphis Commercial Appeal,* 4 March 1935, 1.

shutdown—for good."[24] Officers were also warned "not to tolerate policy houses on your beats if you value your jobs."[25]

The fines for running a policy game were increased by city court, to "take the profit out of policy writing," according to one judge.[26] Meanwhile, the middle class joined administration efforts to crush gambling. A minister and attorney gathered information on policy writers,[27] while a Parent Teachers Association complaint ended the practice of merchants using pinball machines as gaming devices.[28] Police raids on illegal activities continued through the Summer of 1935, and prostitution rings were also targeted. Notorious madams like "Dutch Mary" Sherron were arrested for running disorderly houses, while individual prostitutes were detained for vagrancy.[29]

By this time, a severe blow had been dealt to the underworld, but crime did not disappear from the streets of Memphis. As already stated, many voters participated in these activities, while funds collected from such activities greased the political machine. Despite this, Crump and his lieutenants decided it was time to sever their alliance with gangsters. To sever such ties, Crump's machine would depend heavily on the police. In years past, the city's leaders were restricted from attacking gangland crime because they had limited control over law enforcement.

Civil service protection had been afforded the Memphis police beginning in 1910, making it difficult to remove officers from the force. In 1927, for example, the names of fifty-one policemen were discovered in a ledger seized during a liquor raid. Beside those names were dollar amounts, suggesting the possibility of bribery. A civil service trial board was convened to judge the "pay-off book scandal," but all policemen were found not guilty and returned to the department.[30]

---

[24] *Memphis Commercial Appeal*, 3 March 1935, 1.

[25] Ibid.

[26] *Memphis Commercial Appeal*, 22 June 1935, 2.

[27] *Memphis Press-Scimitar*, 5 March 1935, 1.

[28] *Memphis Press-Scimitar*, 25 April 1935, 1.

[29] *Memphis Press-Scimitar*, 17 June 1935, 1, *Memphis Commercial Appeal*, 22 June 1935, 2.

[30] *Memphis Evening Appeal*, 19 November 1927, 1.

BEAUTIFYING BARKSDALE DISTRICT STATION 1936

Hon. WATKINS OVERTON
present Mayor

Hon. E.H. CRUMP
then mayor who built
this Station 1910

Hon. CLIFFORD DAVIS
present vice-mayor
Fire & Police Commissioner

BARKSDALE MOUNTED POLICE STATION

Beauty Spot
from another angle

Rose
Garden

Gateway
with Lantana
bed on left
and Zenia
bed on right

Mr. WILL LEE
Chief of
Police

Photos by
Tuttle
Police
Photographer

Rockery in
Rose Garden

Designed by
Harry E. Northrup

Rose Garden South Side

Cannas

Criticism of Memphis law enforcement by the national media pressured city leaders (upper right-hand corner) to move against organized crime. Photo courtesy of the Memphis/Shelby County Public Library and Information Center.

Although not in power at the time, the Crump machine must have been influenced by this scandal. Mayor Overton and Police Commissioner Davis inherited these officers and thus were aware of corruption in the ranks of law enforcement. That is not to say they were powerless. Shortly after Overton took office in 1928, every officer was moved to a different patrol area. In the midst of their war against the underworld, the machine took further steps to increase control over the police.

Shelby County legislators pushed through the Tennessee General Assembly an omnibus bill that included among its new mandates the elimination of civil service protection for Memphis police.[31] Before the bill passed in February 1935, a suspected officer was entitled to a trial by his superiors, and was granted the right to appeal the decision to the city commission and the courts.[32] The new "merit" law gave the police commissioner authority to dismiss officers at will, without the right of employee appeal.[33] Thereafter, individual officers were described as "frightened" and "jumpy" as they made their rounds,[34] while the leaders of the machine kept a watchful eye.

In conjunction with the establishment of a "merit" system, some officers were transferred, while others were demoted or forced to retire.[35] The abolition of civil service thwarted gangsters' attempts to purchase cooperation from the police while at the same time politicized the operation of law enforcement. No doubt any policeman who dared support a political candidate not chosen by the machine quickly found himself unemployed. However, it is also true that victory over the policy racket was in large part due to the "merit" system.

---

[31] *Memphis Commercial Appeal*, 11 February 1935, 13.

[32] *Memphis Commercial Appeal*, 12 April 1935, 1.

[33] *Memphis Press Scimitar*, 5 May 1935, 1.

[34] Ibid.

[35] *Memphis Commercial Appeal*, 11 February 1935, 13.

As the drive against organized crime got underway, the city court clerk, it was soon discovered, was returning fines to those who had been found guilty of violating the state liquor law. Although the United States had abandoned prohibition in 1933, the State of Tennessee had not. Mayor Overton forced the resignation of that clerk, W. L. Clark, in spite of objections from city court judge Lewis T. Fitzhugh. Revealing that he had ordered Clark to remit the fines, Fitzhugh vowed to continue the practice whenever "a mistake of judgment has been made."[36]

Fitzhugh had enjoyed machine support since 1927, but that ended when Overton accused the judge of keeping the fines for himself rather than returning them as reported in court records.[37] Describing the situation as a "racket," Overton vowed to drive out "crookedness in the city government."[38] Fitzhugh countered that every Memphian knew "there is a corrupt alliance between…the political machine and the criminal classes," and by attacking him they were diverting attention from this fact.[39] The judge also argued that the machine wanted to replace him with someone who would cooperate more fully in the law enforcement drive.

In response to the mayor's accusations, the Shelby County Grand Jury indicted Fitzhugh and Clark for larceny and receiving stolen property. Fitzhugh lashed out by stating he was being "railroaded through a controlled grand jury upon perjured evidence procured by this conscienceless machine."[40] This statement landed Fitzhugh in jail when criminal court judge Phil H. Wallace had him arrested for contempt of court. After posting a $250 bond, Fitzhugh proclaimed to a packed courtroom: "Conscious of the rectitude of my official conduct, and confident, therefore, of absolute vindication, I will retire temporarily from the bench."[41] A guilty verdict was handed down in Fitzhugh's contempt

---

[36] *Memphis Commercial Appeal,* 16 August 1935, 18

[37] *Memphis Commercial Appeal,* 30 March 1935, 1.

[38] Ibid.

[39] Ibid.

[40] *Memphis Commercial Appeal,* 11 April 1935, 1.

[41] *Memphis Commercial Appeal,* 16 May 1935, 9.

trial despite the fact that he claimed that he meant no disrespect to the courts.[42]

Attorney General W. Tyler McLain and City Attorney Will Gerber argued at Fitzhugh's larceny trial that the former judge had stolen $32,000 of forfeited fees. Ledger books in which fees were recorded, along with witnesses who did not receive their remitted fines, were introduced as evidence, while the defense argued that no money had been found in Fitzhugh's possession.[43] The jury deliberated for over forty hours before reporting they were deadlocked nine to three for Fitzhugh's acquittal. With no choice left to him, the presiding judge declared a mistrial.[44] Attorney General McLain vowed to try Fitzhugh again, but the former judge died less than a year later.[45]

The Fitzhugh trial, while on the surface a defeat for the machine, did help in the machine's war on the underworld. According to one newspaper account, bootleggers attributed the police departments' zeal to the fate of Judge Fitzhugh.[46] No doubt, many officers felt the need to be more diligent and honest since the fall of Judge Fitzhugh as well as the implementation of the "merit" system.

But what of Lewis Fitzhugh—was he a crooked judge? Based on evidence discussed in the newspaper accounts, it is probable that Fitzhugh was targeted for removal only after he refused to cease remitting fines for state liquor-law violations. The machine leadership was certainly not above creating scapegoats to deflect attention from the appalling crime rate. Apparently, the leadership chose court clerk W. L. Clark for that role, and when Fitzhugh stood by him, Fitzhugh was targeted as well.

No doubt Crump and his stalwarts—wanting to communicate to the city bureaucracy that the crackdown on the underworld was real—chose the fine-remitting practice as a way of sending this directive. Had

---

[42] *Memphis Commercial Appeal,* 16 August 1935, 18.

[43] *Memphis Press-Scimitar,* 12 August 1935, 1.

[44] *Memphis Commercial Appeal,* 16 August 1935, 18.

[45] *Memphis Press-Scimitar,* 30 April 1936, 16.

[46] *Memphis Press-Scimitar,* 17 June 1935, 1.

Fitzhugh stayed out of the controversy surrounding Clark's dismissal, he perhaps would have remained on the bench. Given that Attorney General McLain was a member of the Crump inner circle, it is not hard to imagine that the machine persuaded the Shelby County Grand Jury to indict Fitzhugh in order to eliminate a recalcitrant judge.

The offensive directed at the underworld was successful in crushing the policy racket while curbing other forms of gambling. One area of crime that was more difficult to address was homicide. In 1934, for example, ninety-three Memphians were murdered.[47] The majority were shot with pistols, though eight were killed with shotguns, twenty were mortally stabbed with knives, and five were clubbed to death.[48] As previously mentioned, the Overton administration vehemently argued that Memphis was unfairly labeled "murder capitol" of the nation, but, as the number of deaths rose from sixty in 1928 to 105 in 1932,[49] it became more difficult to combat that image.

In January 1935, just before the "Sinners in Dixie" article was published in *Colliers*, Overton began carefully scrutinizing police reports for ways to curb the homicide rate. Writing to Police Commissioner Davis and Attorney General McLain, Overton stated, "I think by making a very careful analysis of these places we can find out the cause of these homicides and correct the conditions which are causing them." The mayor then chided the homicide bureau for not making a more detailed investigation.[50]

Chief Inspector W. T. Griffin suggested to the mayor that adding a bureau of ballistics would "add to the effectiveness of prosecutions of homicide cases."[51] But to Overton, Griffin was missing the point. The mayor was amenable to the idea of a ballistics department, but he wrote:

---

[47] *Memphis Commercial Appeal,* 5 January 1936, I, 7.
[48] Memphis Police Department, Homicide Bureau Annual Report, 1934, Watkins Overton Papers (Memphis/Shelby Public Library and Information Center, Memphis TN).
[49] *Memphis Commercial Appeal,* 5 January 1936, I, 7.
[50] Watkins Overton to Clifford Davis, 10 January 1935, Overton Papers.
[51] W. T. Griffin to Watkins Overton, 2 February 1935, Overton papers.

"prosecution of these cases is much better at present than our efforts to analyze the causes of our high homicide rate."[52] Overton was no doubt sincere in his desire to root out the causes of murder, which further explains the 1935 underworld crackdown. But it was a difficult problem, much more so than shutting down a criminal enterprise. Despite the zealousness with which the city government attacked organized crime, the murder rate soared to 103 deaths in 1935.[53]

Homicide reports forwarded to the mayor revealed the depths of Memphis' culture of violence. Most of the murders were not the result of premeditation, but rather were crimes of passion committed without forethought. An angry confrontation between people, exacerbated by liquor, was the standard reason Memphians turned to violence. In 1937, an inebriated laborer came home and crawled into bed fully clothed with his common-law wife. She insisted that he take his clothes off; in response, he got out of bed, grabbed a shovel, and beat the woman to death.[54] In a similar vein, a man was stabbed to death after attempting to stop an argument between a drunken common-law husband and wife.[55]

It was obvious to the Crump machine that vice contributed to the appalling murder rate. Throughout the rest of the 1930s, the police continued to exert pressure on the criminal element. Dice games were broken up,[56] while businesses were investigated for possible liquor violations.[57] The homicide rate, however, remained an intractable problem, seemingly unsolvable.

In 1939, the local war on organized crime received state support when Representative Lon Austin of Lexington, Tennessee, introduced a bill in the state's General Assembly giving counties the option to sell

---

[52] Watkins Overton to W. T. Griffin, 6 February 1935, Overton Papers.

[53] *Memphis Commercial Appeal,* 5 January 1936, I, 7.

[54] Captain W. F. Glisson to Chief Inspector William T. Griffin, 30 March 1937, Overton Papers.

[55] W. F. Glisson to William T. Griffin, 6 April 1937, Overton Papers.

[56] Clifford Davis to Watkins Overton, 2 May 1936, Overton Papers.

[57] Sergeant E. L. McCarty to Captain J. Cross, 2 April 1938, Overton papers.

liquor, which would end Tennessee's thirty-year experiment in prohibition. Guiding the bill through the Tennessee House of Representatives was Memphis representative Charles Brown, which suggested that the machine was in part responsible for the bill's introduction. The proposal wound its way through the state House and Senate with little opposition.[58]

Governor Prentice Cooper vetoed the measure, reasoning that the "bill does not conform to my platform pledge made to the people of this state." Over-riding the governor's veto, Tennessee became the forty-fifth state in the union to allow the sale of liquor within its borders.[59] By vetoing the measure, Cooper was able to appear independent of Crump while keeping ties to anti-machine prohibitionists. It is likely that Crump acquiesced to the governor's action because support for the bill was stronger than Cooper's objection.

Shelby voters went to the polls in May 1939 and overwhelmingly voted for the legalizing of alcohol.[60] Selling liquor legally gave city and county governments the power to regulate the industry, ostensibly replacing gangsters with law abiding merchants. The new law also brought in needed revenue for public services; $10,883 was added to government coffers in the first month of operation.[61] With Memphians once again buying liquor from government-sanctioned dealers, the underworld saw its major cash business evaporate. Organized crime thus found itself in a vulnerable position. Recognizing this fact, the city bureaucracy focused attention on the remaining criminal enterprises.

The final offensive in Memphis' war against organized crime began in the Spring of 1940. That year, newly appointed Mayor Walter Chandler and Police Commissioner Joseph Boyle expanded the law

---

[58] *Memphis Commercial Appeal*, 3 March 1939, 1.

[59] Ibid.

[60] *Memphis Press-Scimitar*, 26 May 1939, 1.

[61] *Memphis Commercial Appeal*, 13 July 1939, 1.

enforcement drive begun by Overton.[62] Patrolmen were ordered to step up raids against gambling and prostitution, while bookmakers were rounded up, and all known brothels were closed.[63] "We're just enforcing laws," Boyle declared, but it was clear to sophisticated observers that the final push against organized crime had begun.

Writing in the *Press-Scimitar*, reporter Clark Porteous declared victory over prostitution: "Like turning off a faucet that has been dripping steadily for more than a century, Commissioner Joe Boyle has cut off vice."[64] Gambling was attacked just as effectively. Bingo was banned, as well as gambling on pinball machines, baseball games, and slot machines.[65] Even those who placed bets on horse races were aggressively prosecuted, much to the surprise of four bookies arrested twelve hours after opening a downtown office.[66] New forms of illegal activity, such as obscene literature, were introduced but were swiftly dismantled with the help of white civic organizations.[67] In an effort to discourage gang leaders from reestablishing their enterprises, the city commission appropriated $4,488 to augment the armaments of the police. Machine guns, grenades, and gas masks were purchased, in Boyle's words, "to meet any emergency."[68]

Close ties between police officials and the underworld continued to embarrass efforts to contain illegal activity. Captain Lee Boyles, who headed the "purity squad" responsible for enforcing anti-prostitution measures, was dismissed after he allegedly allowed two brothels to reopen.[69] Upon further investigation, it was learned that Boyles and Sergeant A. M. Perry, son-in-law of Police Chief Will Lee, had failed to

---

[62] Wayne Dowdy, "E. H. Crump and the Mayors of Memphis," *West Tennessee Historical Society papers*, 53 (1999): 89–91.

[63] *Memphis Press-Scimitar*, 25 April 1940, 1.

[64] *Memphis Press-Scimitar*, 7 May 1940, 1.

[65] Ibid.

[66] *Memphis Press-Scimitar*, 26 April 1940, 1.

[67] *Memphis Commercial Appeal*, 19 May 1940, 1.

[68] *Memphis Commercial Appeal*, 12 June 1940, 23.

[69] *Memphis Commercial Appeal*, 25 May 1940, 1.

Mayor Walter Chandler and Police Commissioner Joseph Boyle (center) directed the final assault on organized crime in Memphis. Photo courtesy of the Memphis/Shelby County Public Library and Information Center.

report the existence of several houses of ill fame.[70] Despite his family connection, Perry was also dismissed.[71] The swift action by the administration blunted any charge that corruption was rampant in the Memphis Police Department. A much more serious scandal, however, erupted in the wake of a shooting over a gambling debt, calling into question the ability of the machine to suppress corruption as well as terminate organized crime.

In May 1940, James Knight (alias "Race Riot"), an African American gambler from West Memphis, Arkansas, pulled a pistol and shot Jim Ivy Smith in the arm during an argument. Quickly picked up by the police, Knight was arrested and held in city jail. "Race Riot" was no stranger to Memphis. He was well known to police and his mother in law, Lois Bass, owned a restaurant frequented by high-ranking police officials.

While Knight languished in the calaboose, Bass summoned homicide captain W. F. Glisson to her home. Glisson also met with C. C. Culp, West Memphis Town Marshal, who pleaded for the gambler's release. Knight operated a dice game for Culp in West Memphis and was no doubt a valuable asset to the marshal. Shortly after the two visits, Knight was released from jail. Meanwhile, Bass approached Jim Ivy Smith, brokering an agreement in which Bass would give the victim $50 and would pay his medical expenses in exchange for Smith promising to drop the charges.[72]

The homicide bureau continued to gather evidence against Knight, angering his patron Culp. The town marshal visited police headquarters, where he reported that Knight had paid Glisson $200 to end the investigation, but the homicide captain reneged on the deal and was asking for $50 more. The Crump machine was outraged by these revelations; in

---

[70] *Memphis Commercial Appeal,* 14 July 1940, I, 7.
[71] *Memphis Commercial Appeal,* 20 June 1940, 1.
[72] *Memphis Press-Scimitar,* 5 August 1940, 1.

response, the city commission met in special session to hear the evidence against Glisson.[73]

Testimony given at the hearing revealed deep connections between Lois Bass and elements of law enforcement—connections that included free meals given to Police Chief Will Lee, Inspector Clegg D. Richards, and Glisson. Perhaps not surprisingly, the city commission learned that Lee and Richards had agreed with Glisson that Knight should be released. City leaders ruled the officers "were derelict in their respective duties in ordering the release of the negro," and suspended them for thirty days without pay until a more detailed investigation could take place.[74] Releasing their findings in September 1940, the commission condemned each man for dereliction of duty; Chief Lee retired, while Glisson and Richards were reduced in rank.[75]

The incidents involving Lieutenant Boyles and "Race Riot" Knight were covered extensively in local newspapers, suggesting that the actions taken by the administration were motivated by public scrutiny as well as by the machine's intent to root out corruption. Not all inappropriate conduct by police officers made newspaper headlines, however. The way that government officials handled smaller but no less serious offenses reveals the extent of the commitment of the Crump machine to punishing errant behavior within the ranks of law enforcement.

On the evening of August 19, 1940, Herman Mitchell, a twenty-nine-year-old African American, walked out of a downtown cafe and was detained by two plain-clothes detectives. While searching him, Detective Sergeants H. D. Turner and W. A. Anderson asked Mitchell if he had ever been arrested. The African American told them he had once been arrested by a "speed cop" for driving too fast. According to Mitchell, after he said "speed cop," he was struck by Turner. "It's police officer, not

---

[73] Ibid.

[74] Ibid.

[75] Statement of the Memphis Board of Commissioners, 3 September 1940, loose papers of the Memphis Board of Commissioners (Shelby County Archives, Memphis TN).

speed cop," Turner reportedly yelled while hitting Mitchell with his fist. Escaping from the two detectives, Mitchell fled to police headquarters where he made a formal complaint.[76]

On duty that evening was Acting Chief Inspector M. A. Hinds who, after hearing the complaint, ordered the two men to report to him immediately. When Turner and Anderson arrived, Hinds ushered them into his office where he asked them "if they had had any trouble with a negro." Both reported there had been no incidents. Hinds told them of Mitchell's complaint; Turner "stated they had not even been in that vicinity." Confronting the two detectives, Mitchell identified Turner as the one who had struck him.[77]

Both parties were instructed to report the next morning for an interview with Acting Chief of Police Carroll Seabrook. Later in the evening, as Hinds was leaving headquarters, he was approached by Sergeant Anderson, who was "very much distressed." Reminded that "they had all been warned about the treatment of citizens and prisoners," Hinds advised Anderson to tell the truth. No doubt concerned about his future, the detective sergeant reported that Turner had assaulted Mitchell.[78]

The next morning, however, Anderson had a change of heart. He and Turner asserted in a written statement that Mitchell was attempting to steal an automobile and that Turner only swung at Mitchell after the latter man refused to call police officers by their correct title. The report conceded that Turner "swung at" Mitchell, but denied that contact was made.[79] Ultimately, Hinds did not believe the two detectives. For their actions and disingenuous statements, Turner was fined two days pay while Anderson lost one, a decision sanctioned by the mayor.[80]

---

[76] Statement of Herman Mitchell, 19 August 1940 and acting chief inspector M. A. Hinds to acting chief of police Carroll Seabrook, 20 August 1940, Walter Chandler papers (Memphis/Shelby County Public Library and Information Center, Memphis TN).

[77] M. A. Hinds to Carroll Seabrook, 20 August 1940, Chandler Papers.

[78] Ibid.

[79] H. D. Turner and W. A. Anderson to M. A. Hinds, 19 August 1940, Chandler Papers.

[80] Walter Chandler to M. A. Hinds, 22 August 1940, Chandler Papers.

The Mitchell situation was certainly more than a routine police brutality case. For one thing, Herman Mitchell was a very brave man since he had ample reason to fear retaliation. Also, the white power structure, represented by Hinds and Mayor Chandler, took the word of an African American over that of two white men, an event almost unheard of in the segregated South. This is not to suggest that justice was colorblind or that politics were equal in Memphis. Comprising 41 percent of the population,[81] African Americans were important to the operation of the machine because of their large numbers, but the Mitchell situation did not fundamentally change their second-class status.

The administration's preoccupation with police brutality did not divert from the anti-crime offensive but instead was an integral part of that effort. In a further attempt to curb the murder rate, police raided establishments on Beale Street looking for concealed weapons. Many African Americans were arrested for carrying long-bladed knives, commonly referred to as "Arkansas toothpicks."[82] Commissioner Boyle also sought the help of federal law enforcement to address illegal narcotics trafficking in Memphis. "I received the assurance that I would receive full co-operation," the commissioner reported.[83]

The measures taken in 1940 effectively ended organized crime in Memphis. Major criminal enterprises were moved just outside of Shelby County; prostitution flourished across the Mississippi River in West Memphis, Arkansas,[84] while gamblers relocated to Desoto County, Mississippi.[85] To be sure, crime continued in Memphis, but gambling, illegal liquor, and prostitution virtually disappeared from the city's streets. Murder, while not eliminated, decreased significantly in

---

[81] G. Wayne Dowdy, "The White Rose Mammy: Racial Culture and Politics in World War II Memphis," *Journal of Negro History,*(Fall 2000): 310.

[82] *Memphis Press-Scimitar,* 15 November 1940, 1.

[83] *Memphis Press-Scimitar,* 4 December 1940, 1–2.

[84] Ibid.

[85] *Memphis Press-Scimitar,* 6 June 1940, 1.

Memphis. Thirty-two people were killed in 1941, and that number remained below fifty through 1946.[86]

Despite reductions in the crime rate, many African Americans during this period felt that war was being waged against them rather than against gangsters. Collins George, LeMoyne College professor, described local conditions in a letter to NAACP headquarters: "Negroes are stopped on the street, cursed, beat, kicked; they are pulled off of street cars for the dire offense of not rising to give the very last seat in a car to a white, and likewise arrested if they dare to make a comment about it."[87] To George and many other African Americans, the anti-crime drive was a smokescreen, obscuring the machine's attempt to subordinate black political independence.

Two other incidents further convinced many black Memphians that they were the intended victims of renewed law enforcement. First, the longstanding alliance between Crump and black Republican leader Robert Church Jr. ended when Church and his lieutenant J. B. Martin were pressured into leaving Memphis.[88] Church's Republican organization was supplanted by the Colored Democrats Club, which bound the black vote more securely to the Crump machine.[89] Secondly, Commissioner Boyle cautioned African Americans to remember that Memphis "is a white man's country."[90]

The bitterness engendered by these actions remained a powerful force in the African American community. Many blacks continued to vote for Crump candidates because they were encouraged to participate, and the machine rewarded supporters with patronage and services.

CROSSROADS

---

[86] *Memphis Press-Scimitar,* 7 January 1947, 11.

[87] Michael Honey, *Southern Labor and Black Civil Rights: Organizing Memphis Workers* (Urbana: University of Illinois Press, 1993), 165.

[88] Laurie Beth Green, "Battling the Plantation Mentality: Consciousness, Culture and the Politics of Race, Class and Gender in Memphis, 1940–1968" (Ph.D. diss., University of Chicago, 1999), 74–77.

[89] J. E. Walker, Chairman of the Colored Democrats Club, to Shelby County Commissioner E. W. Hale, 31 October 1940, E. W. Hale Collection (Memphis/Shelby County Public Library and Information Center, Memphis TN).

[90] Biles, 89.

African Americans, though, were under no illusions. Despite their support, many black Memphians remained wary of Crump and his political organization.[91]

Historians have accepted this interpretation of the machine's anti-crime measures. Scholar Michel Honey, in his book *Southern Labor and Black Civil Rights*, goes so far as to describe these events as a "reign of terror" against the black community.[92] While race played an important role in machine rule, the evidence suggests that many other factors were involved.

Arguably the most important reason to reevaluate the "reign of terror" thesis is the Herman Mitchell police brutality case. If African Americans were being terrorized on a wide scale, then why did Mitchell feel he could report that a white police officer had hit him? Perhaps Mitchell was not aware of what was going on, or perhaps he was simply determined to exercise his rights no matter the cost. Regardless of the reason, it would seem that in Mitchell's case the use of white terror on blacks failed. This suggests the racial situation in Memphis during the 1930s and early 1940s was far more complicated than many historians have asserted. No doubt that the inner circles of the Crump organization desired to quash black hopes for equality. This attitude was tempered, however, by the machine's need for African American support during elections.

Several factors drove the machine's war against organized crime in Memphis: negative publicity, corruption, the tenacity of the underworld, and police brutality. Perhaps the single greatest factor, however, was the fear that the 1935 *Colliers* article by Owen P. White might threaten the Crump machine's hegemony. It was thus necessary to eradicate the source of the criticism that Memphis was a lawless city. The degree of success achieved by the machine in combating this image can

---

[91] Randolph Meade Walker, "The Role of the Black Clergy in Memphis," *West Tennessee Historical Society Papers,* 33 (1979): 39–42.
[92] Honey, 165.

be detected in the national press coverage of Memphis once organized crime was eliminated.

In June 1940, *Time* magazine reported: "Last week Memphis had the cold-water blues. Gone from hotel lobbies were the expectant blondes. Brothels were closed; their staffs had fled. Bookies had shut up shop."[93] Six years later, in a cover story on Crump, *Time* described him as "the most absolute political boss in the U.S." The correspondent also made note that "there were no prostitutes, gamblers, policy games or gunmen. Crump had simply banished them."[94]

The marriage between organized crime and machine politics was not unique to Memphis. Tammany Hall in New York City had an "arrangement" with the underworld, culminating in a virtual mob takeover of the Democratic organization in the mid-1940s.[95] In Chicago, the "syndicate" controlled votes in the 1st ward, making it an important ally of the Cook County Democratic machine.[96] Although these examples of machine politics were not unlike the machine in Memphis, Crump's machine was far more successful in eradicating gangsters—not only within its organization, but also from its city streets.

Machine politics had a great deal of influence on the success of the law enforcement drive, but so did Southern culture. Historically, Southerners have held contradictory views of crime. Natives of the region have often condoned personal violence while insisting that persons committing illegal behavior be severely punished.[97] This conflicted view of antisocial behavior strongly influenced the rise of organized crime in Memphis. However, it also impacted the direction taken by city officials in ridding Memphis of its entrenched criminal class between the

CROSSROADS

---

[93] *Time,* 10 June 1940, 22–23.

[94] *Time,* 27 May 1946, 20–21.

[95] Warren Moscow, *The Last of the Big-Time Bosses: The Life and Times of Carmine DeSapio and the Decline and Fall of Tammany Hall* (New York: Stein and Day, 1971) 51–54.

[96] Adam Cohen and Elizabeth Taylor, *American Pharaoh: Mayor Richard J. Daley His Battle for Chicago and the Nation* (New York: Back Bay Books, 2000): 190–91.

[97] Henry Lundsgaarde, "Crime, Attitudes Toward," in *Encyclopedia of Southern Culture,* ed. Charles Reagan Wilson and William Ferris (Chapel Hill: University of North Carolina Press, 1989): 1478–79.

years 1935 and 1940. Although the gangster purge during this period weakened the multi-ethnic nature of the Crump machine, most Memphians continued to be involved in the political process. African Americans, in particular, remained members of Memphis' Democratic Party coalition despite the heavy-handed tactics employed against some of the city's black leaders. For this reason, 1930s Memphis was unique for a Southern city, in that disenfranchisement did not exist there and in that the one-party system actually represented all Southerners, albeit unequally.

Dorothy with staff and kids.

Southern Hospitality

BY DOROTHY HAMPTON MARCUS

"It's not that they are inferior; they just have a different nature," I heard my Mama say more than once as I was growing up in Winston-Salem, North Carolina, during the 1930s and 1940s. She was talking about "colored folks" or "Nigras," as they were called. Mama. Mama, who never wore make-up. Mama, who wore her straight black hair pulled back in a knot at the back of her neck. Mama, the seamstress, who wore simple "house dresses" that she could make in an hour flat. Mama, who could stretch a dollar further than anybody, during hard times or otherwise. Mama, who didn't know that there were lies our Southern culture had taught her and that she was passing them on. The lies, as I learned them, were not overt straight-out lies. They were subtle… benign…infectious. It was just the way things were. We caught the lies by osmosis.

Mama didn't know what she didn't know. When she began to know, to get some glimmer of the lies, to recognize there was something wrong with the culture, she set out to change things where she lived the best way she could. Based on what I was beginning to learn in college about the lies, Mama and I discussed how we hadn't questioned the way things were—such as the Southern way of Negro women always eating separately in the kitchen or after the white family ate. Mama decided to change things with the woman who came weekly to clean our house.

"Now, Ellamae, we want you to come sit down at the table and eat with us."

Ellamae plopped the platter she was holding on the kitchen counter with a thud to keep from dropping it. "Oh, no Ma'am, I couldn't do that. I ain't used to eatin' with the folks I works for," Ellamae said, hugging her crossed arms close to her breast and shaking her head as she looked down at the linoleum she had just scrubbed and waxed. "It just ain't right."

"Well, Ellamae, I think maybe it ain't right the way we've always done things."

I honestly don't remember if Mama persuaded Ellamae to sit down and eat with us. What I do remember is the terrible awkwardness we all felt as we tried to undo a little piece of our lying culture. Now I know that it was not such a little piece and that we were asking Ellamae to fix it. We were asking her to sit down and break bread with us when she didn't even have a last name, much less a title, in our house.

As I look back now, I can begin to imagine how she might have felt: "They don't even know me. They don't know how I loves my children. They don't know that I's the president of the usher board at my church and that my husband and I works with the youth fellowship. And that I'm taking care of my ailing Mama and her sister. And… And…And…And here they wants me to set down with them like I's their friend. I know they means well, but they just don't understan' how I feel. They don't know me."

We didn't know how little we knew. We didn't know how to let each other know what we didn't know about the lies our culture had taught us and about what those lies had done to all of us on both sides of the chasm. We were just beginning to recognize the chasm, from our side.

As a child of the '30s and '40s, I didn't know (and it never occurred to me to ask), "How come the colored girls who work in our home have only first names?" So, why would I ask, "How come I call women at church Miss Proctor or Mrs. Carter and I don't use Miss or Mrs. for the colored girls at home?" And, "Oh, by the way, how come the women at church are women, and the women who work at home are girls?" Nor did I ask: "What do WHITE and COLORED water fountains, restrooms, and waiting rooms mean?" "How come the colored people sit in the back of the bus?" "Why do all the colored people live in East Winston ('Nigger Town')?" "How come the colored children go to different schools?" It was just the way things were. It was the way the lies permeated the culture.

In high school, I began to have some inkling that things should be different. My senior year, in 1950, we had a six-week "race unit" in our sociology course. All I remember from that unit was a field trip to Adkins, the colored high school in Winston-Salem, and the snide comments from my classmates, such as "Their school is nicer than our school," "Their lockers are bigger than ours," and "The floors are all shiny"—the implication being that their school shouldn't be better than our school. Perhaps the colored school was newer than ours to make the then legal "Separate but Equal" doctrine more believable. Of course, we knew nothing of such politics. Nor did we know the NAACP was in the process of challenging that doctrine in the courts. Little did we know that in four short years the U.S. Supreme Court would rule in *Brown vs. Board of Education* that "Separate but Equal is inherently unequal."

After entering college in the early 1950s, I was embarrassed to recognize how I had been allowed as a child to participate in the lying culture when I called an elder Negro woman "Laura" while she addressed me as "Miss Pete." For many years, Laura had worked in my Aunt Husie's boarding house and had worked for my family once in a while. I remember my sisters telling me how as children, long before I was born, they learned one day that Laura had a last name. It was funny to them then, and they danced around the ironing board and Laura, singing "Miz Dunlap, Miz Dunlap, Miz Dunlap." I wonder how she felt as she continued ironing?

With my embarrassment about the past and my new righteousness, I went home for spring break determined to address the current cleaning woman with her proper title and last name. The day before she came,

I asked Mama for Maggie's last name and was all ready to call her "Mrs. Jackson" at my first opportunity—very naturally, of course. In the afternoon, after she arrived, I went upstairs to take a nap. When the doorbell rang, I sprang from my bed to let Mrs. Jackson know that I was not downstairs to answer the door,

"Maggie! Can you…"

Oops. My righteousness and good intentions had succumbed to the "natural" habit of calling her "Maggie." Change don't come easy.

I went to Meredith College, a Southern Baptist women's school in Raleigh, North Carolina, a hundred miles from home. It was for whites, of course. I was the youngest of six in my family and the only one to know from a young age that I would go to college. Evelyn, the oldest of six children, went to Meredith six years after graduating from high school and decided that her baby sister would go to college, too—and she saw to it that I did, paying for most of my tuition.

Meredith College had always been a little ahead of its time. The Baptist Student Union (BSU) helped us begin to question our segregated culture through joint meetings with students from Shaw University, a Negro college across town. For the first time we met and shared common interests with our peers across racial lines. It was exciting to be a part of those first interracial experiences. We didn't know what we didn't know. Excited about what we were beginning to know and experience, we were very aware that we were being interracial, and we were very careful not to entertain a negative thought about any of our new Negro friends. It didn't occur to us then, but it does occur to me now that they just might have entertained a negative thought or two about us. They knew a whole lot of what we did not know. It would be forty years before I would hear the term "white privilege." We hadn't the faintest concept of how much more freely we, being white, could move about in Raleigh, or anywhere else, compared to the uneasiness our Negro friends had to live with. I'm still working on recognizing and understanding how, where, and when my white privilege plays out in my life—a large part of not knowing what I didn't and still don't know.

Campers at Camp Rabbit Hollow, 1953.

We thought we were solving the problems of the world. And we had a good time. The only Shaw student whose name I remember is Lucius Walker. He was a good-looking fellow of average height, a natural leader who was lots of fun. I remember some of us playing with his name, calling him "Luscious." When I spoke with him recently about our experiences in 1950–51, he said, "It seemed natural for us to be together. We were aware of the historical significance; we knew we were opening new ground. It was a bold exercise in being natural." Lucius added, "We were ahead of the times." He gave another example: he and some of the other Shaw students had sat toward the front of the bus en route to and from their jobs in Cameron Village, a mall in a white area not far from Meredith. While they were aware of "a few scowls," they did not have the kind of experience Rosa Parks had that sparked the Montgomery bus boycott and the civil rights movement.

The Rev. Lucius Walker Jr. would become a leading social justice activist. In 1967, he founded (and served as Executive Director of) the Interreligious Foundation for Community Organization, which "assists the poor and disenfranchised in developing and sustaining community organizations to fight human and civil rights injustices."

We may have relaxed and forgotten about race momentarily when we as Meredith and Shaw students talked for countless hours on the long bus ride from Raleigh, North Carolina, to Nashville, Tennessee. We knew we couldn't stop en route because there was no place that would accommodate an interracial group. We were on our way to the National Baptist Student Union Convention at Fisk University, one of the foremost traditional Negro colleges. Lucius told me that they deliberately did not use "Negro" in the title of their BSU because they were hoping to make it truly national. I'm sure I enjoyed some fine speeches at that convention. But what I really remember is sharing a room with a Negro girl and chattering away on our bunk beds about our schools, friends, clothes, the Convention, and maybe even boys! I realized as I drifted off to sleep that this was the same as drifting off to sleep in any other dorm…and that I was excited about the sameness.

In the Fall of 1953, my senior year, the North Carolina Baptist Student Union Convention was held in Winston-Salem, my hometown. That weekend event was memorable on many levels. For the first time, Negro students attended "our" Convention.

There was a big brouhaha about one of the speakers. The NCBSU staff invited Nels Ferre, a well-known theologian and author from Andover-Newton Seminary in New England, to lead the worship services at the convention. The top North Carolina Baptist officials found some of Dr. Ferre's writing to be too "liberal," too "dangerous" for "raising too many questions." One of the books they cited was *The Sun and the Umbrella* in which Dr. Ferre discussed some aspects of Christianity that people sometimes deify into "umbrellas" that shield them from the Deity, such as the Church, the Trinity, and the Virgin Birth. The Baptist officials saw Ferre's various scholarly theories about the conception of

Jesus (such as the possibility that Mary might have had an "affair" with a soldier at a military base near Nazareth) as his personal denial of the Virgin Birth. The state Baptist officials felt that one of their "umbrellas" had been attacked. Those officials requested the NCBSU staff to withdraw Ferre's invitation lest he corrupt our young minds. The BSU staff refused.

Nels Ferre, a gentle, unassuming, fairly short man with thinning sandy hair, quietly led several thought-provoking, worshipful and non-controversial meditations at the beginning of each convention session. The next week, Meredith College students who hadn't read a theological book since the required freshman religion course were seen in the cafeteria line reading *The Sun and the Umbrella*. Baptist officials in North Carolina were determined that the BSU staff had to go. In the Spring of 1954, a busload of Meredith students traveled to Greensboro for the "mock trial" of the three men who had invited Nels Ferre and helped to open our minds, our hearts, and our worlds. All three were fired. While Nels Ferre's "liberal" theology was undoubtedly offensive to the conservative Baptists, we were convinced that the efforts of our BSU leaders to enable us to challenge the racial lies of our culture played a large part in their "excommunication." In our recent conversation, Lucius confirmed to me that "the Shaw students were certain that these men were fired because they had engineered our interracial activities." We were heart-broken, angry, and...changed. The Baptist officials may have thought they were protecting us. What they did was to politicize us.

Another memorable aspect of the BSU Convention was the post session party one night at my house. It was a simple event, not that different from the "fellowship hours" we had at our house on many Sunday evenings after church when I was in high school. Mama made cookies and her famous non-alcoholic punch. People were milling around in our good-sized living room and spilling over into the dining room. Some good conversation, with lots of laughs. What was different about this event was that for the first time we were having Negro guests. And while it was clear to my parents, my friends, and me that we were breaking new ground by having an interracial social event in my home, I don't remember any objections. I talked to Mama beforehand, and I guess she talked to Daddy—or maybe she didn't! Yes, it was a simple event, and for me it was spectacular. That night for the first time in his 67 years, my Daddy, who routinely used "Nigger" in referring to Negroes, with no negative connotation (to him), reached out and shook the hand of a Negro, Lucius Walker. That night, my Daddy expanded the meaning of Southern hospitality. Tears of joy welled up in me as I witnessed this simple gesture.

Parallel to my college experiences were my summer adventures. The Summer of 1952, I worked in New York City and lived with my sister Evelyn, who had migrated there after fleeing Southern Baptist land. We took advantage of every free event the city had to offer. Twice I was overwhelmed with awe. One night we walked west on a poorly lit 47th Street talking about our day. Suddenly, we saw Times Square, with all its lights. And there was this tremendous billboard with a man's face bigger than our apartment blowing real smoke rings from his huge mouth and holding a Camel cigarette a couple of yards long. Camels were made in li'l ole Winston-Salem, my hometown. My hometown up in lights in Times Square in New York City!

The second awesome event: we went to church. Back in Winston-Salem, we were proud of the lovely church we had built a few years before, with its tower that was taller than both the Methodist and Moravian churches a couple of blocks away. Instead of the traditional brown pews, our new sanctuary had white pews trimmed in maroon to match the carpet and the drapes adorning the big clear windows that let the sun come streaming in, giving a light and airy aura.

Then one Sunday, my big sister took me to church in New York City. We walked into the Nave of the Riverside Church. I was dumbstruck—flabbergasted—overwhelmed. It was magnificent in size and beauty. At least four of my down-home churches could have fit in that sanctuary, two stacked on top of two. Here were glorious stained glass windows two stories high, and the ceiling kept reaching up higher. A huge gold cross hung over the altar, flanked with screens of carvings on both sides and above. And there were magnificent chandeliers with tiers of twenty-five or fifty lights that looked like candles.

Through Riverside's Guild for young adults, we visited other churches in the city to learn how they were serving their communities, including the Negro Presbyterian Church of the Master, a small stone structure directly down the hill from Riverside and on the other side of Morningside Park at 122nd Street in the heart of Harlem. There the renowned Rev. Dr. James H. Robinson told us about their programs through the Morningside Community Center, including the interracial camps in New Hampshire where they took Negro, white, and Spanish kids away from the hot inner city streets for two weeks of outdoor life.

After his talk, I approached this gentle, dynamic man with trepidation: "Dr. Robinson, my name is Dorothy Hampton, and I wonder if I might be able to work in one of those camps next summer?"

He said, "That might be possible. Let me give you the name and number to call for an application," probably hiring my Southern white accent in his head on the spot.

After I returned to Meredith for my junior year, I got the application, sent it back and haunted the campus post office, holding my breath as I waited for a reply. In my innocence I didn't realize that, of course, they would snatch up this Southern white girl with no camping experience just to educate her. They did!

The Summer of 1953 was the major turning point of my life. For the first time, I lived in an interracial community long enough to forget that it was interracial. It was a long way from my native segregated North Carolina to Camps Rabbit Hollow and Forest Lake—600 miles by train to New York City and another 250 miles by bus to Winchester, New Hampshire. Eight hundred fifty miles and several light years.

After a few days of orientation at Forest Lake, the girls' camp, which was prettier and more intimate than the boys' camp, I moved (with the male staff) to Rabbit Hollow, the boys' camp, where I was assigned to work in the office. Rabbit Hollow had a rough terrain, with white frame cabins scattered on a hill on one side of the big old frame farmhouse that served as the office and as sleeping quarters for the non-counselor staff. The dining hall was way up a rutted dirt road on the other side of the farmhouse. Later, when the guys and I traveled over to Forest Lake for Saturday evening fun and games, the female staff would tease, "Here comes 'Pete' with her harem!"

Very soon after joining the staff of Negro and white American and international college students, the skin color of my new friends became unimportant to me. There were times when I forgot about it altogether. As I looked around the table at staff gatherings, I would think "Now Eddie and John are really very conscientious counselors, and sometimes Mack and Allen seem to slack off a little." And I would realize later that one of each pair was Negro and one white. I saw them as individuals. I no longer had to censor a negative thought about a Negro or to compare people on the basis of race. I could just see them as people with different personalities, different approaches, different ways of expressing their commitments. It's entirely possible that I fell into the trap that we white folks often fall into, believing and saying "we're all just alike." I was beginning to know and appreciate how we are alike in our humanity. I didn't know how much I had to learn about the impact slavery and its legacy made—and still makes.

One day I leaned back in my battered, creaking swivel chair, with my feet on my desk (Mama had been trying for years to get me to keep my feet below my head). I looked across to Brad, the camp director and my summer crush, sitting at his mismatched desk facing mine. I asked, "What color is Jackie, that mischievous kid who is always up to something, trying to con me out of a candy bar at canteen time or chasing somebody around the tables in the dining hall when we're trying to say grace?"

He did a double take, "I know the kid you're talking about, and I can't remember either. Is he Negro or white?"

I had a revelation rather suddenly one day as I walked down the hill from the camp dining hall, my ears still ringing from 100 boys singing the old camp songs at the top of their lungs. I had my hands on the shoulders of two of those campers, as we talked about the songs and their hopes it wouldn't rain so they could go swimming after "rest time." There I was, just walking down the dusty, gravelly, rutted road with two little boys. No big deal. Then it slowly began to seep into my consciousness that one of those little boys had coarse black hair curled close to his scalp and the other little boy had very straight blond hair hanging in his eyes. And that it didn't make any difference to me. I was free. I had been released from what my segregated culture had done to me. I was aware that I had been unaware of the difference in their hair and skin— then aware—then delighted that I had been unaware.

One Sunday afternoon, I climbed up on a huge boulder across the narrow dirt road from the old farmhouse to wait for the summer's last batch of inner-city darlings to tumble off the bus. I had a book to read. It fell from my hands as I found myself reveling in the liberation this summer had brought me:

"The shackles of my Southern culture have been broken," I thought. "I want to go home and share this exhilaration with my family and friends back home who don't know they have shackles." I made a commitment that day that would shape my future. "I am going to do something on the interracial level." I had found my "mission in life." I vowed to challenge the lying culture I had grown up accepting as "just the way things are." I had no idea what I was talking about. Race relations jobs weren't exactly listed in the classifieds of the day.

When I got off the train back home, I saw the WHITE and COLORED signs as if for the first time. I had seen these signs all my life. Why were they jumping off the walls at me now? For a moment, I stopped and stared at the signs. I considered going into the COLORED waiting room. Then I realized that I did not know what I would do if I were challenged—that it just might be a good idea to have a plan. So I sadly went into the WHITE waiting room as usual. This was eight years before the Freedom Rides of 1961 that would deliberately challenge the continuing segregation of buses and terminals despite the Supreme

Court decision in *Boynton v. Virginia*, which prohibited segregation in interstate travel.

I returned to Meredith for my senior year, telling everybody who would listen about the new freedom I felt, sharing my exhilaration from the summer with my classmates. I have found notes and a scribbled speech that I probably made at the Sunday evening student gathering at Pullen Memorial Baptist Church. As far as I could tell, all of my classmates were quite enthusiastic about my summer. My roommate decided she wanted to go to "my" camp the following summer. She did.

I often wondered if some of my classmates might have been less supportive than those who expressed their excitement and approval of my summer adventure. Recently, I asked some of those who had expressed support if they were aware of any negative comments behind my back. They remembered none. Meredith was still a little ahead of its time.

One Monday night in May 1954, three weeks before graduation, we heard singing from the other end of the dining hall: "Congratulations to you, Congratulations to you…." We wondered who had become pinned or engaged over the weekend. The singing continued, "Congratulations Supreme Court…." The U.S. Supreme Court had that day declared segregation in public schools unconstitutional. I'm proud that at my college there was a small celebration for this event, when most of the rest of the white South would launch a mighty resistance to the ruling. I know now that some Negroes and their allies then questioned whether that decision was for the best. Some still do.

Upon graduation, most of my classmates planned to be teachers in North Carolina. I was excited to go back to New York City to work for the National Council of Churches, and to be paid $400 a year more than those North Carolina teachers. The first summer I participated in a "Church and City" project at Judson Church in the heart of Greenwich Village and then moved in with Evelyn. I attended Church of the Master. Although it may seem strange for a white girl right out of the South to attend church in Harlem, it seemed perfectly natural to me.

That was where my friends from camp were. I became active in the young adult group and taught a Sunday school class.

After trying to teach that obstreperous bunch of eighth graders for almost a year, I learned that the church had been unable to keep a teacher for that particular class for more than a few weeks since kindergarten. So I guess if they didn't pay attention to me after all my late Saturday night preparation, it was not necessarily because I was white. One Sunday when I planned to be away, I arranged for a substitute. When my plans changed, I decided to look in on the class. It was bedlam. Not one adult in sight. Kids were running around, noisy beyond belief, and one big kid was holding a heavy chair over his head like he was going to bring it down on somebody. I slowly and deliberately walked up to him. "Jimmy, put the chair down." He did. I was surprised when I realized later that I had not been afraid. I had established some kind of rapport. Did he put the chair down because I was white? I

Campers swimming at Camp Rabbit Hollow, 1953.

choose to believe he did it because I had earned his respect. At the very least, he knew I was not afraid of him.

Among the young adults group, we talked about race some, but mostly we did Bible study, had programs of interest to young people, went on outings, held retreats, and had parties. We were young, sometimes serious, sometimes frivolous, sometimes bouncing back and forth between the two.

One Sunday an especially attractive young woman told us about being rejected after applying to be an airline stewardess. In those days, only white women of specified dimensions held those very glamorous jobs. Someone asked her what they said when they turned her down. She replied coyly, "They said it was my legs," lifting her skirt slightly to reveal her gorgeous legs. Stewardesses had to be attractive back then—and white! We laughed to keep from crying. I learned later that Dr. Robinson had asked her to apply for the job in order to develop a test case.

I was surprised to find myself being pursued by perhaps the loudest and most militant black man in the group. Since I had not dated much in college, I enjoyed having more attention from this gregarious man than I had had from any other man. Maybe he was trying to prove something, and maybe I was too. It didn't seem so at the time. I found a note he wrote to me dated March 10, 1956, which seems to indicate some depth in our relationship. He wrote: "Rapport and empathy developed between us naturally and quickly, the ease and speed with which we were able to exchange our frank and honest opinions."

One rainy day as we boarded his car for some church outing, I remember his teasing a Negro woman and me, as we were both concerned about our hair. She was worried that the rain was going to make her hair kinky, and I was concerned that it was going to make mine straight.

When I told Evelyn about my new boyfriend, she said, "Well, if you decide to marry him, Paul and I will support you, but it might kill Daddy." I don't think I ever thought I would marry him. Of course, people tend to anticipate that possibility, especially if the couple is interracial. As it happened, some time after I went back South, he married the woman with the other kind of hair.

Yen and Muriel Whitney were the one married couple in the young adults group. One day they were taking some of us to a church function in their car. I'll never forget Yen's statement in the midst of our conversation: "It's easier to be a Negro in the South than in the North. In the South we know where we can go and be accepted. In the North, we never can be sure where we will be insulted or refused service or worse." This was not idle speculation on my part or something I had read. This was my dear friend's pain.

As I went to church and made friends with young people who experienced life differently in many ways because they were Negro, my race relations education progressed. If there were formal race relations courses available in the mid-'50's, I was unaware of them. As far as I know, most of us who worked in the field in the '50's and '60's got our education from each other and from reading (and teaching as we read) Benjamin Mays, Gunnar Myrdal, Liston Pope, Gordon Allport, and assorted pamphlets. I remember reading something by Benjamin Mays and thinking, "He's saying the same thing I've been saying," and then realizing that I had read his work earlier, absorbed it, and forgotten that he was the source of my brilliance!

On December 1, 1955, Rosa Parks kept her seat on a bus in Montgomery, Alabama, and the civil rights era was launched. As the Montgomery bus boycott and subsequent events began making national news, I was champing at the bit and telling everybody I knew about my passion to go back to my beloved South and "do something." I still had no idea what that something might be.

I did have a fantasy about a few white Southerners poking their heads out of their windows looking for other people who also wanted to do something about race relations, every one of them scared they were the only one and that if they stuck their necks out too far, their heads would be chopped off. My fantasy was that several would stick their necks out at the same time and discover each other—or that maybe I would somehow be able to help them find each other. One of the categories on my resume in later years would be "Bringing People Together," alluding to the most satisfying aspect of my career.

One Wednesday afternoon, one of my New York colleagues came back to our office and said to me, "I just had lunch with Galen Weaver from the Council for Christian Social Action of the United Church of Christ. They are looking for a white Southern woman to work on race relations in North Carolina and Virginia."

Had it finally happened? It sounded like they were looking for me. I was ecstatic. I called Galen and raced up the street to his office that very afternoon.

A new Protestant denomination was forming. The Congregational Christian Churches and the Evangelical and Reformed Church were in the process of becoming the United Church of Christ, still considered as among the most "liberal" of the Protestant denominations. The new Church was not going to allow the segregated regional bodies that existed in the South to continue. The social action bodies of the two denominations had designed the Race Relations Project to enable their churches in North Carolina and Virginia to begin to accept and move toward a non-segregated regional body. The Project involved sending an interracial team to North Carolina and Virginia to prepare the way for that transition—to help the people accept what most of the white folks considered an unnecessary edict imposed by a national church that didn't understand the South.

The Negro woman for the interracial team had already been hired and the "white" job had been offered to a middle-aged, well-respected member of one of the churches in Virginia. She would be much more acceptable to the white leaders of the area than I, a twenty-four-year-old who had been raised a Southern Baptist and had been attending a Negro Presbyterian Church in Harlem. It was bad enough that the national church was perceived as imposing this race relations project on the churches in North Carolina and Virginia. To have outsiders staffing the project would be even worse. There was some question about whether this very acceptable woman would take the job. She was to decide by Sunday. If she didn't take it, the job was mine. So I held my breath again.

Come Sunday I exhaled. The acceptable woman did not take the job. I finally had my job "on the interracial level" in my beloved Southland.

The next four years would be among the most difficult and the most satisfying years of my career. It took eighteen months for me to feel that I had any real support from the leaders of the top white regional bodies. There were only four white ministers who fully supported us from the beginning. It was very difficult for this white twenty-four-year-old woman and the Negro sixty-something woman to become a "team." I was spared from really dealing with that issue when her husband became ill and she had to resign. All the traveling—at first to meet strangers, some of whom were dead-set against what we were trying to do and many more who were scared to help us do it—was stressful; I came back from many trips to wake up the next morning with a migraine. The travel didn't lend itself to my developing much of a social life.

After a year or so, I began to fill up my calendar without begging. I spoke in many churches and led workshops, usually with rather small groups. By the second summer, we formed a committee from the three regional bodies through which we pulled off an interracial senior high camp, the most visible accomplishment of the four years and the most satisfying. This was 1957. This camp continued even after I left the job. We also formed a United Committee for Campus Ministry, through which we organized an interracial state organization of students from several Negro and white colleges; those students gathered occasionally and went to national conferences.

Looking back over those four years, I believe they were where I made my most valuable contribution, primarily through the hundreds, perhaps thousands of individual conversations that may have moved those good people along in their journey to know what they didn't know about the lies our Southern culture had taught them, and to expand the meaning of Southern hospitality.

The Shellman Story

BY HENRY A. BUCHANAN

I went to Shellman, Georgia, to be pastor of the Baptist church there because Dr. Spright Dowell was President of Mercer University, and he told the people at Shellman that I would be the right man for the job. Dr. Dowell had a good impression of me because I was the only man in the graduating class of 1945 who showed up in short sleeves for the reception at the President's home. It was a hot, humid June day, in Macon, and even the President's home was not air-conditioned in 1945.

Dr. Dowell knew about me because he had helped to get me through school, but he also knew about Shellman. A wealthy man named Riley Curry lived in Shellman. He was getting old and near the end of his life, and Dr. Dowell convinced him that he should give a part of his wealth to Mercer University to endow a chair of Christian Studies. The story got out, told by a Negro manservant in the Curry home. "Y'all know what? A man come down here an' he got Mister Riley Curry to give a hundert thousand dollars for a mercy seat in heab'n."

Well, this was the legend I heard when I arrived in Shellman in the Summer of 1951, a recent graduate of the Southern Baptist Theological Seminary in Louisville, Kentucky. I preached a "trial sermon" entitled "The Integrated Man." The congregation was pleased with Dr. Dowell's choice of man for their pulpit. They offered me the church and showed me the house where I and my wife MarthaLee would live. They were pleased, I learned later, that she had not come with me for the "trial sermon" because it signified that I was a man who could make up his own mind about matters of great importance.

I told them I would consider the offer prayerfully, went back to Louisville and asked MarthaLee what she thought about it. She thought I should accept an appointment to the Air Force Chaplaincy, but she consented to go to Shellman, and I informed the people there that we would come as soon as we could pack and move. We arrived two weeks before our furniture did, and when the Shellman people saw what we owned, they wondered why we had bothered to wait for it.

For three years the people of Shellman were happy with both me and my wife. She was employed to teach second grade in the elementary school. Two small country churches, Friendship Baptist and Brooksville Baptist, sought my service; I held worship services at these two churches on Sunday afternoons. It seemed that Dr. Dowell had sent them a good man, and that they even had a better bargain in my wife, and the only concern they had was that some larger church would steal me away from them with a better offer. It was only when we became embroiled in the racial issue that the people of Shellman wished some other church had me.

In May 1954 the Supreme Court of the United States handed down the decision that became known as *Brown vs. Board of Education*. It not only outlawed racial segregation in public schools across the United States; it also ended the halcyon days of my ministry at Shellman, and ushered in seven months of bitter conflict between me and the people of the Shellman Baptist Church and the whole community around Shellman.

Just about everybody in Georgia was unhappy with the Court's decision. The Governor, Herman Talmadge, was the chief spokesman for the opposition, but there were plenty of others who were outspoken on the issue. Against it.

Just about everybody, but not quite. I wrote a letter to the editor of the *Atlanta Journal* & *Constitution*, saying that the decision of the Court was right and ought to be accepted and obeyed, and that refusal to do so

Henry A. Buchanan reflecting upon his experiences in Shellman, Georgia during the early 1950s.

could result in great damage to the school system. And that it was the Christian thing to do. "The *Journal* covers Dixie like the dew," but when the people of Shellman saw their pastor's name attached to this unacceptable statement, it was as if frost settled in May on that little farming center.

They reacted with great displeasure to the publicity their town was getting as a result of my letter. The AP got hold of it, and every newspaper in the U.S. spread the word that the quiet little town of Shellman, Georgia, had a Baptist minister who was out of step with Southern tradition. Mr. Riley Curry had "bought hisself a mercy seat in heab'n for a hunnert thousand dollars," but I had got myself a peck of trouble with a letter to the editor of the *Atlanta Journal*.

Signs began appearing on utility poles, warning people that they were approaching the abode of the most notorious "nigger lover" who was intent upon bringing great harm to his own good Southern people. Georgia born, but educated out of state, I must have seemed worse than a Yankee interloper to those people.

I was urged by some of the deacons and leaders in the church to be quiet, but I did not heed their warnings and even set forth my views from the pulpit, saying that the Christian view of the Fatherhood of God and the Brotherhood of believers in Christ laid on the Church the responsibility to take the lead in bringing the white and black races together. The upshot of this was that I was hanged in effigy in the town hall and buried downtown with a poetic epitaph that also covered a couple of deacons who had not been sufficiently outspoken in their disapproval of my views on racial integration of the schools.

The town hall was the place where the sheets for the Ku Klux Klan were stored, and this is what gave rise to a story that the KKK was responsible for the hanging. The sheriff, at the urging of the chairman of the deacons of the Baptist church, cut me down, and I was told that he lost seventy-five votes in the upcoming election as the result of this action. I never knew what they did with the mound that served as a grave, but when this symbolic threat failed to move me, the opposition sent a messenger to me to inform me that I would be taken for a midnight ride in the country. But when I informed the bearer of this message that I would not be the only man who would fail to return from this ride, then hedged my bet by loading my shotgun, nobody showed up to take me for a ride. But lots of people did show up for the vote that was held on Sunday morning, June 27, 1954, in the Shellman Baptist Church.

It appeared at first that I would be voted out, but Mrs. Mae White, the wife of one of the older deacons, J. A. White, rose in church to defend me. Her defense of me was so strong, and her attack on the ones who had instigated the move to oust me was so damaging, that I was sustained by a vote of sixty-six to thirty-seven. The ballots had been marked STAY or GO, and it now appeared that I would stay.

Well, I had won the day, but not the war, for my opponents gathered their forces and began working to force my resignation. I, on the other hand, fully intended to strengthen further my position by clarifying for the public just what my position was. And for this, I intended to speak on radio at station WDWD in Dawson, which lies between Shellman and Albany, Georgia, and in this address I made an even stronger appeal for acceptance of the Christian ideal of acceptance of all men as brothers and equals in the Lord Jesus Christ.

The radio station manager told me that he had received a threatening call warning him not to let me speak, but he assured me that I was free to speak on his station at any time. In my address, I warned that if the Church remained silent in that crucial hour, it might as well keep silent for the next twenty years, that if Christians embraced the principle of enforced separateness at that point, they would discover that the universal Christ had passed them by, and "that he who has some Truth to teach, but turns away those who would learn because they are of another color, will presently find that the Truth itself has also fled from him."

When I had finished speaking, Mr. James Woodall, the station manager, was again gracious to me. I went home to Shellman to find that the other ministers in town, the Methodist Frank Gilmore and the Baptist E. A. Cline, were happy that I had spoken, but they showed no inclination to speak themselves. Miss Susie May Brown and Mrs. Mae White were ecstatic over my address, and, best of all, MarthaLee hugged me happily.

So I had gone public with my views, had won a vote of confidence in the church, and had the most important people in my life on my side. I would take a little vacation. MarthaLee and I would drive to Louisville where I would find some quiet, peaceful place to think and study and write and plan for the future. Was I in for a surprise! I had hardly settled into the routine of work in the library there when I began to get mail from home. And the mail all brought bad news. First, the two country churches had voted to ask for my resignation. Then MarthaLee got a letter from the school superintendent asking for her resignation. There was nothing I could do to fight the accomplished vote of the two country churches. There was something to be done about MarthaLee's job.

MarthaLee refused to resign and threw the responsibility for dismissing her back into the lap of the superintendent. He, realizing that his only ground for action lay in the fact that she was married to me, backed down, and she kept her teaching position. But our vacation was spoiled. We returned home to the loving embrace of our supporters and to the hostile stares of our opponents. Miss Susie May Brown and Mrs. Mae White proved to be our valiant lieutenants, but there was a hard core of people in the Shellman Baptist Church, supported by some in both the Friendship and Brooksville churches, who were determined to stand by us with loyal support.

Deacon Manry Stewart led the opposition, threatening secession from the union, and George Robinette ordered me to leave his house "by the back door like a nigger." I had become *persona non grata*—thank you Miss Florrie for making me study Latin—in town. Most disappointing was my discovery that I did not have the support of other clergymen in my fight for racial equality. Some Baptist ministers were willing to be identified with me. Jim Coker and Ed Straney at Columbus were with me. Waldo Harris made a statement at the morning service in his church—I don't recall where he was—and was fired at the evening session. But most of the ministers wanted to be as far away as possible when the stones began to fly. One minister spoke for all when he was asked for his position; he said, "It is a good time to pray about it and a bad time to talk about it." Most of the ministers I had known did not want to talk about the issue publicly. The pastor at Cuthbert, a town only a few miles from Shellman, informed me that people in the area suspected that I had lost my mind, and if I insisted on continuing to speak on the subject of race I would remove any remaining doubt they might have about it.

You may think that because I was minister of the Baptist church in Shellman, my troubles would be limited to the Baptist people in town. Not so. Baptists and Methodists were intermarried, and they did business with one another, and there could be no clear line of demarcation between them. I got in hot water with the Methodists in town by offending a respected and retired Methodist minister whom I never met, because he wrote a strong defense of racial segregation for the official Methodist periodical; his statement was given to me by a prominent Methodist, Mr. Land, who invited me to respond to what the writer, Mr. Davenport, had written, which was that the ruling white race had treated the subject black race in America better than ever before anywhere or anytime in history. And he bolstered his view of separateness as the ideal with an appeal to Scripture.

Reading Mr. Davenport's article in the Methodist journal, I replied that we live in a democratic republic that does not recognize ruling and subject races. Then, as if that were not enough to say, I gave the journal back to Mr. Land with the comment that "the writer's racial prejudice is exceeded only by his ignorance of the Scripture." I believe Mr. Davenport had taken the drunken Noah's curse on his son Ham as divine approval for black slavery. My harsh treatment of his article did me in with the Methodists in town, though. But the conflict was not limited to the Methodist retired clergy. I came into conflict with a retired Baptist minister who was more highly revered in Shellman than anyone, with the possible exception of Jesus Christ himself. This was Dr. John E. Martin, kin to half the people in Shellman and looked upon as an authority in matters religious and theological by all of them. Here is the way I got into it with Dr. Martin and with his followers in town.

On the Sunday when Dr. Martin was in town, I invited him to speak at the morning worship service. He did, and did not say anything about the conflict we were having in the church over race. In the evening I spoke on the storm that was gathering over the Southland, and urged the people to stand ready to meet the gale force of it with Christian fortitude, issuing a strong warning against those who refused to accept change. The next day Dr. Martin and I were invited to eat lunch with a pair of elderly ladies who lived across the street from me. They were kinswomen of his, and as might be expected with two preachers present, the conversation turned to religious questions. I have forgotten just what the questions were, but it seems to have been whether the whale swallowed Jonah, then regurgitated him three days later on dry ground.

In any case, I learned after he had left town that Dr. Martin had found me unsound in doctrine and had stated that I ought to be silenced. I refused to be silenced, but I didn't care whether the whale swallowed Jonah or Jonah swallowed the whale. I thought the question totally irrelevant to the issues facing us in the church and in the nation. I was concerned about whether the Church was willing to follow what I considered the dictates of the Christian ethic in the matter of race relations, or whether the people of Shellman and of Georgia, and of the whole Southland, would insist on preserving their own hallowed traditions in defiance of God and the Court.

But the people who wanted to be rid of me had found what they wanted: a highly respected clergyman of the Baptist faith who would say that I was wrong. In Dr. Martin they had what they wanted, and he had done his work while quietly avoiding a direct controversy with me. Now the noose was tightening about my neck as the opposition planned to bring my ministry there to an end.

All through the Summer of 1954, the pressure was building up toward a second vote to oust me from the pulpit of the Shellman Baptist Church. But my opponents were hoping to convince me to resign and leave town without the second vote because of the uncertainty of its outcome.

Baptists don't have bishops, and each Baptist church is independent and self-governing, but they cooperate to do many good works, such as schools, orphanages, and foreign missions where they preach the gospel of love and brotherhood to blacks in Africa. And for these endeavors they get together in state conventions and even in the larger Southern Baptist Convention. The Georgia Baptist Convention met in the Fall of 1954, and though I had been urged, entreated, even warned to keep my mouth shut on the matter of race relations, I determined that I would go to the Georgia Baptist Convention meeting in Augusta, Georgia, and that I would find or make an opportunity to speak there on the matter of race relations facing the Baptist churches of Georgia. The occasion was provided by the report of the Social Service Commission, a committee formed for the very purpose of making statements on issues of this nature.

The report was read by Judge Humphrey Dukes, and it said that we were faced with a grave situation that we ought to pray about and try to do the Christian thing about, when we were forced to do it and after God had indicated (in answer to our prayers) what we ought to do in Christian love. The report did not say that we ought to do anything that would upset anybody.

I didn't think the report said anything one way or the other on the issue, but Hugh Grant, who claimed to be a former envoy to Ethiopia, thought the report was a rebuke to Governor Talmadge and that it opened the way for integration of all facilities and that it was a direct violation of the fundamental rules of the Baptist faith and philosophy. He considered the Court's decision political and a conspiracy between Communists and the NAACP, and said that if we passed the resolution of the Social Service Commission we were approving the Supreme Court's decision and repudiating the Governor.

I made my passage to the speaker's platform and was grudgingly granted one minute to reply to Mr. Grant. I said that we were not concerned with the repudiation of the Governor, but that we were in danger of repudiating Jesus Christ if we advocated the separation of the races, and that we were faced with a moral issue we had to deal with courageously, even though it meant that we would be fired from our pulpits when we returned home.

The report was approved, though it did not say much, and nobody did anything about it subsequently. I went home to Shellman, and I found that I had spoken a self-fulfilling prophecy. The people who were opposed to me were fully intending to fire me if they could not get me to resign in the face of being fired, which amounted to the same thing.

I still didn't resign, though the pressure was being applied from all sides. The people who were loyal to me continued to be loyal and true, though, and even Julian Gill's midnight telephone call in which he cursed me and told me I was insane did not convince me that I ought to resign. Julian Gill was a Methodist and didn't have a vote. He ran the Shellman drug store, but Mr. Jones was a Baptist, and he had a drug store too, so we quit buying medicine from Julian Gill and bought our aspirin from Mr. Jones.

Johnny Curry was a Baptist, and he was alcoholic; he was loyal to me and he never got too drunk to know which side he was on. He would fight for me, and then come to tell me about the fight, and we would drink coffee until Johnny was steady enough on his feet to walk home.

Zack Crittenden was a Methodist who gave me lessons in theology. He did not consider the doctorate in theology conferred on me by the Baptist seminary sufficient for me to understand what God was doing in the world. Zack told me that "God never intended for white men to work. That's what He created niggers for." Zack was a living embodiment of his theology, but my cat Romulus evened the score with Zack's old bird-dog whose name I never learned, so I will just call him

Nameless. Now, Nameless was devoted to his master, Zack, and he ran home at noon every day when Zack drove home for lunch, but Nameless took the short cut along the alley that ran past my house. Running along with his hind legs slewed out of line, Nameless was unaware of Romulus waiting under the Forsythia bush. Romulus leaped onto the back of Nameless, sank his claws in and rode him to within sight of Zack Crittenden's farm implement shop, but Romulus dropped off just in time, returned home and lay licking himself on the back porch.

Romulus was given to me by Truitt Martin as a sort of incentive to make me feel favorable toward coming to be pastor of the church. Another way to look at it is that I promised to take Romulus off Truitt Martin's hands—Romulus was just a kitten then—if the church called me as pastor. After both Romulus and I were installed in the church-owned pastor's home with MarthaLee, who viewed Romulus more realistically than I did, he came to church to attend the Sunday evening services. He would leap onto the organ, stretch and lick himself, and watch me preach. This sent Miss Alma Martin, the organist, into hysterics, but she got even with both me and Romulus by voting against me in the end. Her husband, Francis Martin, a retired medical doctor, even voted against me by proxy because he was not inclined to leave the house except to visit the barber shop for his daily shave.

Romulus and I got into trouble with Jimmy Nix, too. Jimmy Nix lived next door to me, and he kept a pack of bird dogs that he would turn loose so that they could get some exercise. Their favorite place to run was my back yard, where they found Romulus relaxing, and they chased him up a big pecan tree. I chased the dogs away and rescued Romulus, but this was not what brought about the rift between me and Jimmy Nix. He had small children who were enrolled in the Sunday school, and he came to me and expressed his concern that they might be contaminated by exposure to my beliefs on race. He asked me if I thought he was sinning to let them attend the Sunday school, and I told him that I thought he could do no better than send them to Sunday school where they would learn that Jesus loves the little children of the world, especially the little black and white ones.

The reader will see that with Baptists and Methodists both involved, and with a cat and dog fight going on inside the big church fight, things would go from bad to worse, and they did, for when I came home from the Georgia Baptist Convention where I did just what I had been warned not to do, and the people in Shellman read all about it in the newspaper, the deacons met and voted to give me until the first Sunday in December to resign, or else, the "or else" being that they would ask the church to fire me.

I told the deacons that I would not resign, and that they would find their own duties spelled out for them in Holy Writ, "but firing the preacher is not one of them."

Matters in Shellman continued to go from bad to worse, as I have already said. The people who wanted me to leave were becoming nastier. Manry Stewart got my salary cut in half, claiming that I was being paid by the NAACP and that I didn't need what the church was paying me. The people who were loyal to me stuck more tightly with me and MarthaLee, whose salary was not cut by the school board that had failed to get her to resign. Our friends assured us every day and in every way that they would stick to us to the very end, which was not far off because December 5, 1954, had been set for the church to hear the proposal of the deacons to fire me, and this the church congregation did by an overwhelming vote of seventy-eight to seventeen.

This action was to be effective on January 1, 1955, so I was still pastor for three weeks, and I took advantage of this office to preach my farewell sermon on that Sunday morning following the action of the church in firing me. The sermon was a bit harsh, to say the kindest thing I can say about it. Some of the people who had voted against me got up and walked out, but enough remained to report what I said to them. And all of the people who had voted for me had remained, out of loyalty to me and possibly to hear what I would say about the firing.

I took the church roll into the pulpit with me and wrote "Cast Out" by my name and MarthaLee's. Then I told them that they had declared themselves heretical because their action was a refusal to accept the plain teaching of the Bible. They might as well drop out of the Southern Baptist Convention as well, since they did not intend to follow the policies accepted and proclaimed by that body.

This served well for a starter. After this I told them that they were in rebellion against their nation because they refused to accept the Supreme Court's decision on racial segregation as binding upon them, and that their action was contradictory to the practice in our armed forces where their sons served.

After this I said that they were in denial of the Church of Jesus Christ and ought to call themselves the Shellman Community Club instead of a church since they had renounced the teachings of the Bible and since they had recognized no divine authority for the preaching of the Word of Truth. As a consequence, I said that they would suffer a famine of the preaching of the Word of God.

My final message was so harsh I wonder why they did not bodily eject me from the church building. They did not. Instead, MarthaLee and I walked out. We stored our furniture, moved into Miss Susie May Brown's house at her gracious invitation, and I prepared to drive back to Louisville to see if I might find a new direction for my activities. That is to say, to look for work.

While I was in Louisville, Martin Luther King Jr. called me and asked me to join his Southern Christian Leadership Conference, but I turned him down. I had been hanged, buried, and fired by three churches. I did not want to get shot.

I found a basement apartment close to Cherokee Park, drove back to Shellman to be reunited with MarthaLee at Miss Susie May's house, and we returned together to Louisville, where the seventeen loyalists supported us with their prayers, assurances, and money for living expenses. I was looking for work, but I had to turn down the offer of a reputable distiller who thought I might be just the man to promote his product in the face of clerical and ecclesiastical closed-mindedness. Hugh Peterson, registrar at the seminary, came up with something that was more in my line. He sent me to Parkersburg, West Virginia, to preach a "trial sermon" at the Old North Baptist Church.

After an all-night ride on a train, I gave Old North the best I had, and the pulpit committee met that afternoon and invited me to answer questions. They showed no great concern over my racial views, but they balked at my failure to see the story of Jesus' walking on the water of the Sea of Galilee literally. I tried to explain it in symbolic terms, but they pressed me so hard that I was forced to say that unless the water was frozen over, I did not believe He did, IN FACT, walk on the surface of the water.

My next chance at getting back into the work of pastor was at Hurricane, West Virginia. The church leaders there did not raise the question of miracles, but they wanted to know just why the church in Georgia fired me, and when I replied that it was because I had preached that Negroes ought to be treated like white folk, they decided that they had heard enough. So I was back at the seminary looking for work when Bill Mitchell showed up at the barbershop there and told me that a chaplain was needed at the Veterans Hospital in Lexington, Kentucky.

Bill and I had been students together at the seminary; he was now pastor of a small country church near Lexington, and he knew Harry Alexander, the senior chaplain at the hospital, which was a center for the treatment of neuropsychiatric diseases of veterans of both World War II and Korea. I went to see Chaplain Alexander, got the job as his assistant, went to work, and loved it. Some of the men were very sick, a few were dangerous, but even the most dangerous among them vowed that they "liked me because they felt that I was just one of them." It was a comfort to me to know that the mentally sick people I was working with were behind closed doors instead of out there plotting ways to fire the preacher. I was also grateful that I had a key to the doors.

Then, the newly opened Baptist Hospital needed a chaplain; a friend recommended me, and I went to work there. One of my assignments was to integrate the hospital, both patients and workers, and I struck up a friendship with Bob Brown, a local pastor; together we wrote an article called "Why the Churches Don't Integrate," and it was published by *Ebony*, which was the black counterpart of *Life*.

After my retirement, I wrote a little book of Southern tales called *And the Goat Cried*. It was while I was traveling about over the Southland and the Midwest doing book signings that I decided to revisit Shellman. It had been forty-four years, and I went back to Shellman, wondering if anybody would recognize me and what would happen to me if someone did recognize me. When I arrived in Shellman, I had been driving since early morning, and I stopped at a little coffee shop that had not even been there when I left. I asked the woman who ran the shop "How long have you been in Shellman?" She answered that she had been there three or four years, and I asked why she had come to Shellman to operate a coffee shop. She replied, "Shellman is a quiet little town where nothing much ever happens, and I thought it would be a good place to bring up the kids."

I asked her where I could find the Baptist preacher, and she pointed across to the City Park, which was also new, with a new brick building called the City Hall. She said "That's the Baptist preacher over there working with the children who are running for a charity of some kind." I drove over to the City Park, walked up to the man who was counting the number of times the kids circled the area, and introduced myself.

He studied my face and said "Buchanan. Seems like I heard that name somewhere but I can't remember…"

When I told him I had been pastor of the Shellman Baptist Church forty-five years ago, he became very thoughtful and said "I have told them that when I am eligible for Social Security and the Baptist Retirement, I will retire, and they won't have to fire me."

We went over the list of the people I remembered, those who had supported me and those who had opposed me, and as I called the names, he would say "dead" or "moved away." But he said, "Miss Mattie Weathers is still alive. You remember where she lives? Her granddaughter Byrd is there with her. Miss Mattie is deaf. You will have to knock loud and yell because she can't hear it thunder."

Miss Mattie couldn't hear me, so I gave up knocking and went inside; I found her and Byrd in a sitting room near the back of the house. They recognized me, even though I didn't have the beard when I was in Shellman; they threw their arms around me, hugging me and laughing. Miss Mattie said, "Byrd has had brain surgery for cancer and she can't remember anything. I can't hear, but I remember everything." Apparently she had forgotten that they didn't vote for me forty-four years ago, and I did not remind them of it. We talked of old times, and I reminded Byrd that when she was an airline hostess she met me when I got off her plane in St. Louis, and she took me to a bar, where I ordered a Seven Up, and then she took me to an unusual restaurant, where they threw bread at us. Miss Mattie said, "Byrd can't remember anything." Byrd laughed and seemed to remember everything. We hugged again, and I drove down the street past the new brick home for the preacher and parked near the Baptist church.

Jane and Brooks Wooten lived across the street from the church. Jane was outside by the edge of the street, putting out the garbage. She dropped the garbage can, yelled "Brother Buck," and then said, "Come on in the house and see Brooks." Brooks was sitting in his easy chair, looking very much the way his father, Jim Wooten, had looked forty-four years ago. Brooks told me he had tried to get in touch with me for the church's anniversary. I am not sure which one. Maybe it was two hundred. But he couldn't find me. I wondered what I would have said if I had come and they had asked me to speak. Well, things look about the same as when you fired me, and I told you that you were all hell-bound. But they did not even remember that they didn't vote for me, and we hugged again and they said, "Sarah Curry lives right up Pearl Street on the left. She will be happy to see you. Stop and visit her."

Sarah Curry was out in the front yard doing "nigger work." She was raking up the broken tree limbs and debris from the rainstorm of the night before, but she dropped the rake and ran to me, throwing her arms around me and laughing and crying at the same time. She was no longer the slender, red-headed young mother I had known, but she was a thin old woman and very beautiful. She said, "I have felt guilty all these years about what we did to you here. Can you forgive us?"

I felt guilty about all the harsh things I had said to them, and hoped that she could forgive me, but I don't think she even thought I needed forgiveness because she said that all the things I had said had come true in Shellman and that everybody had accepted the changes. She was just happy that God had spared her and her house in the storm that had struck during the night. We hugged again, and I got into the car and drove west to Cuthbert, the county seat of Randolph County where the alcoholic lawyer practiced and got drunk to celebrate when he won a case and got drunk to commiserate when he lost. It was where Dick Allman was pastor of the Baptist church forty-five years earlier when he urged me not to speak and remove any doubts that people might be harboring about whether I was crazy or not.

I ate lunch in Cuthbert, at a little hot dog and hamburger place. When I sat down at a table alone, I saw several young workmen sitting together, eating, joking, and laughing. Some of them were white and some were black. I finished my hot dog, paid the cashier, got into the car, and drove toward Alabama, where I was scheduled to sign my book *And the Goat Cried.* But it was at Memphis where I learned how much the world had changed since Shellman had fired me.

Somewhere on the way to Memphis, prompted by an earlier phone conversation with a Memphis newspaper reporter doing a feature story in advance of my bookstore appearance there, I began recalling my early childhood—such thoughts helped to pass the time while driving. I remembered being a very small boy sitting on the back doorstep of the farmhouse where we lived near Macon, eating one of Mama's crusty biscuits with cane syrup in it. Sandy, our mostly-collie dog, was lying in a cool place under the steps. A teenaged Negro girl named Dump came over with a basket of freshly washed and ironed clothes balanced on her head. She was in a teasing mood, and when she saw me sitting there on the step she sang out "Jes' lookit de baby settin' an' eatin' a syrup in de hole." Feeling humiliated, I said, "You shut up, you big black nigger. I ain't no baby and you can't call me a baby neither." At that point, Sandy, sensing that a fight was brewing, rushed out toward Dump and snarled, showing his canine teeth. Dump tried to kick the dog, but succeeded only in spilling the clean clothes onto the ground. Mama then came outside and scolded Dump for spilling the clothes, and Dump said, "He called me a big black nigger an' sicked de dawg on me, an' I ain't gonna stan' fer nobody callin' me a big black nigger." I said, "She called me a baby and made fun of me, and I ain't gonna have no black nigger callin' me a baby." Mama made Dump pick up the clothes and take them back home to wash and iron them again, and Mama washed my mouth out with Octagon soap and switched my bare legs with a stripped peach limb, saying "The very idea, calling somebody a black nigger…"

Then I recalled riding the school bus as a child. Once, when we passed some black children walking to their school who were enveloped in a cloud of our dust, I began throwing shelled corn at them and yelling "Black Nigger! Black Nigger!" The driver stopped the bus and threatened to drop me off in the midst of the angry black children. Instead, he drove on and turned me over to Miss Florrie, the principal at Howard Elementary School, who brought out the orange wood paddle—known as Miss Florrie's Board of Education—and she warmed my backside with it.

Next I revisited a later phase of my life. When I was a bit more grown up, I confided to Uncle Seeb and Aunt Hattie (the terms "Uncle" and "Aunt" were forms of respect used by white youths in addressing elderly black people) that I was going to be a preacher when I was an adult. Uncle Seeb's black face shone like an ebony sun, and he shouted "Praise God! This young man gonna be a preacher for de Lawd." Then Aunt Hattie's chocolate-brown face was wreathed in smiles. She threw some breadcrumbs to the chickens feeding near the doorsteps, singling out a half-grown rooster. "You better git yo' share 'cause you goin' into the ministry. Mist' Alfie heah gonna be a preacher an' you gonna learn him how a preacher eat chicken."

When I reached Memphis, I was still pondering the reporter's question—"Who influenced your thinking on race relations when you were growing up in Georgia?" It was increasingly clear to me how important the people I told the reporter about—"Mama, and Miss Florrie, and Uncle Seeb and Aunt Hattie, and even Fred Powers, the school bus driver"—had been in my life.

I arrived at the bookstore to do the book signing, and I could tell immediately that the manager was a man who knew his business. He placed me where everybody who came into the store would see me and my book. "I want you to talk with everybody who comes in that door. Show them your book. Sell that book. I want everybody who comes in here to buy that book and read it."

No more sitting alone and shuffling the stack of books for me. The autographing went well, and when it was over I looked out and it was dark outside. The darkness had come while I was talking with all those people who wanted to know why the goat cried. Now, how would I ever find my way back to my motel on the other side of town in the darkness? I would surely get lost and spend the night driving all over Memphis, through dark and threatening streets where danger lurked, waiting to pounce out of the darkness onto me like Romulus onto the back of Zack Crittenden's old bird-dog Nameless. I told my problem to one of the clerks, who began to tell me how to get to my motel. Then somebody else started to tell me, until every worker in the bookstore was telling me how to get across town to my motel, all of them telling me different ways. The manager came over again, and this time he said, "All you folks be quiet now." And turning to me he said, "You just follow me. I will lead you to your motel."

We went out to the parking lot. He got into his car, and I got into mine. He said, "You just stay on my tail lights and follow me close." Then he drove away into the darkness with me hugging his tail lights. I followed him through the darkened streets, and I didn't let anybody cut in between us. After some time—at least twelve minutes by the clock in my dashboard—he pulled into the motel parking lot. He rolled down the window and leaned out, a great smile lighting up his face. He said, "Here you are. Thank you for coming to my bookstore. Good night."

He started to draw back inside the car, but I had my face out now, and I said, "Thank you, Good Shepherd. Thank you. And Good Night."

I heard him laugh at being called "Good Shepherd." It was a happy laugh. As when one has come to know that all of life is good and worthwhile. I watched his tail lights as he drove away, and I spoke again, though there was nobody to hear me except myself, but myself was glad to hear me say it: "Now there is a Man, a Black Man, worth getting hanged for."

The Sounds of Friday

BY ALLEAN HALE

Mellora lay back on the tester bed and listened to the Friday night sounds. The high school crowd. They seemed to come from all directions, grinding up on their motor scooters to smash into the curb next door.

"Oh, Junie!" They would call. "Oh, June-ie!" (Youngsters had no manners nowadays.)

Pretty soon Junie would come out—a sweet child, but almost vulgarly attractive—gliding down the walk in that insinuating way. Sometimes she was barefoot, in brief shorts that showed her belly button. Other nights she wore dresses cut low and so thin you could see through them. Often, because she was alone, Mellora would switch off the light and watch through the window: the girl, with her high breasts and provocative hips, surrounded by the eager boys. Like a pack of dogs, Mellora thought.

But this evening she was content just to lie among the clutter that marked her siesta: a package of menthol cigarettes, scattered magazines, two rumpled stockings, a discarded girdle. This evening there were sounds in her own house, the comforting sounds of a man getting dressed.

"Jimmy Mac," she called to him, "come in here and let me look at you...Darlin'!" She heaved herself to a sitting position, pushing aside the bed curtains and plumping the pillows behind her. "Why, you look simply wonderful."

*And you, Mother. You look like a...*even in his mind he couldn't say the word that had flashed there as he saw her running toward him at the airport. She was pushing and clawing her way to the front of the crowd, banging at them with her bracelets. She had been squealing at him then as she was squealing now: "Jimmy Mac! Baby, Baby Darlin'." Her huge-brimmed hat was knocked over one eye, and the too-bright yellow hair stuck out from under like a fright wig.

It was the hair that made him think of the woman at the Cove, the sailor's joint near the base, always jammed on weekend nights. About nine-thirty she would come in, a large woman, not young, for a moment lighting up the doorway with her blond hair and shiny red blouse, strained tightly over big breasts. Then as glasses clinked down on the bar she would walk slowly, deliberately, the length of the room. The guys used to make bets on how old she was.... To shut out the picture, Jimmy Mac had stooped and kissed the face under the straw-brittle hair, the (after all) dear face of his mother. It was a round face, bland as vanilla pudding; a face, he realized, much like his own.

She was beaming up at him now, one rather dirty bare foot lolling from the tumble of bedclothes. "Turn around, Darlin'," she ordered. "I declare, do you realize this is the first time I've ever seen you in tails?"

He revolved slowly. "We didn't have much use for tails in the Navy."

"And they cost me a fortune. But they're an investment, really. There'll be lots of parties this winter. There's little Susan Moberly making her debut—they say her grandfather is the wealthiest man in New Orleans. You know, Jimmy Mac, I used to think that Susan was quite serious about you."

"That was in high school." (High school, Jimmy Mac thought, seemed almost as unreal as this crazy suit.)

"Nevertheless...and the Carrière girl is making her debut. She's almost certain to be Queen of Comus this year. You must keep your head, Darlin'. There'll be lots of pretty girls after my big, tall boy."

"I don't know. They all seem to be engaged or married—or just kids." He frowned into the crazed mirrored door of the armoire, adjusting his tie.

"You haven't had time to look around yet, Dear. Wait till the season starts. Look, I believe we'll have a little welcome home party for you next week. We can have it out on the patio…"

"Listen, Mother," he jerked at the tie, "I can't stick around here forever. I've got to get a job."

"Oh, for Heaven's sake! You've got plenty of time for that. You need a good rest first. Honestly, you don't look well. I don't mind telling you, now that you're back: I used to lie awake at night fretting myself sick over your asthma."

"I didn't have asthma in the Navy, Mother." He said it in spite of himself. "The only place I have asthma is at home."

"Ridiculous. Either you have it or you don't have it. No, I'm going to insist that you take it easy this fall. I'm going to put my foot down, for once."

"Look here." He started toward the door.

"Oh, Honey, I'm only foolin', really. You're a man, now. You'll have to make your own decisions. Only don't forget you have a mother. It's like Monsieur Duchesne said—that poet who spoke at the Vieux Carré Club Thursday: 'Every mother's heart is a battleground.'"

"I know you've had a rough time alone." He paused.

"I'm not complaining. I'm not the complaining type, you know that. Just a few weeks, Darlin'. That's all I ask."

"I just wanted you to understand—."

"That's right," Mellora rushed on, "it's the sensible thing to do. You can party around, maybe take a few lessons on your horn from Professor Olivier. He always said you had talent. That will give you time to find yourself, decide whether you want to be an engineer—or go into business."

"Mother, you don't just go into business," Jimmy Mac protested.

"And when you're not too busy, maybe you can take your mother some of the places she has to go. You won't feel foolish, will you, being my escort tonight at the Opera League Ball?"

"Why should I?"

"I could go with Mathilde and Lyle, but I'd much rather go with you. All the young girls will be eating their hearts out when they see us."

"You'll be the youngest one there," said Jimmy Mac. She laughed with pleasure. Reaching up for one gleaming coattail, she drew him down to sit stiffly on the bed beside her.

"Jimmy Mac, do you remember when I had Miss Hazel Deane do that portrait of you?" He looked upward with her, over the bedroom fireplace with its cast iron grate, to the almost life-size figure of a tow-headed child with round china-blue eyes.

"I insisted on the white middy suit because they never go out of style. You were handsome even then, Honey. People used to stop me in Audubon Park just to look at you, so blond among all those little Creole children...I never dreamed then that you'd go into the Navy. Your father, being a Major in the Air Force, naturally expected that you'd follow him. And you were always crazy to fly—but then there was that unfortunate vision test—."

"Yeah," he remembered, all right. He scooped up his coat tails, moving farther away. "The nearest I got to a plane was on an aircraft carrier."

"Not your fault, Darlin'. I'm afraid weak eyes come from my side of the family. None of the MacNeeleys could see from here to yonder. But you wouldn't know that from that portrait, would you, Sweetie? She's given you such expression. And see, she even painted your toy."

It was an airplane he had tried to build out of balsa wood. He had worked on it for days, Mellora remembered, but somehow when he aimed it into the air it would always crash. Like his plans to fly, to be like his father. He had enlisted the minute Frank died—just when she needed him most, her only son. But now Jimmy Mac was back in her bedroom, just like the little boy in the picture.

He had risen and was examining the portrait. "Wasn't I a little old for a middy suit?"

"Not at all, Darlin'. You were six. And were you jealous! One morning you climbed into bed between your father and me—this same old creaky antique bed—and you said, 'Go away, Daddy. You get to sleep with Mommy ever night. Why can't I sleep with her on Sunday?' We laughed a long time over that."

"Mother, for God's sake—." He turned on her.

"Don't be cross with me, Baby. Now run on, I've got to get dressed." But he was already out of the room and half-way down the stairs. "You don't have to slam it," she called, as the front door banged. "I declare, the Navy has done something to him."

On the porch Jimmy Mac paused to light a cigarette, his match flame exploding into the dark. "That does it," he muttered. He felt pulled this way and that, between love and revulsion, and guilt at his revulsion. Why couldn't they be friends, he wondered, just two separate individuals in the world? All the time he'd been away he'd been sick for home, forgetting the old pressures that were there, smothering him. Roughly he pushed aside the fingers of the bougainvillaea vine that reached down, sweet and tenacious, from the gallery under his mother's window. A large cockroach scuttled out of his way on the walk.

Mellora lay in bed and thought, *I must get up, must get up, must get up*. Strange how much harder it got each time. She reached along the marble top of the bed-table for a small gilt clock, knocking a sherry glass onto the carpet. "I can't go like I used to," she murmured. Luncheon at the Club, a committee meeting, on for bridge or cocktails, home for a snack or a tiny nap before dressing for the theatre or the opera or a concert. More and more she would forgo food for bed. She would lie limp, frightened sometimes by little pains that would not be allayed by any of the pills on her dresser.

"How do you do it?" people asked. "Every place I go I see you." "Miz Mellora," said her cleaning woman, "Las' night I see yo' picture in the papah."

When she burst into a room, she knew that people smiled, if ironically; it mattered little to Mellora so long as they saw her entrance. Nor did she mind if, in a city that fed on Carnival, her role was often the clown. She had neither wealth nor family (Mellora MacNeeley from East Tennessee), yet in the Crescent City everyone who was anyone knew her by name. (Not that "MacNeeley" was exactly hillbilly, either, or she would never have wished it on her son.) If anything, Frank had been the one without "family." But being a Major had helped—and getting that position as head of protocol at the University had given him an entrée. When they'd moved to New Orleans, she had quickly sized up a society where one was either Bourbon or trash, and had determined her goal. The zenith was to sit on the gallery of the Boston Club on Mardi Gras day when Rex, King of Carnival, paused on his float for the champagne toasts. Finally she had been invited, and now she was one of the aristocrats…by the name of Botts. It was an achievement.

Mellora sighed. Jimmy Mac must be made to realize how important it all was to his future. Now, had he been a girl…she shivered as from a slight draft. A young girl in the house makes you feel your age. A tall, handsome son—a son keeps you young. But she'd have to go easy, she cautioned herself. He was all she had. Mellora climbed heavily out of bed and gathered up the castoff garments, retrieving her slippers from under a rosewood chair. Oh, it would be a gay season. Heavenly to have someone to take you places. Not to be forever telephoning, wheedling another woman's husband to pick you up. Not that they minded, she assured herself. Sitting down at the dressing table, she daubed a triangle of rouge on each cheek and powdered her face, avoiding the mirror.

And Jimmy Mac would be going to the few places she wasn't invited, with the younger crowd, dancing at the Carnival balls, sitting at the Queens' suppers. Mellora saw herself waiting up for him, calling him to her bedside to ask what the girls wore, what they had to eat, whether they had served champagne. Dear child, she sighed. If only he could learn to be more attentive to those details…. She went to the armoire and took out a long dress splashed with purple flowers. *It doesn't suit me*, she thought despondently. With effort she pulled it over her head.

"Damned zipper," Mellora said aloud. "Now that I've put on just a teensy bit of weight...." She twisted and struggled, becoming quite warm. Then she remembered she didn't have to do for herself any more. She had Jimmy Mac! It was time he was coming in, anyhow. She went to the tall open window. "Jimmy Mac," she called, as she had to the little boy in the middy suit when he had wandered too far down the street.

There was no answer. From habit she flicked off the light, and the night came in languorously between the shutters. There was no light in the house next door. What was keeping the boy, anyway? All the Friday sounds were gone, except—she bent to the screen as she heard a movement on the verandah below. In the dark she could make out two heads, the small dark one of Junie, and above it one that was familiar, masculine, and, she knew, blond. As she watched, the heads drew together slowly in the absence of sound that was a kiss. Mellora backed away from the window. With shaking hands she groped for the light, as if the flood of it could blot out what she had seen.

"No, no, no," she said aloud, commencing to pace up and down. *I mustn't let myself*, she thought. *It's bad for me. My head feels like it will blow off. But how could he...with that trash! Rita Carroll's daughter, I've watched her grow up, and she's common, common as pig's tracks. Trashy little high school slut!* Saying the word several time made her feel better. *Poor lamb, he doesn't realize.* She thought out her strategy. She would finish dressing and just step over there casually as if she didn't know a thing. Or wait—maybe he hadn't even heard her call? Again she went to the window, and this time her voice was carefully clear and sweet.

"Jimmy. Oh, Jimmy Mac! Are you over there?" For a moment, silence; then the girl's low laughter, smothered abruptly, and her son's voice saying "Shhhh." And again silence, humid and seductive as the night air. Mellora clutched at her dressing table. *I could just go back to bed*, she thought. *My head aches bad enough. I could go to bed and act like nothing ever happened.* She lifted her head and was caught by her reflection in the mirror: the pudgy body squeezed into the odious dress, the flamboyant hair showing dark at the roots, the map of wrinkles across the throat, the too-bright lipstick, a trifle crooked.

"But I won't." She defied the image. "It isn't good for me to brood. I need something to cheer me up." Her fingers slipped on the phone, so that she had to dial three times.

"Mathilde," she said; "Good evenin', Dear. Mathilde, could you and Lyle be sweet enough to stop by for me after all. Because it looks like I won't have an escort this time. Jimmy Mac has been unavoidably detained."

This time, Mellora grimaced as she cradled the receiver. *But don't think I'm giving up, James MacNeeley Botts,* she vowed silently; *because mothers just don't give up when it comes to the welfare of their children.*

A wave of maternal indignation washed over Mellora, so violent that it felt like rage. The least he could do—she wanted to throw back the shutters and scream—if he didn't care for himself or his mother, the very least he could do was to come on home and take off those tails before they got mussed. If worst came to worst—for one moment a long lonely future stretched ahead of her—if worst came to absolute worst, she thought, maybe she could talk the store into taking them back.

The Lunchroom Victory: A Memoir

BY ROBERT MORGAN

In the Winter of 1956, when I was in Miss MacDonald's fifth grade class at Tuxedo Elementary School in Henderson County, North Carolina, my mother lost her job at the cotton mill. It had been a bad year for farming, and my father had no money and no job either. Things got lean, and my mother had trouble finding the quarter each day for lunch money for me. Knowing that some students worked for their lunches at the cafeteria, she called Mrs. Barnett, who managed the lunchroom, and arranged for me to work for my noon meal.

Miss MacDonald, my teacher, was not pleased when I told her I would have to leave class early every day to go to the lunchroom. Lunch period began at 11:30, but I had to leave at 11:00 to refill sugar jars and salt shakers for each table in the cafeteria. Also, I stacked milk in cartons on the counter where students passing with their trays could easily reach them. The three girls who also worked for their lunches did similar tasks. I was the only boy serving in the lunchroom.

The two Anders sisters who worked in the kitchen for Mrs. Barnett—Elise and Estelle, elderly and unmarried women of liberal girth—were very kind to me. They showed me where everything was, and heaped my plate for the lunch I had to eat quickly before the other students arrived. The students came to the cafeteria in shifts, beginning with the first and second grades at exactly 11:30.

My main job was to clean the plates for Estelle, who was the dish-washer. I had to grab the silverware off each plate and toss it into a separate pan, throw the wadded napkins into a trash can, and scrape the plate into a garbage barrel. At first I tried to clean the plates with a spoon, but Estelle, a huge woman with black eyes and heavy brows, told me that was too slow. I had to work fast to keep up with the volume of dishes handed through the window.

"Just use your hand," she said.

I was reluctant, but the plates heavy with leftovers piled up quickly as students hurried to play before classes started again. I rolled up my sleeves and wiped a dish with the heel of my palm. It worked as if my palm had been designed for the purpose. I wiped off rice, and mashed potatoes, half-eaten beets, coleslaw, and pinto beans. Some of the food was still warm. I scraped away cornbread and broken crackers. Hardest to clean were gravy and smeared filling from pies. It took skill to wipe jelly or ketchup off the china. The dishes had to be clean before Estelle would accept them for the wire basket that she lowered in boiling water, then lifted out smoking to be rinsed with a hose and left to drain and dry.

At first I was ashamed to be seen by the other students, scraping their leavings into the barrel. "Hey Bud," they would say through the window as they tossed the soiled plates on the heap. Some said, "How do you like your new job, Robert?" I especially dreaded facing my friends through that cafeteria window, my hands covered with the muck of half-eaten lunches. Some of my friends, though warned not to, put chewing gum on their plates. Chewing gum was almost impossible to wipe off a dish, and Estelle made me check the bottom of each plate. Bubble gum was the worst, for it melted in the boiling water and left pink strings stuck to all the dishes in the wire basket.

As I got into the work, I began to take pride in cleaning each plate quickly. I got faster and faster. Most of the time I could wipe the plate clean with two sweeps of my hand. In two or three days I learned to clean plates as fast as they were handed through the window. After the second day I did not let a single wad of gum get by to foul the washed dishes.

Estelle and I sweated and laughed as we worked side by side. I cleaned hundreds of plates and handed them to her. I never dropped a single one on the cement floor. I learned to watch out for bits of sweet potato or juice or gravy that would splash onto my shirt and pants.

After all the plates were scraped and the students had left the cafeteria, my work was still not done. While the girls who worked for their lunches swept the cafeteria, mopped, cleaned all the tables, and gathered up the sugar jars and salt shakers, I had to take the barrel of paper trash out to the wire incinerator behind the school and make sure all the napkins and paper cups and wrappers were burned. I sometimes struck match after match to get wet napkins to kindle.

When I finally brought the barrel and matchbox back into the lunchroom, Elise or Estelle would give me a sweet roll or sweet potato they had saved for me. And then I would hurry back to the classroom.

By the time I reached Miss MacDonald's room, I would have been gone about two hours. She would glare at me as I entered and would tell me to take my place. When I'd sit at my desk, I'd notice that my hands, though I had washed them, still smelled of cinnamon or sweet potato, butter or vanilla, and my pants were spotted with flecks of dried food. Miss MacDonald would frown at me all afternoon. The other students would mostly ignore me, jealous that I had been able to get away from class so long.

The strangest part of my work in the lunchroom occurred later that winter. I had been working for my lunch about two months when Mrs. Barnett called the four student assistants to a conference. She said the county health department required all employees of restaurants and cafeterias in the county to take a course in safety and sanitation, to be taught each day for two weeks in the city hall.

"I know this sounds silly, but it's required," she said.

The classes were to be taught at 10:00 in the morning and at 4:00 in the afternoon. We students would attend the morning sessions, and she and Estelle and Elise would go in the afternoon.

One of the girls, Mary Gladys, asked how we would get to the city hall eight miles away at 10:00 in the morning. Mrs. Barnett said she had solved that problem. The driver of the bread truck who delivered loaves to the cafeteria each morning at 9:30 had agreed to let us ride in his truck to town. And when the class was over at 11:00, Mary Gladys's father, who drove a school bus, would pick us up at the city hall in his car and drive us back to school in time to work for the lunch hour. We would have to eat our own lunches after we finished working each day.

It was thrilling to get to go to town each morning. When I told Miss MacDonald I'd be leaving the classroom each day at 9:30 instead of at 11:00, she frowned even harder than usual.

"Might as well not come to school at all," she said.

I told her the sanitation classes would last only two weeks. All the other students looked at me with envy as I swaggered out of the classroom at 9:30 in the morning.

It was a real adventure to ride in the bread truck every morning to town. We did not get to go to town all that often. There was only one seat in the truck—for the driver—so we students had to stand, holding onto the racks where the bread was stacked in wire boxes. The driver ignored us as he whipped the wide truck around curves, but he warned us to stand back from the window so no one could see us and tell his boss.

The classes at the city hall were an odd affair. They were held in a basement room and were taught by a very glib man in a brown suit, who worked for the State Board of Health in Raleigh. We four were the only children in the class. The rest of the participants were waiters and waitresses, cooks and managers of cafeterias. Everyone smiled at us on the first day of class and then mostly ignored us.

The instructor welcomed every one, and then said, "Last night I ate at a restaurant in this county, and the waitress who served me spat in my food."

Everybody in the class gasped.

He looked at a smartly dressed woman in the front row and said, "No, Mrs. Clemson, it wasn't your restaurant." There was laughter.

The instructor then explained that the waitress who took his order licked the tip of her finger before turning a page on her check pad. And then she served his food with the hand she had licked. Her spit may have gotten into his food and on his plate.

He said a hundred people in Charlotte had almost died of poisoning because a baker had made cream puffs without washing his hands. Germs from an infected sore had gotten into the cream puffs.

The instructor told us to always wash our hands and to always wear hair nets or caps when working in a kitchen. He told us not to serve food that had been left out of a refrigerator. He told us he had found rats in bread safes and milk cans, and he had seen ovens so filthy they turned his stomach.

When the class was over, we ran out to the street where Mary Gladys's mother and father waited in a long black car. Mary Gladys had eight younger brothers and sisters, and we climbed into the back and held young children on our laps as we rode back to Tuxedo. Mary Gladys's mom and dad sang gospel songs all the way to school.

Because we were late getting back from town, I had to hurry through my chores faster than usual. And I was later still getting back to the classroom. As the sanitation class wore into its second week, Miss MacDonald's frown got darker and darker as I'd slink back into her classroom, and the other students giggled when Miss MacDonald said, "Welcome back, world traveler."

When it rained I couldn't use the incinerator behind the school, but had to burn the paper trash in the school furnace located in the basement. The janitor had showed me how to put on the heavy glove and how to swing open the iron door to reach the blaze. But when I used the glove and tossed paper into the fire, I seemed to always get soot on my clothes or on my face.

On the last day of the sanitation class it was raining hard, and I was late getting the trash to the basement. I must have brushed my face with the sooty glove, for when I got back to Miss MacDonald's room and crept to my desk the other students began laughing. I looked around and saw they were all laughing at me.

"Come up here, Robert," Miss MacDonald said.

I walked up to her desk, and she took a tissue from a drawer and wiped my face. When she got the soot off my cheek, she turned me around to face the class.

"This is what you get for gallivanting all over the county instead of coming to class," she said, and then she spanked me hard on the seat of my pants.

The class laughed again, but this time it was a laugh of solidarity. I grinned at them and felt good, because in some way that I could not name I had won. I had earned my lunch. I had gallivanted around the county, I had missed classes, I had irritated Miss MacDonald, and I had gotten away with it.

Incident at Lake Manageechee

BY JACLYN WELDON WHITE

Sometimes with no warning an incident occurs that turns an innocent person into an accomplice of an act that is less than innocent. Much later come the questions. What sparked the incident? Was that person's capacity for violence always present, or was it created whole in one hot, sun-blinded moment? I didn't know the answers then, and I don't know the answers now.

Summer was the grail we chased through the other nine months of the year. When June finally arrived in all its warm, green glory, it brought with it an overwhelming urge to do everything at once. Catching lightning bugs, sleeping late, camping out in the backyard, and swimming were the stuff of our dreams during the cold months, but swimming was, hands-down, the favorite. That was why Margie McClain and I were sharing the back seat of a 1960 Oldsmobile 98 with Mary Catherine Rogers and her little sister Doreen that Saturday morning in late June, 1963.

Margie and I had been best friends since the first grade, but we had only known Mary Catherine for a year or so. To tell the truth, we didn't really like her that much. She had been in Miss Stovall's 7th grade class with us, but she had never quite fit in with the other kids. Taller than any of the boys in the class, Mary Catherine was pale and blonde and always knew the right answers in math. She never hesitated to say exactly what she thought, even when it was rude. And she was from somewhere up north. Not only did she speak with a harsh accent that was sometimes hard to understand, she never missed an opportunity to tell us how much better things were where she used to live.

Finally, she was Catholic—a religion as exotic as Buddhism to those of us brought up Baptist. When Mary Catherine talked about confession, rosaries, and Stations of the Cross, she might as well have been speaking a foreign language. I didn't know much about Catholics, but Margie's Aunt Lela had once heard at one of her missionary society meetings that Catholic priests sacrificed babies! Mary Catherine had never said or done anything that suggested she was interested in human sacrifice, and the story did seem unlikely, but it still added fuel to our fire of distrust.

That morning, however, we were able to put our feelings aside because Mary Catherine had one redeeming quality: parents who were willing to make the 30-mile drive to Lake Manageechee on the south side of Atlanta. Our own parents were of the collective opinion that the county-operated pool a mile from our houses offered everything we needed. They didn't understand the attraction of a big lake with a real sand beach and a raft you could swim out to and back from. When Mary Catherine invited us to go along with her and her family, Margie and I jumped at the chance.

The drive that morning was exhausting. The open windows channeled in the over-heated air from outside, and Doreen never stopped complaining. She was eight years old and well-padded with baby fat, and she seemed to have a never-ending supply of things she didn't like and didn't want to do. Her whining was all we had to listen to because Mr. Rogers refused to turn on the radio.

"How am I supposed to concentrate with that noise you kids call music? There will be no rock and roll in this car," he had said.

When we finally arrived and Mr. Rogers steered the big car into the gravel parking lot, I was anxious to get out and away, but Mrs. Rogers wouldn't let us go until she established the rules. She turned in her seat to face us. The heat had turned her face damp and red.

"Now, girls," she said, "I want you to stay in the beach area. Don't go wandering off. And there's no need for you to buy any of the junk they sell at the refreshment counter."

"But I want a hunkie," Doreen complained.

"You don't need any ice cream. We have plenty of sandwiches and pop for lunch."

Margie cut her eyes at me when Mrs. Rogers said "pop," but I determinedly looked away. I knew if our eyes met, I'd burst out laughing. There were Cokes and Dr. Peppers and even generic soft drinks, but we knew Lake Manageechee would not be selling "pop." That was something you'd have to travel to the North to find.

"What kind of sandwiches?" Doreen wanted to know.

"Egg salad."

"Yuck, I don't like egg salad."

"Well, that's what we're having. If you don't want to eat, that's your business."

I didn't much like egg salad either, but I knew to keep my opinions to myself.

We got out of the car, gingerly unsticking bare legs from the vinyl upholstery, and followed Mr. and Mrs. Rogers across the lot. Mrs. Rogers covered her bathing suit with a white, knee-length terry cloth robe and had a wide-brimmed straw hat jammed down over her hair. Mr. Rogers wore striped Bermuda shorts, sandals, and black socks. He couldn't have been more obviously a Yankee if he had carried a sign.

It was already hot, even at 10:30 in the morning. The sun beat down from a cloudless sky. As we crunched our way across the gravel, I could see the lake, silver and sparkling, in the distance beyond the cyclone fence. A bright red tin roof over to the right marked the concession booth where the delights Mrs. Rogers called "junk" were sold. Like Doreen, I'd not be sampling any of those delicacies that day. After my mama talked to Mrs. Rogers and found out my lunch would be provided, she had given me only 50 cents—just enough money for admission into the Lake Manageechee Recreational Park. I held the coins tightly in my sweaty fist until I relinquished them to the man at the gate and was granted admission.

The park was a magical place. White sand stretched out before us all the way to the water's edge. It looked like the pictures I had seen of tropical paradises, except there were straggly pines instead of palm trees and the only exotic music to be heard was Chubby Checkers' hit "Let's Twist Again (Like We Did Last Summer)" blaring from the loud speakers above our heads.

The beach was already crowded. Families had claimed spaces with blankets and umbrellas stuck at odd angles in the sand. Portable radios competed unsuccessfully with the loud speakers. Small groups of teenagers posed and postured to impress each other, and younger children shouted and ran around wildly. Mr. and Mrs. Rogers spread a big red blanket on the sand and began rubbing lotion on their arms and legs. Margie, Mary Catherine, and I dropped our beach bags, kicked off our flip-flops, and ran for the water. Only Doreen, chubby and sulky in her skirted suit, was left behind, squirming in the determined grasp of a mother armed with suntan lotion.

The water was cool, a milky, brownish-green that obscured our feet and legs as we waded in. We ventured into deeper water, and the sand beneath our feet gradually turned to mud, but no one complained. We were too busy treading water, trying different swimming strokes, and turning underwater flips. Between our aquatic exercises, we speculated in whispers and giggles about the boys around us. Mary Catherine, not as interested in that activity as Margie and I were, suggested that we swim out to the raft.

It looked a long way off, and I wasn't much of a swimmer, but I figured I could make it if we took it slow. We set off together, but soon Mary Catherine was several yards ahead. Her long, thin arms sliced effortlessly through the water, and her legs kicked smoothly and didn't splash much. Margie and I paddled along in her wake. When we reached the raft, Mary Catherine was sitting on the platform, feet dangling in the water. Two boys who were about Doreen's age stood on the opposite side of the raft, daring each other to jump.

"You go first!" the black-haired boy said.

"No, *you*," his blond companion replied.

Margie and I climbed the ladder, a little out of breath, and sat beside Mary Catherine.

"What a glorious day!" she blurted.

Margie and I didn't talk that way, and neither of us had anything to add about the quality of the day.

"You first," the black-haired boy said again.

The other boy settled the matter by shoving his friend into the water, then jumping in after him. The resulting splash sprinkled all of us girls.

"Hey, Mary Catherine," Margie asked, "where'd you learn to swim like that?"

"I took lessons when we lived in Chicago. All the high schools up there have swim teams and I was going to be on one. But then we moved *here*." Mary Catherine made Georgia sound like the other side of nowhere. "All they have here is basketball and football. It's positively uncivilized." She got to her feet. "Want to race back?"

"Not right now," I answered.

She dove off the raft and glided away toward the beach. I watched her with a mixture of irritation and envy. I hadn't worked up the courage yet to learn how to dive.

"All they have here is basketball and football. It's positively uncivilized," Margie said, mimicking Mary Catherine's flat, Midwestern accent. "Why doesn't she just go back to Chicago where everything's perfect?"

"Yeah," I agreed. "Who needs a swimming team?"

When Margie and I trudged out of the water onto the beach a few minutes later, Mary Catherine was standing near the concession stand talking to a real cute redheaded boy who must have been at least fifteen. He was trying to impress her, smiling and talking fast. I had to admit Mary Catherine looked pretty good right then. Her hair was drying into little feminine ringlets, shining in the sun, and her pink-and-white-checked, two-piece bathing suit made her look at least two years older than she was. I coveted that suit. I was pretty sure Sandra Dee had worn one just like it in *A Summer Place*. My one-piece Janzen felt suddenly dowdy.

Lunchtime came. We all walked up and over a small hill to a shady area where several wooden picnic tables were arranged. Mrs. Rogers spread a plastic cloth, and we helped set the table. Soon we were all eating egg salad sandwiches and potato chips, even Doreen. She might not have liked egg salad, but she managed to put away two sandwiches in no time. When the meal was over, Mrs. Rogers wouldn't allow any of us to go back into the lake.

"You have to wait half an hour or you'll get cramps and drown," she warned.

We passed the time in the adjoining playground. While the swings got quite a workout, none of us chanced the tall slide. Its gleaming metal surface, heated by the June sun, would have seared the skin right off our bare legs. At one o'clock, Mrs. Rogers announced that the time was up.

"All right, girls, you may go back to the lake, but I want you to keep an eye on Doreen."

"They won't play with me," Doreen whined. She was right, of course. We had done our best to avoid her all morning. "Make them play with me."

Mrs. Rogers assured her daughter, "I'm sure they will, dear."

"No, they won't." Doreen pouted. "I don't want to go back in swimming. I want to stay here and swing."

So Mr. and Mrs. Rogers stayed with Doreen, sitting in the shade while she played on the swings.

"When we come back down to the beach, I expect you girls to play with Doreen," Mrs. Rogers yelled as we hurried away.

We had been in the water only a few minutes when Mary Catherine stated that she wanted to go back out to the raft.

"It's so far," Margie complained.

"No, it's not. Besides, you could use the exercise. You're getting a little pot belly."

Margie stared daggers at Mary Catherine's retreating back, and then we were off thrashing through the water. Once again, Mary Catherine was waiting for us when we got to the raft, stretched out on her back, eyes closed. I lay down beside her on the hot wooden planks, and Margie plopped down next to me, sitting with her arms around her knees. We were alone on the raft. The only sounds were snatches of music from the beach—I thought it was the Everly Brothers, but couldn't be sure—and the occasional slap of a wave against the raft's pilings. Far off in the west, thunderheads had begun to build, hinting that we might be in store for a late afternoon storm.

Mary Catherine sat up and held her arms out in front of her. "I wish I could tan darker. I've tried and tried, but I just turn a kind of pinky beige." She gave a theatrical sigh.

I wasn't in the mood to debate shades of tanning because I hated sunbathing. It was the most boring activity I knew, except for sitting through a church sermon.

"Who was that boy you were talking to?" I asked Mary Catherine.

"What boy? Oh, before lunch? Just a boy. I don't remember his name. He was nice, I guess, but I don't think he was very smart."

I looked up at Margie, and she shrugged. Neither of us had ever had a boyfriend, though getting one was a frequent topic of conversation between us, and dismissing someone as cute as that boy had been on the grounds that he wasn't very smart seemed unimaginable.

Mary Catherine stretched, arching her back.

"I don't think I'd turn him down just because he's not brilliant," Margie said.

Mary Catherine shrugged. "You probably wouldn't, but I'm looking for someone really special." She stood up. "It's so hot. I'm going to cool off." She walked to the edge of the raft, stepped out into the air, and dropped straight down, momentarily disappearing beneath the water's surface.

"Bitch," Margie muttered, so low I could hardly hear her.

I had never heard her talk like that before, but I understood that Mary Catherine could cause a lapse into cussing. She seemed to take special pleasure in being ugly to Margie.

A splashing sound to my left signaled Mary Catherine's return to the surface. Margie jumped to her feet and was over to the edge of the raft like a shot. She dropped to her knees, then went down on her stomach, her arms extended past the raft. By the time I had crossed the raft to stand beside Margie, both of her hands were tangled in the wet hair on Mary Catherine's head, and Margie was pushing down. Mary Catherine's face was just visible beneath the water. From the wild thrashing, it was clear that Mary Catherine was fighting hard to get away.

In the past I had been around people who enjoyed pulling other people underwater, but I had never participated. The few times I had been the victim of that kind of horseplay, it had scared me half to death, so I can't explain what happened next. Over the years, I've spent a lot of time wondering why, but right then I never questioned my actions. One second I was standing on the raft, the next I was laying beside Margie. Mary Catherine managed to get her head above the surface for a few seconds, gasping for breath. Then my hands joined Margie's, and we thrust Mary Catherine under once more. Our fingers gripped her hair, so she couldn't simply sink lower in the water and swim away from us. She could only push desperately upwards against the joint strength of our hands.

The bubbles bursting on the surface must have made us realize what we were doing. We let go of her head as if it had burned our hands. Mary Catherine's face broke the surface of the water—blotchy red and furious. She coughed and sputtered, then swam clumsily the few feet to the ladder, taking care to keep well out of our reach.

"What's wrong with you? Are you crazy?" Her voice was shaky. "You could have killed me!"

"We were just playing," Margie said scornfully. "Can't you take a joke?"

Mary Catherine made her slow way up the ladder and sat on the raft, still breathing hard. She gave us a wary look, then transferred it toward the beach, which now looked miles away.

I turned over on my back and threw my arm over my face to block the blazing sun. My heart hammered in my chest as I waited for Mary Catherine to say more, but she didn't. A few minutes later, when the pounding had eased and my breathing had slowed, I sat up and looked around, feeling like a dreamer just coming to consciousness. Mary Catherine was gone. I searched the dazzling water until I spied her swimming toward the beach. Margie sat motionless beside me, her eyes likewise on Mary Catherine.

We didn't say a word about what had happened—then or ever. And I still don't know if Mary Catherine told her parents. If not, perhaps she believed it had been a prank as Margie had told her. But I doubt it. That "joke" had felt deadly serious to me.

The clouds continued to mass, and the threatened thunderstorm arrived about the time we got back to the car. Rain poured on us during the long drive home. We four girls in the back seat were very quiet. Doreen had stopped her whining. Mary Catherine stared out the side window, and Margie kept her eyes straight ahead, watching the wet road ahead. Crowded between Doreen and Margie, I sat motionless, trying to find room in my skin for the new person now living there.

The summer went on just as we had anticipated, with backyard cookouts and watermelons and drives up to the mountains, but I never went back to Lake Manageechee. In the fall, we learned that Mary Catherine had transferred to a parochial school. I think about her from time to time, and I wonder if she, too, looks back on that hot day at the lake and wonders what happened and why.

Reunion of Fugitive/Agrarian Group, Nashville, TN, 1956

Agrarians All!
Or, Southerners Without Masters

BY M. THOMAS INGE

In recent years, certain literary critics have seen in the writings of Southern literary scholars who began to publish in or shortly after the 1960s a kind of critical conspiracy under the immediate influence of Louis D. Rubin Jr. and more generally under the influence of the Fugitive/Agrarian poets and their followers who dominated Southern letters after 1930. The criticism began with what I suspect was intended as a figurative and innocent remark by Lewis P. Simpson in an essay for the Spring 1988 issue of *The Southern Review* on the state of Southern literary scholarship. In discussing the recently published *History of Southern Literature* edited by five senior scholars, including Simpson himself, and taking note of the general absence of the use of European critical theory in the book, he saw this as a generational limitation of what he called the "Rubin generation."[1]

Perhaps Simpson was primarily thinking of the senior editors, who were mainly of the same chronological generation, with Blyden Jackson born in 1910, Simpson himself born in 1916, Thomas Daniel Young born in 1919, Rayburn S. Moore in 1920, and Rubin in 1923. At the

---

[1] Lewis P. Simpson, "The State of Southern Literary Scholarship," *The Southern Review* 24 (Spring 1988): 2502.

time of its publication, the forty-four other contributors to the *History of Southern Literature* ranged in age from seventy-nine (Lewis Leary) to thirty-seven (Mark Winchell and Michael Kreyling), so clearly there was no true generation here in terms of chronology.

Writing almost simultaneously with Simpson, in an essay for *American Literature* published in March 1988, Michael Kreyling faulted the contributors to the *History* for keeping the discussion of Southern writing apart from the larger context of American literature and for heeding what he saw as an "orthodox critical practice" or consensus at work established by "soldiers in the Agrarian cause."[2] It was Kreyling's "conviction that awareness of one's politics and the political climate of one's time is both inescapable and necessary to the writing of literary history" and that this has been "edited out" by the authors of the *History*. He then continued:

> Signs of this editing appear in M. Thomas Inge's "Appendix A: The Study of Southern Literature." Inge's opinion of Richard King's *A Southern Renaissance* (1980) is the specific occasion. King's study, Inge argues, errs methodologically and ideologically when it "moves beyond history and sociology into cultural anthropology and psychoanalysis, which in conjunction with his sympathy for the liberal tradition makes a balanced treatment of the literature [of the Southern renascence] impossible" (p. 595). This is a clear warning: the study of Southern literature shall be reserved for the community of the faithful who believe in the South as icon above and beyond history and intellect, who eschew literary approaches through alien territory occupied by the tribes of Levi-Strauss and Freud, and who espouse a con-

---

[2] Michael Kreyling, "Southern Literature: Consensus and Dissensus," *American Literature* 60 (March 1988): 89.

servative intellectual tradition as far to the right as T. S. Eliot. If we were to heed this warning there would be one, fixed, academized Southern literature, hostile to the new and different, reserved for believers.[3]

When I first read this, I was startled both to find myself a major spokesperson for the entire body of contributors to the *History* and their "orthodox consensus hold on Southern literary study"[4] and to witness how such a body of opinion so foreign to my own beliefs could be extracted from such a single sentence.

But I will return to that in a moment in order first to trace the continuation of this debate as camps are established and battle lines are drawn, to retain Kreyling's military metaphor. In opposition to the Rubin generation, Jefferson Humphries assembled a like-minded set of contributors for a book published in 1990 called *Southern Literature and Literary Theory*, which oddly enough included two contributors to the *History* (Kreyling and Craig Werner, both now apparently feeling free to quote Fredric Jameson or Jacques Derrida to their heart's content), with the entire endeavor dedicated to the second-most senior of the Rubin generation, Lewis P. Simpson, rescued from that camp by Humphries because "in spirit, he is one of us."[5] While speaking in the name of dissensus and diversity, and turning to deconstructionist, feminist, and Marxist theory, it appears that another kind of orthodoxy is being established in its "us" and "them" mentality that may be no less exclusionary than the first. As James Mellard very aptly observed in his review of the book for the *Mississippi Quarterly*:

---

[3] Ibid., 94–95.
[4] Ibid., 95.
[5] Jefferson Humphries, ed. *Southern Literature and Literary Theory* (Athens: University of Georgia Press, 1990) xvii.

One of the "truths" of postmodern theory [which *Southern Literature and Literary Theory* is meant to represent] is that no text can escape ideology. No text, that is, can avoid exhibiting some governing philosophy or conceptual framework ("ideology" becomes the favored term because all such frameworks are regarded as retaining "power" and so are "political" in some fashion). Humphries's book is no more able to escape an ideology than any other.[6]

In other words, it makes a difference who writes literary history, and the authors will inevitably reflect their own social, political, and aesthetic biases. Yet hasn't this always been evident, and how exactly is history to be written otherwise? (I must confess here to a small degree of satisfaction that Mellard commented in a footnote about my contentious essay in the *History* that it was "excellent.")[7]

At this point Michael Kreyling once again stepped forward to reclaim his command of the newly organized Army of Critical Theory in an essay for the *Mississippi Quarterly* on "Southern Anthologies in an Age of Political Correctness" to note that "No literature anthology, Southern included, is innocent of a political agenda."[8] Here he surveyed the several anthologies designed for classroom use, with a focus on the major one, *The Literature of the South* edited in 1952 by Richmond Croom Beatty, Floyd C. Watkins, and Thomas Daniel Young, and revised in 1968. Like most of the others, Kreyling said, "this anthology set out to valorize the neo-Agrarian understanding of Southern cultural meaning."[9]

---

[6] James M. Mellard, "Lists, Stories, and Granny's Quilt: Writing—and Rewriting—Southern Cultural and Literary History," *Mississippi Quarterly* 44 (Fall 1991): 471.

[7] Ibid., 466, n2.

[8] Michael Kreyling, "Southern Anthologies in an Age of Political Correctness," *Mississippi Quarterly* 44 (Fall 1991): 443.

[9] Ibid., 447.

By now chafing at this and several other essays in the same issue of the *Mississippi Quarterly,* which seemed to blame him and his "generation" for an alleged orthodoxy in Southern literary scholarship, Louis D. Rubin Jr. responded the following spring with "A Letter to the Editor," in which he commented, "First of all, I wish to say that assertions by Mr. T. Jefferson Humphries to the contrary notwithstanding, the idea that such a thing as a 'Rubin Generation' of monolithic Southern literature scholars exists or has existed is so much tommyrot."[10] Without responding to the larger theoretical issues or denying the influence of politics on how one teaches or writes about Southern literature, Rubin injected some common sense into the discussion. He recognized that he was *necessarily* ignorant of modern critical theory in the 1950s because it was unavailable then. Rubin claimed that his main intention was to create a legitimate place for the study of writing by Southerners as a distinct phenomenon in the academy. He concluded:

> As a card-carrying Democrat I am far from denying the importance of ideas and the usefulness of schematizations, but I shall go to my cremation insisting that (a) no idea or schematization can do justice to the complexities of human experience, that (b) novels and poems provide a unique way of examining those complexities, and that (c) one need not apologize for devoting one's professional life to reading, teaching, or writing about novels and poems *as* the novels and poems that they are.[11]

To assume an affiliation between Rubin and the Agrarians is itself problematic. They did not see eye to eye about a good many things. Donald Davidson, for example, told me that he disagreed with Rubin's notion that Agrarianism was meant to be taken metaphorically rather

[10] Louis D. Rubin Jr., "A Letter to the Editor," *Mississippi Quarterly* 45 (Spring 1992): 189.
[11] Ibid., 192.

than literally since the Agrarians were mainly creative writers. Davidson also disagreed with Virginia Rock's argument in her dissertation that the Agrarians were actually "Utopians."

Not to be deterred, Kreyling in an essay specifically on Rubin argued that Rubin contributed to a sort of post-modern anti-Agrarian version of *I'll Take My Stand* assembled by twelve Vanderbilt faculty members and friends called *The South as an American Problem* (the connection is noted in the introduction, though they claim "no intention of either echoing or answering our predecessors."[12]) When I see a book title including some form of the phrase "the problem of the South," I am reminded of a comment by an African-American friend and scholar who once asked, "Why do white people always talk about the 'problem of the Negro'? We are not the ones who have the problem."

Without explicitly saying so, in this essay Kreyling accuses Rubin, as "the primary architect and developer of Southern literary study in this century,"[13] of a kind of waffling racism in what he reads as support of "the politics and thematics inherent in Agrarianism"[14] that refused to recognize slavery as the heart of the Southern dilemma. Kreyling also widens the definition of the "Rubin generation" to include his "fraternity of friends," all those who studied under him at the University of North Carolina in Chapel Hill, and the authors of books published under his editorship in the Southern Literary Studies series for Louisiana State University Press.[15] Kreyling then adds sarcastically, "Since it is now the case that scholars whom Rubin has helped to train at the University of North Carolina are now training others, it might be correct to speak of a Rubin dynasty."[16] Following this same logic, since Rubin was one

---

[12] Larry L. Griffin and Don H. Doyle, ed., *The South as an American Problem*. ed. Larry L. Griffin and Don H. Doyle (Athens: University of Georgia Press, 1995) 3.

[13] Michael Kreyling, "Race and Southern Literature: 'The Problem' in the Work of Louis D. Rubin, Jr.," *The South as an American Problem*, 242.

[14] Ibid., 237.

[15] Ibid., 242, 256 n17.

[16] Ibid., 256 n17.

of the founders of the American Studies movement in the 1950s and served while teaching at the University of Pennsylvania as one of the first executive secretaries of the American Studies Association in 1954–55, are we to assume that all members of that group are part of the Rubin generation?

Kreyling revised and brought together his several essays on the topic, along with some new ones, in 1998 in his book *Inventing Southern Literature*. Although it adds appreciably little to his earlier arguments, the book does provide an open and extended arena in which to work and usefully examine more extensively the fiction of Faulkner as well as selected female and African-American writers in the South.

Jefferson Humphries returned to many of these themes in his essay on "The Discourse of Southernness" in his book *The Future of Southern Letters* (co-edited by John Lowe), and Humphries called once again for younger scholars untainted by the elders of the Rubin orthodoxy to "bring recent European philosophy and theories to bear on southern texts and the text of the South."[17] Of course, one need not have called for this, given the tendency of critical theory to spread on its own like wildfire in all areas of cultural and intellectual inquiry. It was inevitable. The truth of this is demonstrated in the June 2001 special issue of *American Literature* devoted to "Violence, the Body, and the 'South,'" edited by Houston A. Baker and Dana D. Nelson. All the discourses of recent critical theory were employed in this issue, often brilliantly, by the six contributors, without a mention anywhere in the text or notes of Humphries, of Kreyling, or of any of the discussion outlined above. Derrida, Foucault, and company have a way of getting ahead on their own, and the application of their ideas to Southern letters was just a matter of time.

---

[17] Jefferson Humphries, "The Discourse of Southernness, or How We Can Know There Will Still Be Such a Thing as the South and Southern Literary Culture in the Twenty-First Century," *The Future of Southern Letters*, ed. Jefferson Humphries and John Lowe (New York: Oxford University Press, 1996) 131.

It is perhaps a sign of tolerance on the part of Humphries that he allowed into *The Future of Southern Letters* "Of Canons and Cultural Wars: Southern Literature and Literary Scholarship after Midcentury," an essay by Fred Hobson, who had been identified by Kreyling as a member of the "Rubin dynasty." Hobson, like Rubin, is a former editorial writer who abandoned journalism for the academy (Rubin at the Richmond *Times-Dispatch* and Hobson at the Winston-Salem *Journal and Sentinel*). Hobson completed his doctorate under Rubin, was editor of *The Southern Review*, and eventually inherited his mentor's mantle as a professor at Chapel Hill, editor of the Southern Literary Studies series at Louisiana State University Press, and co-editor of the *Southern Literary Journal*. If anyone belongs to a Rubin dynasty, it would surely be Hobson, and while he does not deny the affiliation, he is clearly his own person in intellectual matters, as anyone who has read his work knows. Hobson insists in his essay, however, that it should be called, if anything, the "Rubin-Simpson generation" since both have been called "the pillars of the Southern literary establishment."[18] Thus Simpson, kidnapped earlier by the Army of Critical Theory, has been stolen and seemingly returned to the reputed Agrarian camp, probably like Criseyde without being consulted about his preference.

Hobson does mount a counterattack on Kreyling by denying the existence of some sort of neo-Agrarian conspiracy or monolithic conservative consensus among the editors and contributors to *The History of Southern Literature*. Hobson goes on to note:

> Kreyling is justified in raising the broad issue—in questioning whether we have too readily accepted the Agrarian definition of the South and the southerner, and thus the Agrarian definition of southern literature—but

---

[18] Fred Hobson, "Of Canons and Cultural Wars: Southern Literature and Southern Literary Scholarship after Midcentury," *The Future of Southern Letters*, ed. Jefferson Humphries and John Lowe (New York: Oxford University Press, 1996) 76.

I believe he is excessive in presuming a conservative bias on the part of the editors of *The History of Southern Literature,* or, in other particulars, making them overly responsible for the sins of some of their contributors. Kreyling focuses, for example, on an ill-considered remark by M. Thomas Inge in an appendix that serves as a survey of southern literary scholarship. In considering Richard H. King's *Southern Renaissance* (1980), Inge charges that King "moves beyond history and sociology into cultural anthropology and psychoanalysis, which in conjunction with the sympathy for the liberal tradition makes a balanced treatment of the literature impossible." This is hardly the case: King's book, in fact, adds much to the discussion of twentieth-century southern letters— partly *because* of his use of psychology and his "sympathy for the liberal tradition"—and Kreyling is right to contest Inge's evaluation. But he also seems to suggest that Inge speaks for the editors and the general philosophy of *The History of Southern Literature.*[19]

Which brings us back to my essay, except now I am identified as a "sinner" and author of an "ill-considered remark." Exactly how "ill-considered" was it? (For a continuation of the debate, see the reviews of *The Future of Southern Letters* by Kreyling in the Winter 1996–97 issue of the *Mississippi Quarterly* and by Scott Romine in the Fall 1997 issue of the *Southern Literary Journal,* as well as Kreyling's continuing diatribes against those with "deep University of North Carolina at Chapel Hill connections" [as opposed to shallow connections?] as found in reviews such as those published in the Summer 2001 issue of the *Mississippi Quarterly* and the Fall 2003 issue of *Southern Cultures.*)

---

[19] Ibid.

I wrote my essay for the *History of Southern Literature* in the Summer of 1982 while on a fellowship at the Institute for Southern Studies at the University of South Carolina, the only place in the country where all the necessary resources were assembled. I had read King's book when it appeared two years earlier and felt then that while it was full of useful insights, he had carried his own political, sociological, and psychological agendas too far and had often forgotten he was dealing with products of the imagination that also had aesthetic values. All texts seemed to become equally valid social documents, and there were few efforts to consider their imaginative power. I have reread the book for this occasion, and I think better of the book than I did twenty years ago, perhaps because many of the new critical perspectives he was establishing now appear unexceptional. In comparison with some more radical recent criticism, King seems downright common-sensical in fact, and I derived much pleasure from the clarity and intelligence of his prose. If I failed to appreciate or misrepresented King's intention, I apologize.

Now, however, I find another problem that I did not note the first time. Because King decides to focus only on what he calls the "Southern family romance" and themes related to that mythic concept, he is forced to exclude any attention, he says, to "black writers such as Richard Wright or Ralph Ellison or … women writers such as Eudora Welty, Carson McCullers, Flannery O'Connor, and Katherine Anne Porter … because … they were not concerned primarily with the larger cultural, racial, and political themes that I take as my focus."[20] Were I reviewing the book today, I would suggest that any study that omits women and African-American writers in the South cannot bear up under the title *A Southern Renaissance: The Cultural Awakening of the American South, 1930–1955*, which suggests a comprehensiveness not to be had without them. The study of the family romance is a central and important part

---

[20] Richard H. King, *The Southern Renaissance: The Cultural Awakening of the American South, 1930–1995* (New York: Oxford University Press, 1980) 8–9.

of understanding Southern culture, but it is not the whole of it or the only reason for the Renaissance having occurred.

My own feeling is that we must not simply find a place for blacks and women within the traditional views of Southern literature but totally redefine the tradition with them there at the start, not ill-fitting appendages but an essential part of the definition. We must re-imagine Southern literature from the inside, as if the paternalistic view had never been articulated, so that all perspectives are valorized. In a sense an example of this may be Alice Randall's re-imagining of Margaret Mitchell's *Gone with the Wind* from the point of view of Scarlett O'Hara's mulatto half-sister and the slaves in *The Wind Done Gone*. Only the point of view of the Slatterys and the poor whites remains unarticulated. If King's emphasis on the family romance had been made explicit in his title, I would not make this criticism. In any case, I do not want to hold him responsible for what he did not intend to do.

However fair or unfair my assessment of the book in 1982, or unclear what I was trying to say, in no case should I have been taken as a spokesperson for some conservative consensus on the part of the senior editors. As any of the contributors know, including Kreyling who was among them, no editorial guidelines were issued or statement of principles made by Rubin or his colleagues, and to my knowledge no private discussions or committee meetings were held to determine an agenda. I suspect I was an afterthought anyway, since the invitation to contribute came late after all the other topics on which I might have claimed some expertise had already been assigned. When they realized there was no room for a bibliography, someone—my guess is Dan Young—thought of asking me to write a brief survey of the scholarship on Southern literature instead. Rubin's only response to my manuscript on submission was that it mentioned him too frequently.

Looking at the larger body of my own work, it would be difficult to argue that I am an enemy to Levi-Strauss and Freud or a camp follower of T. S. Eliot. I helped organize the first interdisciplinary American Studies programs at Michigan State University and Virginia

Commonwealth University. Among things for which I have been held responsible is helping to open the academy to the study of all forms of popular culture, including comic strips and comic books, considered the veriest trash by the guardians of the conservative Western tradition and high culture (though T. S. Eliot was known to admire Walt Kelly's comic strip *Pogo*). I taught the first course in American humor, subversive by its very nature, to a mainly conservative student body at Michigan State University, as well as to Marxist-trained students at Moscow State University in the former Soviet Union, no less ideologically-bound and threatened by the arts of sarcasm and satire. I offered the first course in ethnic-American literature taught at Virginia Commonwealth University in 1972. Over 200 students attempted to enroll, but I was only allowed to keep forty, and I was appropriately challenged by black and Hispanic students over my ability as a white to understand their cultures. I helped challenge the canon by editing with Maurice Duke and Jackson R. Bryer the first scholarly guides to research and writing on African-American and women writers.

For me, any mode of criticism or critical theory is but one of many tools through which a reader can come better to understand and appreciate the full complexity of a piece of literature. No one tool can do the job on its own, and if one theory is pressed to an extreme, it serves only to distort and obscure the work. There is no single critical avenue to truth or a definitive reading of a text, nor should one adopt a theory as if it were a religion exclusive of all others. Theoreticians are not gods, nor are critics members of a priesthood, though this often appears to become the end result. Our profession has never been lacking in intellectual arrogance. Criticism has its usefulness and when well-practiced can be an art form itself, but I would never consider a piece of criticism as equal in value to the creative act or the ability to produce an effective poem, play, story, or novel.

I have little or no claim to being a member of a Rubin generation or dynasty, if there are such things. I did not study with Rubin at Chapel Hill. I will confess to great admiration for his essay "The Great American

Joke," the most influential piece ever written on the subject of American humor, an opinion shared by almost everyone in humor studies. Edgar MacDonald and I did edit a collection of essays on James Branch Cabell that appeared in Rubin's Southern Literary Studies series, but I never contributed to the *Southern Literary Journal* until recently (when I submitted a book review). Long before I knew of Rubin, I knew of his father, Louis D. Rubin Sr., who was famous when I grew up in Richmond because of his amateur but highly accurate method of predicting the weather. I knew about "Rubin days" long before I knew that James Branch Cabell and Ellen Glasgow lived in Richmond.

It is my Vanderbilt credentials, I am sure, that make me more suspect than any connection with Rubin. I should state up front that I am not and never have been a member of the Agrarian party. I have been interested in Agrarianism as a cultural and literary phenomenon, and while I have written about the Nashville group individually and collectively, I have always viewed them as part of a much larger and lengthier tradition that descends from classical times. I tried to make clear in a small textbook I edited in 1969, *Agrarianism in American Literature*, that patterns of such romantic thought are as characteristic of writers from the North and Midwest as from the South (perhaps one of the reasons Robert Frost and Donald Davidson were such good friends and lived near each other in Vermont during the summers when Davidson escaped the heat of Nashville). Indeed, Agrarianism is arguably one of the defining traditions of American civilization. Personally, however, I am very much a city person who prefers to be near the bright lights and commercial conveniences of large urban centers. I place no stock in the earth as some source of spirituality and morality, and I once irritated my father-in-law, a farmer, by saying that I planned to follow some line of work in which I would not get my hands dirty.

Charlotte H. Beck, in her book *The Fugitive Legacy: A Critical History*, has argued persuasively and with convincing documentation that Southern letters and criticism have been more influenced by an aesthetic network rather than by a conservative conspiracy. As she tells the story, what began as a local and regional movement in Nashville with the publication of *The Fugitive* poetry magazine in 1922 soon became a national phenomenon, and its primary instruments were the university classroom and the subsidized academic literary quarterly.

The primary figure and teacher was John Crowe Ransom, who came to Vanderbilt as an instructor in English in 1914, soon to be joined by Donald Davidson, at first a student and after 1920 a fellow faculty member. Their shared passion for poetry was widened to include several younger students, such as Allen Tate, Robert Penn Warren, and Andrew Lytle, though their magazine *The Fugitive* would eventually reach out to a national circle of poets and readers and include among its contributors Hart Crane, John Gould Fletcher, Robert Graves, and Laura Riding. In their gatherings, the young poets passed around, read aloud, commented on, and borrowed from each other's work, establishing a pattern of collaboration that would last a lifetime. They were also developing through their close analytic scrutiny the seeds of what would become the New Criticism, though Beck rightly locates its origins in the practices of the Methodist ministers of the time whose sermons were based on careful rhetorical and semantic explications of biblical phrases and texts. Both Ransom and Warren were sons of Methodist clergymen and undoubtedly heard many such sermons. It should also be noted that Vanderbilt University was originally established in 1875 by the Methodist Church, with Cornelius Vanderbilt as the financial founder, though by 1920 the affiliation had been formally ended.

As the members of the group graduated and moved on to other institutions to study or teach, they soon picked up new student followers, mentored them into artistic maturity, published them in quarterlies they edited or established, and encouraged contacts with numerous other writers through friendship and correspondence. On the surface, this may appear to be simply a "good-old-boys" (and sometimes "girls") network functioning to get each other into print, but it was not a matter of merely doing each other favors. Indeed they subjected each other's work to the severest kind of criticism, required extensive revision, and as often as not rejected it out of hand. The quarterlies they edited— *The Southern Review, The Kenyon Review, The Sewanee Review,* and *Hound and Horn* among them—set new standards for American poetry, fiction, and criticism, and with such success that the writers found it easier to gain entrance to the high-paying prestigious publications where they had no personal influence, like *The New Yorker, Harper's, Scribner's, Atlantic, Mademoiselle,* and *Esquire.* A roster of the names who emerged from this collaborative network also dispels any notion of cronyism at work: Randall Jarrell, John Berryman, Robert Lowell, Caroline Gordon, Katherine Anne Porter, Eudora Welty, Peter Taylor, and Flannery O'Connor. Then there were the people they in turn tutored or influenced, like James Dickey, Jesse Hill Ford, Elizabeth Spencer, Walter Sullivan, Madison Jones, Edwin Godsey, and Robert Drake, as well as such critics as Cleanth Brooks, Lewis P. Simpson, Thomas Daniel Young, Louise Cowan, and Ashley Brown.

By all rights, I suppose that I too should have become one of the Fugitive legatees, but when I came to Vanderbilt in the Fall of 1959 as a graduate student in English, I had no idea that it was the site of such major developments in American literature. I knew nothing of *The Fugitive* magazine and of the poets who published there and their influence (not only on poetry but also on modern fiction and literary criticism). I knew little about politics and had never heard of the Nashville Agrarians or *I'll Take My Stand,* though in coming to know about them I would find myself diametrically opposed to their opinions on matters of race and public policy. I had not taken the only course Randolph-Macon College offered in American literature because it was taught by a brilliantly eccentric teacher who was incomprehensible and interminable in his lectures. Instead, during the summer before I entered graduate school, I undertook to read on my own the entire two volumes of the 1953 second edition of *The Literature of the United States,* edited by Walter Blair, Theodore Hornberger, and Randall Stewart. Since I had done poorly on the Graduate Record Examination in English because it was oriented towards New Criticism, something else to which I had not been introduced, I also read both *Understanding Poetry* and *Understanding Fiction* by Brooks and Warren (fortunately, Vanderbilt placed more stock in the Miller Analogies test, on which I did quite well).

My going to Vanderbilt was largely an accident. I had won a grant from the Southern Fellowships Fund that would underwrite three years of graduate study at any university that would have me, with the understanding that I would eventually teach in a Southern institution (another one of those Northern philanthropic efforts designed to help the South pull itself up by its own bootstraps, like the ubiquitous Carnegie libraries old Andrew built in major Southern cities beginning in 1899 to help benighted Southerners learn how to read and rescue themselves). I was warned away from the University of Virginia because I was told that a terrible war was being waged in the English department there between Fredson Bowers and his opponents, and graduate students were often caught in the crossfire. The University of North Carolina told me that I would be accepted only on a provisional basis because I did not have a course in American literature on my record as an undergraduate and would have to pass an examination on the subject. The University of Florida accepted me without provision, as did Vanderbilt, which not only accepted me but also offered me a fellowship. Although I did not need the support, it was the offer of a fellowship that made the difference. I wanted to be somewhere I was wanted. Also, in the Vanderbilt English department was Edgar Hill Duncan, himself a graduate of Randolph-Macon and one who personally encouraged me to come to Vanderbilt because he had faith in the kind of well-rounded education I had experienced at a small liberal-arts college (despite my escaping without a course in American literature).

I arrived at Vanderbilt in all my naivete and ignorance and was soon immersed in what I now know was the last days of the Fugitive legacy. I took courses with Donald Davidson in the ballad and folklore, read recent British and American fiction with Walter Sullivan, and studied modern poetry with John Crowe Ransom who was a visiting professor in 1961. One of my delights, in fact, was receiving an "A" from Ransom, because the best grade Allen Tate had reportedly ever been able to earn from Ransom was a "B+" when he had studied with him. Whether or not I deserved it is questionable. When I picked up my final examination paper, I asked Ransom why I had received an "A" on it, since there were no comments. He replied, "Well, I read the first few pages, and you seemed to know what you were talking about."

I also had the opportunity to meet or talk with most of the other contemporaries or legatees of the elders Ransom and Davidson: Tate, Warren, Lytle, Brooks, Jarrell, Lowell, Porter, Dickey, Ford, Spencer, Jones, and Drake among them. I missed Flannery O'Connor by five months since she appeared at one of Vanderbilt's annual literary symposia in April of 1959 before I arrived. Melvin Bradford, who would prove to be probably the very last of the Agrarians, was a fellow graduate student, and poet Edwin Godsey was a fellow instructor. Although I took no courses from him, Thomas Daniel Young, who had just returned to Vanderbilt as an administrator, was the second reader on my dissertation, and we would collaborate on two books about Davidson.

Because I was already publishing after my first year of graduate study, and he had approved of my writing for his course in the ballad, Davidson hired me to write a model research paper about Hawthorne and Melville for the concise edition of his textbook *American Composition and Rhetoric*. This would be my main contact with Davidson until Dan Young and I began conducting interviews with him for the books we were writing about his poetry. My relationship with Davidson remains a complex and enigmatic matter that cannot be fully explored here. Its cordiality may have stemmed from the fact that we *never* discussed politics.

My mentor, however, was not among any of these people. The person who took me in hand and served as my professional model was Randall Stewart, the Hawthorne biographer and editor who spent a large part of his career teaching at Brown University. He encouraged my interest in the unconventional by suggesting I write about George

Washington Harris and humor for my master's thesis and allowing me to complete a 611-page annotated edition and critical introduction to the uncollected writings of Harris for my dissertation. He was the one who steered me away from the narrow aestheticism of New Criticism and showed me how to look at literature in its broadest possible historical, biographical, social, and cultural contexts. He was also the one who wisely counseled me not to transfer to the American Civilization program at Yale University because, he said, a degree in English would guarantee me a job anywhere, whereas there were few American studies programs in the South at that time to go to. So I remained at Vanderbilt to work with him. He was the ultimate scholar and gentleman of the old school and a man of keen wit and good humor. Being racially tolerant and knowing of my liberal disposition, he once encouraged me to consider accepting a teaching position at nearby Fisk University. But his mentorship of me ended when he died unexpectedly in his sleep exactly one month after I defended my dissertation. In a sense, his mentorship continued by virtue of his having left to me and another graduate student his research library, which we easily divided according to our diverse interests (she being interested mainly in Hawthorne, Henry James, and the genteel tradition, and I being interested in Twain, Faulkner, and the frontier tradition). I still occasionally use a volume with his annotations and hear his comments laced with equal amounts of dry sarcasm and common sense. He would have found this entire debate intensely amusing.

What can be concluded about all this? It has always been true and will remain true that the writers of cultural history will inevitably inform their work with their own ideological biases. How else can cultural history be written? It cannot be done scientifically and objectively, and to pretend otherwise is foolish. Like Southern literature itself, the writing of Southern literary history will continue with consensus and dissensus, employing every conceivable mode of literary theory, from New Criticism to New Historicism to theories yet to be developed. We should be cautious when we generalize about a very diverse generation of critics, and we should refrain from employing monolithic ideologies, whether conservative or liberal. We should be wary of selecting one voice as representative of a group—especially on the basis of one comment taken out of the context of a larger body of writing—and we should avoid reaching easy conclusions about what that person believes.

Works Cited

Baker, Houston, and Dana D. Nelson, eds. "Violence, the Body, and 'The South.'" Special issue. *American Literature* 73/2 (June 2001): 231–412.

Beatty, Richmond Croom, Floyd Watkins, and Thomas Daniel Young, eds. *The Literature of the South*. Revised edition. Glenview IL: Scott, Foresman, 1968.

Beck, Charlotte. *The Fugitive Legacy: A Critical History*. Baton Rouge: Louisiana State University Press, 2001.

Blair, Walter, Theodore Hornberger, and Randall Stewart, eds. *The Literature of the United States*. Revised edition. 2 vols. Glenview IL: Scott, Foresman, 1953.

Brooks, Cleanth, and Robert Penn Warren. *Understanding Fiction*. New York: Appleton-Century-Crofts, 1943.

———. *Understanding Poetry*. Revised edition. New York: Henry Holt, 1950.

Hobson, Fred. "Of Canons and Cultural Wars: Southern Literature and Southern Literary Scholarship after Midcentury." *The Future of Southern Letters*. Ed. Jefferson Humphries and John Lowe. New York: Oxford University Press, 1996. 72–86.

Humphries, Jefferson. "The Discourse of Southernness, or How We Can Know There Will Still Be Such a Thing as the South and Southern Literary Culture in the Twenty-First Century." *The Future of Southern Letters*. Ed. Jefferson Humphries and John Lowe. New York: Oxford University Press, 1996. 119–33.

———, ed. *Southern Literature and Literary Theory*. Athens: University of Georgia Press, 1990.

Inge, M. Thomas. "Appendix A: The Study of Southern Literature." *The History of Southern Literature*. Ed. Louis D. Rubin Jr., Blyden Jackson, Rayburn S. Moore, Lewis P. Simpson, and Thomas Daniel Young. Baton Rouge: Louisiana State University Press, 1985. 589–99.

———. "The Friendship Between Hawthorne and Melville." *Concise American Composition and Rhetoric*. By Donald Davidson. New York: Scribner's, 1964. 451–75.

———, ed. *Agrarianism in American Literature*. New York: Odyssey Press, 1969.

King, Richard H. *The Southern Renaissance: The Cultural Awakening of the American South, 1930–1995*. New York: Oxford University Press, 1980.

Kreyling, Michael. *Inventing Southern Literature*. Jackson: University Press of Mississippi, 1998.

———. "Old Lights, New Lights." *Mississippi Quarterly* 50 (Winter 1996–97): 151–57.

———. "Race and Southern Literature: 'The Problem' in the Work of Louis D. Rubin, Jr." *The South as an American Problem*. Ed. Larry L. Griffin and Don H. Doyle. Athens: University of Georgia Press, 1995. 234–58.

———. "South to the Future." *Southern Cultures* 9 (Fall 2003): 107–8.

———. "Southern Anthologies in an Age of Political Correctness." *Mississippi Quarterly* 44 (Fall 1991): 443–61.

———. "Southern Literature: Consensus and Dissensus." *American Literature* 60 (March 1988): 83–95.

_____. "Toward 'A New Southern Studies.'" *Mississippi Quarterly* 54 (Summer 2001): 383–91.

Mellard, James M. "Lists, Stories, and Granny's Quilt: Writing—and Rewriting—Southern Cultural and Literary History." *Mississippi Quarterly* 44 (Fall 1991): 463–80.

Randall, Alice. *The Wind Done Gone*. Boston: Houghton Mifflin, 2001.

Rock, Virginia. "The Making and Meaning of *I'll Take My Stand*." Ph.D. dissertation, University of Minnesota, 1961.

Romine, Scott. "Still Southern After All These Years?" *The Southern Literary Journal* 30 (Fall 1997): 128–36.

Rubin, Louis D., Jr. "A Letter to the Editor." *Mississippi Quarterly* 45 (Spring 1992): 189–93.

———. "The Great American Joke." *What's So Funny? Humor in American Culture*. Ed. Nancy Walker. Wilmington DE: Scholarly Resources, 1998. 107–19.

Simpson, Lewis P. "The State of Southern Literary Scholarship." *The Southern Review* 24 (Spring 1988): 245–52.

Night Fog

BY JON PARRISH PEEDE

When the night fog came
billowing through the window
with the wind,
I thought of my mother,
bent tired over the iron,
preparing my next school day.

In my damp sleep,
the moon pale and hidden,
the night fog tasted
like the Egyptian cotton
of the shirt collars
I sucked on as a boy.

Fundamentals of Baseball

BY J. D. GRAFFAM JR.

I almost didn't want to play today
When I found out my cousin tried to kill himself
With alcohol and muscle relaxers.
My dad told me when we were sitting in the truck
Behind the left field chain-link fence—
I didn't cry, didn't even want to
Because all the other players were walking by.
I didn't hear anything over my dad's voice
But cleats crunching Arkansas rocks:
"You just need to go out there and grit your teeth
And swing that bat as hard as you can.
That's your job. So you do it."
His voice was slow, deep like the diesel that pulled
The team's equipment trailer uphill
Along Tokohama Creek. He told me
About Charlie Grant and how bad—
How bad he wanted to play
But never got to.
During the game, Dad sits on the top bleacher
Gripping burning white aluminum
So he won't lean back too far
And fall—I feel black pine digging
Into my nails. Coach tells me to relax at the plate,
But every time I bat, my dad is hollering
Over my squared shoulders, "Bow up, boy, bow up!"

Falling Star

BY RON RASH

She don't understand what it's like for me when she walks out the door on Monday and Wednesday nights. She don't know how I sit in the dark watching the TV but all the while the most part of me is listening for her car. Or understand I'm not ever certain sure she's coming home till I hear the Chevy's wheels crunching up the gravel drive.

And each time a little less of her does come back, because after she checks on Janie she spreads the books open on the kitchen table, and she may as well still be at that college for her mind is so far inside what she's studying. I nuzzle the back of her neck. I say maybe we could go to bed a little early. I tell her there's lots better things to do than study some old book.

"I've got to finish this chapter," Lynn says, "maybe after that."

But there never is a maybe, leastways nights after class. I go on to bed alone. Pouring concrete is a young man's job and I ain't so young anymore. I need what shut-eye I can get to keep up. "You're getting long in the tooth, Bobby," one of the young bucks told me one afternoon I huffed and puffed to keep up. "You best get you one of them sit-down jobs, maybe test rocking chairs."

They all got a good laugh out of that. Mr. Winchester, the boss, laughed right along with them.

"Bobby's still got some life in him yet, ain't you?" Mr. Winchester said. He smiled when he said it, but there was some serious in his words.

"Yes sir," I said. "I ain't even got my second wind yet."

Mr. Winchester laughed again, but I knew he'd had his eye on me. It won't trouble him much to fire me when I can't pull my weight any more.

The nights Lynn stays up I don't ever go right off to sleep, though I'm about nine ways whipped from work. I lay there in the dark and think about something she said a while back when she first took the notion to go back to school. "You ought to be proud of me for wanting to make something of myself," she'd said.

Maybe it ain't the way she means it to sound, but I can't help thinking she just as well might be saying "Bobby, just because you ain't never made anything of yourself don't mean I'm near sorry enough to do the same."

I think about something else she once told me. It was Christmas our senior year in high school. Lynn's folks and brothers had finally gone to bed, and me and her was on the couch. The lights was all off but for the tree lights glowing and flicking like little stars. I'd already unwrapped the box that had me a sweater. I took the ring out of my front pocket and gave it to her. I tried to act all casual but I could feel my hand trembling. We'd talked some about getting married but it had always been in the far-away, after I got a good job, after she'd got her some more schooling. But I hadn't the notion to wait that long. She'd put it on, and though it was but a single carat she made no notice of that.

"It's so pretty," Lynn had said.

"So will you?" I'd asked.

"Of course," she'd said. "There's nothing in the world I want more than to be your wife."

I lay in the bedroom nights remembering her saying that and knowing in my heart she wouldn't say that now. I'm not more than ten feet away. It's like there's a big glass door between me and that kitchen table, and it's locked on Lynn's side. We just as well might be living in different counties for all the closeness I feel. A diamond can cut through glass, I've heard, but I ain't so sure anymore.

One night I dream I'm falling. There's tree branches all around me but I can't seem to grab hold of one. I just keep falling on, like, for forever. I wake up all sweaty and gasping for breath. My heart pounds like it's some kind of animal trying to tear out my chest.

Lynn's got her back to me, sleeping like she ain't got a care in the world. I look at the clock and see I got thirty minutes before the alarm goes off. I'll sleep no more anyway, so I pull on my work clothes and stumble into the kitchen to make some coffee.

The books are on the kitchen table—big, thick books that don't have many pictures. I open up the least one, a book called *Astronomy Today*. Even the words I know don't seem to lead nowhere. They could be ants scurrying around the page for all the sense they make. But I reckon Lynn understands them. She has to for to make her A's on the tests.

I touch the cigarette lighter in my pocket and think a book is so easy a thing to burn. I think how in five minutes they'd be nothing but ashes, ashes nobody could read. I get up before I dwell on such a thing too long. I check on Janie, and she's managed to kick the covers off the bed. It's been a month since she started second grade, but it seems more like a month since we brought her home from the hospital. Things can change faster than a man can sometimes stand, Daddy used to say, and I'm learning all of the truth of that. Each morning it's like she's done sprouted another inch.

"I'm a big girl now," she tells her grandma, and that always gets a good laugh. I took her the first day of school, and it wasn't like first grade when she was near crying when me and Lynn left her there. Janie was just excited this time. I held her hand when we walked into the classroom. There was other parents milling around, the kids looking for the desk that had their name on it. I looked the room over pretty good. A hornet's nest was stuck on a wall and a fish tank bubbled at the back, and beside it a big, blue globe like I'd had in my second grade room. *Welcome Back* was written in big green letters on the door.

"You need to leave," Janie said, letting go of my hand. It wasn't till then I seen the rest of the parents already had, the kids but for Janie in their desks.

That night in bed I'd told Lynn I thought we ought to have another kid.

"We barely can clothe and feed the one we got," she'd said. "And that's not going to change until I get my degree."

"We could get by. I could get some overtime."

"I don't want to just get by," she'd said. "I won't spend the rest of my life having to check the bank balance before buying my child a pair of shoes or taking her and some friends to a movie."

Then Lynn had turned her back to me and went to sleep.

⚜

It's not something I fret over a few weeks, then decide to do. I don't give myself time to figure out it's a bad idea. I just do it. Soon as Lynn pulls out of the drive I round up Janie's gown and toothbrush.

"You're spending the night with Me-Maw," I tell her.

"What about school?" Janie says.

"I'll come by and get you come morning. I'll bring you some school clothes."

"Do I have to?" Janie says. "Me-Maw snores."

"I don't want none of your lip about this," I tell her. "Get you some shoes on and let's go."

I say it kind of cross, which is a sorry way to act since it ain't Janie that's got me so out of sorts.

When we get to Momma's I say I'm sorry it's all of a sudden, but Momma says there's no bother.

"There ain't no trouble between you and Lynn?" she asks.

"No ma'am," I say, and though she looks doubtful she don't ask nothing else.

I drive the five miles to the community college. I find Lynn's car and park close by. I reckon the classes have all got started for there's not any students in the parking lot. There ain't a security guard around, and it's looking to be an easy thing to get done. I take my barlow knife out of the dash and stick it in my pocket. I keep to the shadows and come close to the building. There's big windows and five different classrooms.

It takes me a minute to find her, right up there on the front row, writing down most every word the teacher says. I'm next to a hedge so it keeps me mostly hid, which is a good thing, for the moon and stars are out tonight. The teacher ain't some old guy with thick glasses and a gray beard, like what I figured him to be. He's got no beard, probably can't even grow one.

He stops his talking and steps out the door, and soon enough he's coming out of the building and I'm thinking he must have seen me. I hunker in the bushes and get ready to make a run to the truck. I'm thinking if I have to knock him on his ass to get there I've got no problem with that.

But he don't come near the bushes where I am. He heads straight to a white Toyota parked between Lynn's Chevy and my truck. He don't get in, just roots around the backseat a minute before grabbing out some books and papers.

He comes back, close enough I can smell whatever it is he splashed on his face that morning. I wonder why he needs to smell so good, who he thinks might like a man who smells like flowers. Back in the classroom he passes the books around. Lynn turns the books' pages slow and careful, like as if they'd break if she wasn't prissy with them.

The parking lot is empty again. I figure I best go ahead and do what I come to do. I walk across the asphalt to the Chevy. I kneel beside the back left tire, the Barlow knife in my fist. I slash it deep and don't stop cutting till I hear air hiss.

I stand up and look around. Pretty sorry security, I'm thinking. I've done what I come for, but I don't close the knife. I kneel beside the white Toyota. I start slashing the tire and for a second it's like I'm slashing that smooth young face of his. Soon enough that tire looks like it's been run through a combine. I get in my truck and drive toward home, driving slow so I don't draw no attention to myself. I'm shaking but don't know what I'm afraid of.

Driving back I think about how Lynn had put on a few pounds after Jamie was born. "I need to know you still think I'm pretty, that you're glad I'm you're wife," she'd said most every day. But she didn't say such things now.

I turn on the TV when I get back, but it's just something to do while I wait for Lynn to call and have me come fix the flat. Only she don't call. Forty-five minutes after her class let out the phone ain't rang. I get a picture in my mind of her in that parking lot, trying to fix that tire while the security guard snores away in some office. I think about some guy spotting her and keeping in the shadows as he moves toward her. I get my truck keys and am halfway out the door when headlights freeze me like a deer.

Lynn don't wait for me to ask.

"I'm late because some asshole slashed my tire," she says.

"Why didn't you call me?" I say.

"The security guard said he'd put on the spare so I let him. That was easier than you driving five miles."

Lynn steps past me and drops her books on the kitchen table.

"Dr. Palmer had a tire slashed too."

"Who changed his tire?" I ask.

Lynn glances up at me.

"He did."

"I wouldn't have reckoned him to have the common sense to."

"Well, he did," Lynn says, and there's some put-out in her voice. "Just because somebody's book-smart doesn't mean that person can't do anything else."

"Where's Janie," Lynn asks when she sees the empty bed.

"She took a notion to spend the night with Momma," I say.

"How's she going to get to school come morning?" Lynn asks.

"I'll get her there," I say.

Lynn sets down her pile of books. They're piled there in front of her like a big plate of food that's making her stronger and stronger.

"I don't reckon they got an idea of who done it," I say, trying to sound all casual.

Lynn gives a smile for the first time since she got out of the car.

"They'll soon enough have a real good idea. The dumb son-of-a-bitch didn't even realize they have security cameras. They got it all on tape, even his license. The cops will have that guy in twenty-four hours. Least that's what the security guard said."

It takes me about two heartbeats to take that in. I feel like somebody just sucker-punched me. But it's a feeling more than that. It's like I'm suddenly outside myself, like I'm watching myself from far away.

I open my mouth, but it takes a while to push some words out.

"I need to tell you something," I say, my voice all whispery like an old sick man's voice.

Lynn doesn't look up. She's already stuck herself deep in a book.

"I got three chapters to read. Can't it wait?"

I know I've lost her, known it for awhile. Me getting caught for slashing those tires won't make it any worse, except maybe at the custody hearing.

"It can wait," I say.

I go out to the deck and sit down. I smell the honeysuckle down by the creek. It's a pretty kind of smell that any other night might ease my mind some. A few bullfrogs grunt, but the rest of the night is still as the bottom of a pond. The stars are out, so many I can't even guess their number, though Lynn and her teacher probably could.

"Make a wish if you see a falling star," Momma would say, but they're all stuck in the sky where they are. I think about what I'd wish, and what comes is a memory of me and Lynn and Janie. Janie was but a baby then and we'd gone out to the river for a picnic. It was April and the river was too high and cold and muddy to swim, but that didn't matter. The sun was out and the dogwoods were starting to white up their branches and you knew warm weather was coming.

After awhile Janie got sleepy, and Lynn laid her in the stroller. She came back to the picnic table where I was and sat down beside me. She laid her head against my shoulder.

"I hope things are always like this," she said. "If there was a falling star that would be all I'd wish for."

Then she kissed me, a kiss that promised more that night after we put Janie to bed.

But there wasn't no falling star that afternoon, and there's not one tonight. I suddenly wish Janie was here, for if she was I'd go inside and lay down beside her. I'd stay there all night just listening to her breathe. You best get used to it, a voice in my head says. There's coming lots of nights you'll not have her in the same place as you, maybe not even in the same town.

I look up at the sky a last time, but nothing falls. I close my eyes and smell the honeysuckle, make believe that Janie is asleep a few feet away, that Lynn will put away her books in a minute and we'll go to bed. I'm making up a memory I'll soon enough need.

Southern Gas Station

BY RENNA TUTEN

In my hometown of Guyton, Georgia, is a gas station where few people buy gasoline. Yes, Mr. Mack has his regulars: men who bring in their 1978 model Ford trucks to have their tanks filled. But there are never enough customers to create a booming business based solely on gasoline sales.

It's a full service station, though. An old black man named Mr. Charley works there—he wears three-piece suits and a hat everyday when he pumps gasoline. Over the suit he wears a big white apron smeared with gas and grease and Lord knows what else. Even in the summer, he'll still wear the vest with his shirt sleeves rolled up, and the hat.

Not much repair work is done on cars and trucks there. The garage is full of old tires and tools, and somewhere in there is the standup of the Standard Oil Company boy—the boy with a white crew cut and a striped shirt looking like he's getting ready to punch something or somebody.

You couldn't pull into that garage now even if you wanted to. Blocking the way are flats of petunias and pansies and tomato plants, along with a clothes rack from which hang ferns and begonias. During summer, a pot of boiled peanuts perpetually sits among the plants. In front of the peanuts, the plants, and the garage is Mr. Mack's son Mike's regular parking place.

Most likely, someone will say "hey" to you while you're on your way inside the station to buy a tomato plant. The odds are one hundred to one that it will be Mr. Vernon, who is sitting on a milk crate outside the station. He'll have a cigarette in one hand, while a can of Pepsi will be resting by his feet on the oil-stained concrete. Other men will be sitting there, too—Mr. Wilbur, Mr. Cletus (not their last names, just their first names with the mister tacked onto the front for respect).

These men are all retired, and they log in at least a few hours each week sitting on those PET milk crates and talking, some taking a break from their wives, and some missing their wives. I don't know what they talk about—wars, football, children perhaps? They always speak in low voices, almost mumbling but not quite.

When they say something to you, you have to do a double-take to make sure that it is you they are talking to. They might be asking you such questions as: "Gonna grow you some 'maters?" or maybe "How's that daddy of yours doin'?" or even "Good preachin' at the revival down there in Pineora?"

You can reply with the following: "Yep, we tried those seeds from Wal-Mart last year and they didn't do anything!" Or "He's working like a dog." Or "Yes sir, six people got saved last night, including those Martin people who just moved into that trailer down off Ozbalt Lane."

After asking about their wives (Ms. Gladys, Ms. Inez, and Ms. Daisy), you can proceed inside to pay for your 'mater plant.

Your eyes adjust to the dimness. The smell is sweet from tobacco and stale snack cakes that haven't been bought or even looked at in a few months or years. There is always a radio on, and, depending on the mood, it will be tuned to country music or to country music. Over the radio can be heard the sound of crickets—hundreds of crickets are singing in a cage to pass the time as they wait to be bought by fishermen.

A window lets in a small amount of light—not too much light, but just enough for the man behind the counter to see what you're buying and to ring it up on the old register. Your conversation with him will go something like this:

"Those tomato plants are good ones. They're called Red Rosies. Got 'em from Wilshire Farms over in Wrens. Be a dollar fifty."

"They look good. We tried some seeds from Wal-Mart last year and got nothin'. Here ya go."

"Thank you, ma'am. How's that daddy of yours doin'?"

"Workin' like a dog. Went in at 5:30 Tuesday mornin' and didn't get in 'til around twelve noon on Wednesday."

"Yep. I see your mama down there at that post office, and she says about the same thing. Is there some good preachin' down in Pineora this week?"

"Yes sir, six people got saved last night, but that might have just been the cookin' beforehand."

"You're right about that! Have a good one."

"You too, Mr. Mack."

When you get outside, the light is so bright that you almost trip over Mr. Wilbur's thick black work shoes.

"Careful, honey," Mr. Wilbur says.

Filling Station, Reedsville, West Virginia, June 1935.

SOUTHERN GAS STATION

Hank Williams Sr.: "I'll Never Get Out of This World Alive"

The Last Ride on the Lost Highway

BY RANDY RUDDER

What *really* happened on the night that Hank Williams Sr. died? More than fifty years after that tragic ride from Montgomery, Alabama, to Oak Hill, West Virginia (en route to Canton, Ohio), there are still as many questions as answers. The misinformation—conflicting accounts and general folklore—surrounding Williams' last ride is quite staggering. Over the years, fans of Williams from Montgomery to Oak Hill have wanted to be part of the legend. As a result, even such details as the time and place of death are still hotly debated. The more years that pass, the less chance there is to discover the truth about Williams' death. Even so, a reconstruction of the events of Williams' last days may help provide clarity.

The days preceding the death of country music's greatest legend transpired as follows. In December 1952, at the age of twenty-nine, Hank Williams was at the apex of his career professionally but was straddling the pits of hell personally. During the week of December 20 alone, he had three hits in the Billboard Top 10: "Jambalaya" was at #1 and had been there for several weeks already. Also in the Top 10 were "Settin' the Woods on Fire" and the eerily prophetic "I'll Never Get Out of This World Alive." It was the fifteenth time in his short career that Williams had three of the Top 10 hits on the country music singles chart maintained by *Billboard*.[1]

---

[1] Arnold Rogers and Bruce Gidoll, *The Life and Times of Hank Williams* (Nashville: Butler Books, Inc., 1993) 168.

As far as his personal life was concerned, Williams had been drinking and missing more shows than usual in the weeks before his death. In August 1952, radio station WSM had severed Williams' Grand Ole Opry contract for missing performance dates. Also, his back pain—stemming from the spinal disorder that had plagued him since childhood—had worsened, forcing him to increase the number of painkillers he was taking. Finally, Williams' "o'er hasty" marriage to Billie Jean Jones in October 1952 appeared to be a means of placating some of his emotional pain (his second divorce from Audrey had just been finalized in July of that year). In fact, the marriage to Billie was performed at a justice of the peace because Audrey had threatened to disrupt any public ceremony. As Colin Escott wrote in *Hank Williams: The Biography*,

> In Nashville, the news of Hank's marriage was seen as evidence of his further disintegration. Billie Jean contends that Audrey flew into Shreveport a day or so before the very public marriage and tried to convince Hank to return to her by threatening that he would never see Hank, Jr., again. According to Billie, they met in a hotel room and Hank emerged with a welt on his forehead as a result of her hitting him. A welt is clearly visible in her wedding photos, although its provenance has never been established beyond doubt.[2]

Escott added that Williams had agreed to a public ceremony partly to spite Audrey, but by now that appeared likely to backfire. As a result, the official ceremony was performed by a justice of the peace in Minden, Louisiana, after the first *Louisiana Hayride* show on October 18. "That

---

[2] Colin Escott, *Hank Williams: The Biography* (Boston: Little, Brown and Company, 1994) 221.

way, if Audrey tried to disrupt the [public] ceremony, Hank and Billie could wave a marriage certificate proving that they were already married."[3] The next day, Williams "married" Billie two more times in elaborate public ceremonies at the New Orleans Municipal Auditorium show (at 3:00 P.M. and again at 7:00 P.M.), for a total of three wedding ceremonies in two days.

Also in the Fall of 1952, Williams began showing signs of the heart disease that would shortly thereafter result in his death. Country music star Red Sovine, who spent a lot of time with Williams those last few months, reported later that his friend had been having severe chest pains several months prior. "We were going off to Oklahoma," Sovine said of one such incident, "and he put both hands on his chest and he says, 'It feels like it's gonna bust, like it's gonna tear open. I couldn't hardly breathe last night.'"[4]

It was on one of his trips to Oklahoma City that Williams met Horace Raphol ("Toby") Marshall, a man posing as a physician with experience in treating alcoholics. On December 22, 1952, Marshall wrote a prescription for chloral hydrate that Williams had filled in Montgomery shortly before he left on his ill-fated trip northward.

Williams' premonitions of death during his last weeks on earth lent a bizarre element to an already unusual series of circumstances. He spoke of these feelings to several people. That fall, Williams told a Nashville *Tennessean* reporter, H. B. Teeter, "I will never live long enough for you to write a story about me."[5] On his last night in Montgomery, December 29, 1952, Williams couldn't sleep. According to his new wife, he even went down to the chapel at St. Jude's hospital that evening. "Ol' Hank needs to straighten some things up with the Man," he told her. Later that night, Billie found him awake, staring into the darkness.

[3] Ibid., 221.
[4] Ibid., 223.
[5] Ibid., 238.

When she asked him what was wrong, he replied, "Every time I close my eyes, I see Jesus coming down the road."[6]

As Williams got ready to leave for Canton, Ohio, on December 30, he sensed that this might be the last time he would ever see his new bride. Billie Jean said he came in and sat down on the edge of the bed near her while she was standing in front of the mirror. When she asked what he was doing, Williams replied, "I just wanted to look at you one more time." Then he kissed her and left.[7]

Promoter A. V. Bamford had booked Williams for a New Year's Eve show in Charleston, West Virginia, and two New Year's Day shows in Canton, Ohio. On the morning of December 30, however, much of the South was blanketed by a snowstorm. Hearing that many of the airports were grounding flights, Williams went looking for a driver to take him to the upcoming shows. Even with the inclement weather, he probably figured, if they started out now, they would have no problems getting to Charleston by the next evening.

On the afternoon of the 30th, Williams drove to Montgomery's Hollywood Drive-In and offered Leo Hudson $250 to drive him to Charleston and then on to Canton. Hudson told him that he could not do that because he had a commitment on New Year's Eve. On previous occasions, Williams had hired Charles Carr, a freshman at Auburn University who worked during breaks for his father at the Lee Street Taxi Company. Williams had reportedly told Hudson, "Charles is a good boy, but I don't trust his driving."[8] Some accounts claim that Williams checked on the availability of a couple of other drivers, but found none, so he went to the Lee Street Taxi Company and hired Carr for the drive.

From this point, many of the details of the next two days are sketchy. Carr's age was reported in different publications as 17, 18, and 19 (Carr was actually 17). Some published accounts also claim the two left

[6] Ibid., 237.

[7] Jay Caress, *Hank Williams: Country Music's Tragic King* (New York: Stein and Day, 1979) 207.

[8] Ibid., 206.

Montgomery on Wednesday, December 31, 1952, which was not true. If they were expected in Charleston, West Virginia, that evening, it would have been impossible to get there before the 7 P.M. show, even in good weather conditions.

The route to the shows in Charleston and Canton would take them through Birmingham, where they would pick up Route 11 and stay on it all the way to Bristol, Virginia. After that, they would pick up Highway 19 and take it to Charleston for the show on New Year's Eve, then on to Canton, Ohio, for the New Year's Day shows. Carr also verified in a personal interview with the author that they left on the 30th to get a few miles behind them, then they stopped in Birmingham for the evening. There, they checked into the Redmont Hotel, and Hank bought a six-pack of beer.

Carr says that Williams was in good spirits when they left Montgomery. However, Williams' mother, Lillie, claimed that he was in a foul mood when he left his home city. According to Arnold Rogers, author of *The Life and Times of Hank Williams*, "Toby Marshall stated under oath that Lillie called him at 4:30 that afternoon (December 30) in Oklahoma City, informing him that Hank had been through some extremely emotional and explosive event—some insist it was an argument with Billie Jean—which caused him to start drinking again and to leave for West Virginia in a car."[9] (Both Escott and Rogers admit that Marshall's account conflicts with Billie Jean's recollection of the peaceful parting, as it does with Carr's story, who remembers Hank even singing a few songs along the way.) Lillie supposedly then asked Marshall to leave immediately for Charleston to meet Hank and stay with him until after New Year's Day.

Sometime on the morning of the 31st, Carr and Williams left the hotel in Birmingham, heading up Highway 11 toward Chattanooga, Tennessee, and on to Knoxville. Junior O'Quinn, president of the

---

[9] Rogers, 172.

International Traditional Country Music Fan Club, confirms that the two men lodged the night of the 30th in Birmingham.[10] (O'Quinn devoted an entire issue of his organization's newsletter a few years ago to Williams' last ride.) Carr says they then stopped in Ft. Payne, Alabama, and had breakfast either there or in Chattanooga. Carr also claims that Williams bought a bottle of bourbon in Fort Payne.[11] This is probably when Williams began taking the chloral hydrate that Marshall had prescribed for him, mixing it with alcohol, while Carr drove.

From here, the weather slowed them down considerably; by the time they got to Knoxville—at 11:00 A.M. on December 31—it was beginning to look like they might not be able to make the 7 P.M. show in Charleston. Carr stopped and checked on flights from Knoxville to Charleston and found that there would be a flight leaving at 3:30 P.M. Williams then called Cas Walker, a Knoxville DJ, and told Walker that he wanted to stop by the radio station and perform a song or two on Walker's noontime show. Williams never showed up.

Not much is known about what happened during the next four hours. At 3:30 that afternoon, Carr and Williams boarded the flight for Charleston. After the plane had been in the air about an hour, the pilot was told that the airport in Charleston was snowed in; returning to Knoxville, the plane landed just before 6:00 P.M. Carr contacted Bamford to let him know they wouldn't be able to make the 7:00 show that evening, and Carr then drove Williams to the Andrew Johnson Hotel in Knoxville, where the two men checked in about 7:00 P.M.

Carr ordered two steaks from room service and called the front desk to ask for a doctor to look at Williams, who by now was feeling the effects of the chloral hydrate and alcohol combination. Carr remembers that Williams also had a severe case of hiccups. A Dr. P. H. Cardwell soon arrived at the hotel and gave the country music star two shots of

---

[10] Junior O'Quinn, "Hank Williams: The Final Journey," *International Traditional Country Music Fan Club Newsletter* 4/3 (1999): 7.

[11] Charles Carr, interview by author, 15 February 2002.

Andrew Johnson Hotel, Knoxville

B12, each containing a quarter grain of morphine for his back pain. At least one account of Williams' death posits that Toby Marshall (who had flown from Oklahoma to Charleston, where he was waiting for Williams) may have sent Dr. Cardwell to the Andrew Johnson Hotel.

George Koon is one of many writers who have questioned why the doctor would have given Williams more drugs, given his condition. "Why didn't Carr and Cardwell get Hank to a hospital? Perhaps they were frightened or perhaps they were disgusted with their obviously inebriated patient," speculates Koon. "Besides, Carr still seemed intent on getting Hank to Canton in time to rest before the show; he was well aware that Hank's contract carried a one-thousand dollar default penalty."[12]

The two checked out of the Andrew Johnson Hotel at about 10:45 P.M., less than four hours after they had checked in. Porters carried Williams to the car and later reported that he twice made a coughing sound.[13] The coughs, of course, could have been the severe hiccups referred to by Carr.

In an article on Williams' trip through Knoxville, published in the Knoxville-based newspaper *Metro Pulse*, writer Jack Neely discusses the "Knoxville Curse" associated with the Andrew Johnson Hotel, citing the fact that several performers and celebrities, including Williams, died soon after staying at the Andrew Johnson. Amelia Earhart was there shortly before her 1937 disappearance. In 1943, the Russian composer and pianist Sergei Rachmaninoff passed away not long after performing at the University of Tennessee's Alumni Hall. Singer and actor Nelson Eddy died in Florida shortly after appearing in Knoxville, as did a musician of a subsequent generation, rock star Ozzy Osbourne's guitarist Randy Rhoads. Neely adds that pianist Vladimir Horowitz refused to play in Knoxville because he felt that the city was bad luck.[14]

---

[12] George Koon, *Hank Williams: A Bio-Bibliography* (Westport, Connecticut: Greenwood Press, 1983) 52.
[13] Escott, 240.
[14] Jack Neely, "Death of a Legend: Hank Williams' Knoxville Demise Surrounded by Mystery Half a Century Later," *Knoxville Metro Pulse*, 12 December 2002.

At 11:45 P.M. on December 31, 1952, one hour after Carr and Williams left the Andrew Johnson, patrolman Swann Kitts stopped Carr and gave him a speeding ticket in Blaine, Tennessee. Carr had attempted to pass a Greyhound bus and had nearly hit Kitts, who was coming from the other direction. After pulling over Carr, Kitts saw Williams and questioned Carr whether Williams was still alive. "That guy looks dead," Kitts told Carr. Carr informed the officer who "that guy" was and asked Kitts not to wake up the country music star as he was trying to rest up for a concert. Kitts finally relented and told Carr to follow him into Rutledge, where they went to the home of Justice of the Peace O. H. Marshall. "He held court at his home," recalls Carr. "That's where the fine was paid." Carr claims the officer and the judge charged him more than the $25 showed in the court record. "He [Kitts] asked me how much money I had, and I said $75 and that's what the fine was. They split the difference between the $25 fine that they said they charged me and the $75 I gave them."[15]

Kitts' original report also mentions that Carr was traveling with a soldier. Who was this "soldier"? Perhaps it was someone who had been home on leave for Christmas during the Korean War and was hitchhiking back to his base? There is no way this alleged soldier could have been the relief driver that Carr had with him later that night, as some have theorized. The relief driver, Don Howard Surface, lived and worked in Bluefield, West Virginia, nearly 200 miles north.

A few days after Williams' death, Captain John Davis of the Tennessee Highway Patrol asked Kitts to write a detailed account of his stop of Carr for speeding, which Kitts did. Its contents, however, did not become public until nearly 30 years later. On December 15, 1982, as the 30th anniversary of Williams' death approached, a Knoxville newspaper printed the account. In it, Kitts had written:

---

[15] Carr interview.

After investigating this matter, I think that Williams was dead when he was dressed and carried out of the hotel. Since he was drunk and was given the injections and could have taken some capsules earlier, with all this he couldn't have lasted more than an hour and a half or two hours. A man drunk or doped will make some movement if you move them [*sic*]. A dead man will make a coughing sound if they [*sic*] are lifted around. Taking all this into consideration, he must have died in Knoxville at the hotel.[16]

Kitts, of course, may have been a competent state trooper, but he was no forensics expert. Furthermore, as Carr pointed out, if Kitts really believed that a 17-year-old boy was driving around with a corpse in his back seat, why wouldn't he have investigated further? Also, if Williams had been on the brink of death at the Andrew Johnson Hotel, why would Carr have ordered the country music star a steak dinner? Kitts' account also conflicts with the testimony of Dr. Diego Nunnari, who pronounced Williams dead at Oak Hill. Nunnari claimed that Williams had only been dead a couple of hours when his body arrived at Oak Hill. Considering the wintry weather, the approximately 200 mile drive into West Virginia would have easily taken another five or six hours from Rutledge.

From Rutledge, Carr continued on Highway 11 toward the border towns of Bristol, Tennessee, and Bristol, Virginia. For years, Carr maintained that Bristol was the place where Hank Williams Sr. spoke for the last time. When Carr stopped to get some food at a restaurant, he asked Williams if he wanted anything to eat, and the latter said no. However, in 1999, Bristol *Herald Courier* writer Joe Tennis speculated that Williams never stopped in Bristol. Carr admitted to Tennis that he (Carr) had been mistaken, that the place was in fact Bluefield, West

---

[16] Rogers, 175.

Virginia, not Bristol. Carr had the cities of Bristol and Bluefield confused, an understandable mistake considering that both cities begin with the same letter and are both on the border between different states (Bluefield straddles West Virginia and Virginia). Carr acknowledged that "For forty years, I said it was Bristol, thinking it was Bristol, and there seems to be a strong possibility we gassed up somewhere other than Bristol." Carr added, "We only gassed up one time. Wherever the restaurant was, I got a burger…. And that's where we gassed up. Wherever that was, is where I got [relief driver] Don Surface."[17] Don Howard Surface did indeed live and work in Bluefield, West Virginia.

Surface was born in Matoka, West Virginia, and spent most of his life in the area, where he worked as a coal miner, construction worker, mechanic, electrician, plumber, and cab driver; he died of leukemia in 1965 at the age of fifty. On December 31, 1952, just coming off duty at the Bluefield Cab Company, he stopped in at the Doughboy Cafe on Bluefield Avenue for a late night snack and a beer. The Doughboy is the site of another of the conflicting stories about the night. While Swann Kitts believed Williams was dead back in Knoxville, a waitress at the Doughboy, Hazel Schultz, claimed that the country music star himself came into the restaurant asking about a relief driver. "This Cadillac pulled into Ike Hoffman's service station across the street, and I saw a man cross the street and enter the café. Strangely, he was not wearing a hat," said Schultz, who passed away a couple of years ago. "After identifying himself as Hank Williams, the man asked me if I knew anyone who could take him to Canton, Ohio. I immediately pointed to Don, who was sitting in a booth."[18] Schultz said the two men had a couple of beers and talked for a few minutes before they left. In Joe Tennis' *Herald Courier* article, Schultz said she remembered the evening because the last two beers she sold in 1952 were to Hank Williams.[19] However, the high-

[17] Joe Tennis, "Community Front," *Bristol Herald-Courier*, 26 December 1999, 1D.
[18] O'Quinn, 13.
[19] Tennis, 1D.

way patrol records verify that Williams was with Carr in Rutledge, Tennessee (200 miles away) at 11:45 P.M. on December 31, 1952. Under those difficult weather conditions, Carr probably got to Bluefield no sooner than 4:00 A.M. Given the shape that Williams was in at the time, it was almost certainly Carr who entered the Doughboy.

Interestingly, though, Carr claims that Williams was not only awake at the time of the stop in Bluefield, but that he even got out of the Cadillac to stretch. "Hank was outside of the car when I was gassing up. I told him I was going over to the diner [the Doughboy] and asked him if he wanted anything, and he said no, he just thought he was going to get in the back and get some rest," remembers Carr. "I went to the office of the cab company first and asked if he [the owner] had anybody that could go with us and give us some relief. At that time, he said Mr. Surface had just finished his shift and was next door at this little diner, and I went in there. Someone told me who he [Don Howard Surface] was, and I spoke with him, and he said he would be interested in driving for a while."[20]

Surface began driving the Cadillac, and the three men headed north on Route 19 toward Beckley and Oak Hill. Carr refutes the claim later made by a Dr. Killorn, a Canadian intern at the Beckley hospital, who maintained that Carr brought Williams to the hospital at Beckley and asked him to check on the country music star. Killorn said that he looked at the body and told Carr that Williams was indeed dead, but that the coroner was not on duty and that Carr should take him up the road to Oak Hill.[21] Carr denies this. Indeed, it would be odd to turn a corpse away from a hospital, especially since the doctor who did the autopsy, Dr. Ivan Malinin, came to Oak Hill from the Beckley Hospital. (Dr. Killorn died in a car accident in Canada in 1992.)

Of all the conflicting accounts of the death of Hank Williams Sr., perhaps the most puzzling is the fact that Carr has always claimed he

[20] Charles Carr interview.
[21] Rogers, 173.

arrived in Oak Hill without Don Howard Surface, even though the officer at Oak Hill recalled that there were two men traveling with Williams.
Several newspaper accounts at the time, including the *Memphis
Commercial Appeal*, concurred. The two men were held in Oak Hill that
morning for a brief inquest, according to a local policeman.[22]

Oak Hill is only about sixty miles north of Bluefield, but Carr claims
Surface got out somewhere along the way. As to why someone would
hire a relief driver and then put him out of the car less than sixty miles
later, Carr says it was because he got carsick in the passenger seat. "He
[Surface] was not with us when we got to Oak Hill. I don't ride well with
somebody else driving, then or now. I thought maybe I could relax while
he was driving, but that wasn't the case, so Don didn't stay with us. He
got out at a place convenient to where he could get back."

Carr continues, "I stopped six miles outside of Oak Hill at an all-
night service station and talked to a man there. He looked at Hank and
he said 'I think you have a problem.' He told me Oak Hill General
[Hospital] was six miles from where we were, so I drove on from
there."[23]

When Carr drove into Oak Hill, probably a little after 6:00 A.M., he
pulled into a parking spot on Main Street, and he walked across the
street to Burdette's Pure Oil Station, where the owner, Glenn Burdette,
was on duty. Burdette called Chief of Police O. H. Stamey. After arriving on the scene and realizing a corpse was involved, Stamey radioed
Officer Howard Janney. When Janney arrived, the group proceeded to
the hospital (Janney's name is misspelled in most previously published
accounts as "Jamey").

"I lifted his [Williams'] arm and saw that he was dead," said Janney.
"By the time I got there, Stamey had already checked him. He told me
he was dead before I even opened the car door. I took a look at him and
said 'Well, let's run him to the hospital.'"[24]

---

[22] Howard Janney, interview by author, 26 January 2002.

[23] Carr interview.

[24] Janney interview.

The Last Journey

The Route of Hank's Last Ride.

Dr. Diego Nunnari pronounced Williams dead at 7:00 A.M. on New Year's Day 1953. The copy of the death certificate lists the cause of death as "acute right ventricular dilation" (heart failure), probably hastened by the combination of alcohol, morphine, and chloral hydrate in his body. The original death certificate and the autopsy report were lost in a fire at Oak Hill several years later.

The Cadillac was then moved to the Tyree Funeral Home on Main Street in Oak Hill. The town was beginning to stir, and word was spreading quickly about the country music star's death. A crowd began to gather at the funeral home, and people began taking things from the car for souvenirs, according to Janney. As a result, the car was moved inside the bay at the Pure Oil Station, while the two drivers were held briefly for questioning. Rachel Surface Orbison, daughter of Don Howard Surface, confirms that her father was held for a short period that morning.

Rigor mortis had not yet set in when Williams' body reached Oak Hill, according to Janney. "I asked the doctor how long he'd been dead, and he said 'I don't know. Two hours. Four hours.' I said 'Well, was it two hours or four hours?' and he said, 'That's all I know. Two to four hours.'"[25] If Williams had been up and around in Bluefield at 4:00 A.M. as Carr claims, and if Nunnari was right about it being a minimum of two hours since his death, then Williams probably passed away at about 5:00 A.M., somewhere along Route 19. The death that Williams had sung about for so long and that he had seemingly foretold came upon him, says Janney, "between here [Oak Hill] and Bluefield. I'm sure of that."[26] (Additionally, Janney is skeptical of Dr. Killorn's story concerning the stop at Beckley Hospital.)

According to Janney, Virgil Lyons, the judge in Oak Hill, ordered the inquest. The welt on Williams' head—probably from a fight he had

---

[25] Ibid.
[26] Ibid.

gotten into a few nights before in Montgomery—was enough to invite the judge's suspicion. The inquest found that there had been no foul play, and Carr and Surface were sent on their way. Later, at the Tyree Funeral Home, an autopsy was performed. Dr. Ivan Malinin, a Russian immigrant, came to Oak Hill from Beckley and performed the autopsy. According to Escott, "Malinin, who spoke almost no English, found hemorrhages in the heart and neck and pronounced that the cause of death was insufficiency of the right ventricle of the heart.... He also found that Hank had been severely beaten and kicked in the groin recently."[27]

In a bizarre twist to the story, Williams' sister, Irene Williams Smith, was in Virginia that night, not far from the route of Williams' last ride. Smith later reported that she had a premonition about her brother's death that evening:

> The night of the 31st, my family and I were invited to spend the evening with another Navy couple and their children. We four adults were laughing and talking. The children had long ago gotten sleepy and had been put to bed. Just as the television announcer said "Happy New Year," I turned to my husband and began to sob. "Please take me home. Hank's dead. I must get packed and ready to leave for Alabama" Of course everyone was shocked, feeling, I am sure, that I had lost my mind.[28]

The next morning, when the state troopers came bearing the news, Irene was sitting on her bed waiting with her suitcase already packed. A long-time student of ESP, Irene felt that her brother died shortly after midnight. If Swann Kitts' account is to be believed, then she was correct.

CROSSROADS

---

[27] Escott, 243.

[28] Junior O'Quinn, "Hank's Final Days," *International Traditional Country Music Fan Club Newsletter* 7/1 (1999), 5.

If Carr and Nunnari are right about the time of Williams' death, she was only a few hours off.

Another intriguing anecdote concerned the disappearance of the country music star's hat. William "Raz" Rogers is a longtime resident of Oak Hill who began working in the coalmines when he was twelve. At fifteen, he became the chauffeur for the town's wealthiest citizen, Herbert Jones, and Rogers worked for Mr. Jones for the next fifty years. Rogers lived in the Jones mansion, which was next door to Burdette's Pure Oil Station, and was on the scene the morning that Williams died. Now in his 90s, Rogers was good friends with Glenn Burdette. According to Rogers, Burdette somehow obtained Williams' cowboy hat and began wearing it around the station regularly. Eventually, Burdette's hair began to fall out, and he told Rogers he thought the hat might be haunted. Rogers says, "I told him, 'Oh, that hat ain't causing you to lose your hair.'" Still, Burdette kept wearing it. A few years later, he died in an apparent suicide behind his gas station.[29] The hat has never been recovered.

After Williams was pronounced dead, Carr contacted Williams' mother and wife in Montgomery. The next day, Lillie and Carr's father flew up to Oak Hill, and those two, along with the younger Carr and Toby Marshall (who had arrived from Charleston), drove the Cadillac from Oak Hill back to Alabama. After the inquest, Don Howard Surface called a relative that lived near Oak Hill, Lake Surface, who eventually drove him back to Bluefield.

Later that day, Hank Williams' fans were already gathering in Canton, Ohio, for the scheduled afternoon show when word reached the auditorium about the star's death. The band there played a musical tribute to Williams while the crowd wept. The funeral was held on January 4, 1953, in Montgomery. Tens of thousands of people showed up to pay their last respects.

---

[29] William Rogers, interview by author, 26 January, 2002.

On the drive from Montgomery to Oak Hill, Hank Williams Sr. may have been composing the last song he ever wrote. In the book *Hank Williams: Snapshots from the Lost Highway,* authors Colin Escott and Kira Florita included this lyric believed to have been in Williams' hand the night he died:

> "We met, we lived
> and dear we loved
> Then came that fatal day
> The love that
> felt so dear fades far
> away
> Tonight we both
> are all alone and here's
> all that I can say
> I love you still and
> always will
> But that's the price
> we have to
> pay." [30]

---

[30] Colin Escott and Kira Florita, *Hank Williams: Snapshots from the Lost Highway* (Cambridge MA: DaCapo Press, 2001) 173.

Remembering Hank, U.S. Postage Stamp, 1993.

Jesse Owens's Alabama Legacy

BY ZACHARY MICHAEL JACK

"'Where's the train gonna take us, Mama?"
She answered only, "It's gonna take us to a better life.'"

—Mary and Jesse Owens upon leaving Alabama, quoted in Tony Gentry's book *Jesse Owens*

On an otherwise quiet Sunday, enthusiasts gather in the north Alabama town of Oakville, birthplace of Jesse Owens, to witness the unveiling of a roadside historical marker commemorating the legendary runner known as the "Buckeye Bullet." That nickname referred to the fact that Owens, from the age of nine, grew up in Cleveland, Ohio, and eventually attended The Ohio State University. The Buckeye State was far from the Lawrence County Seat of Moulton, Alabama, where, today, farmers in bib overalls order Big Macs at the local McDonald's—and where, in 1983, requests for a Jesse Owens monument at the County Courthouse were rejected.

But for the folks gathered on this windy September day at the Jesse Owens Memorial Park and Visitor Center in Oakville, Owens will always be a native son. They remain proud of this American icon—the son of a local black sharecropper—who won four gold medals for track and field events at the 1936 Olympic Games in Nazi Germany.

※

In Lawrence County, the pediment above the courthouse pronounces, "Justice must be observed even to the lowest." Unfortunately, for the man who is arguably Alabama's most internationally-acclaimed native, local justice has been a long time in coming.

On September 12, 1913, the day that Mary Emma Owens gave birth to James Cleveland Owens (Jesse was his nickname), the police blotter in the Decatur *Daily* reported that a black man named John Alexander was arrested and fined for having "offered an insult" to a white woman. As reported to Owens biographer William Baker, Mary considered Jesse a "gift child" because "he [Jesse] was made when he couldn't have been made by us." Jesse and his nine siblings helped their father Henry Owens with the task of sharecropping cotton in fields owned by Big Jim Clannon, a hard-driving but reputedly even-handed Irishman whose house still stands north of the present-day museum site.

Around 1922, Mary moved the Owens family to Cleveland, Ohio, where Jesse's sister, Lillie, had established a foothold. Convinced by Lillie's dispatches and discouraged by the boll weevil and Clannon's growing profits at their expense, the Owenses joined the approximately 65,000 blacks that had migrated from Alabama to the North. Jesse Owens was not yet ten years old.

Afterwards, Owens's memory of Alabama remained riddled with blind spots. Owens's daughter Marlene Owens Rankin, raised in Hyde Park, Illinois, does not recall her father mentioning Alabama much; instead, she remembers him discussing family-specific incidents, most of them unpleasant—for example, how hard his sisters had to work harvesting vegetables and scrubbing floors. As he aged, Owens's boyhood memories hardened further. In a series of interviews granted to Barbara Moro for the Illinois Historical Library, Owens remembered "busting the furrows" behind a mule and picking a hundred pounds of cotton each day. Late in life, he viewed the specter of his impending death, the landscape of it, as "a long, long, long-distance race over hills and through valleys"—a place like north Alabama.

＊

In Oakville, Owens took his first steps, his mother cut painful sores from his legs with a kitchen knife, and the future runner tested his legs in games of tag and keep-away. Such stories about Owens have become legendary, preserved by Owens's fans as well as by his remaining relatives in Alabama. Seventy-year-old Elsie Fitzgerald, significantly younger than her cousin Jesse, remembers her mother complaining of the boy's prankish ways.

Owens's youngest daughter and 1960 homecoming queen at her father's alma mater, Ohio State, Marlene is arguably the most active among her siblings in furthering her father's belief in the ameliorative powers of athletics. Along with John Blalock, an alumnus of the University of Alabama, Marlene helps to run the Owens Foundation, which offers academic scholarships and athletic opportunities to underprivileged youths. From her office at the Jesse Owens Foundation, formed in Chicago after her father's death, Marlene confides, "We don't really know our Alabama relatives. There's some on my grandmother's side, but I can't even think of their name." While names elude her, Marlene speaks of Alabama as "the place where my father's family emanated from." She compares her generation's attitude toward Alabama to an extended family—they feel warmth, but not necessarily closeness toward the state. She points out that there are a number of shirttail relatives living in and around Oakville.

One such relative on hand for the Owens plaque unveiling, Fletcher Owens, who as a youth heard how "Jesse could outrun a horse," admits to having lost track of his famous kin's exploits when World War II erupted, and Fletcher began his military service. He wasn't alone. After World War II Jesse Owens became a peripheral public figure, of marginal political and commercial value.

＊

Stripped by the Amateur Athletic Union (AAU) of his amateur status for dropping out of a series of post-Olympic fund-raising exhibitions in 1936, Owens, when turning pro, had the support of his coach at Ohio State, Larry Snyder, and of the media. "If he can make a little money," the Boston *Herald-American* commented, "more power to him."

But instead of receiving "a little money," Owens experienced a post-Olympic endorsement blitz. He was everywhere people gathered in the years leading up to World War II, whether stumping for Republican Alf Landon in the 1936 presidential campaign, barnstorming with baseball's all-black Indianapolis Clowns, or opening a Cleveland dry-cleaning business billed as "Speedy 7 Hour Service by the World's Fastest Runner." None of these ventures were lucrative for Owens, who knew he could not afford to stay home and manage his investments. From 1940-42 he served as national physical education director for African Americans, largely an honorary position sponsored by the federal Civilian Defense office. On the heels of a Treasury Department audit which forced Owens to pay an estimated $20,000 in unpaid income tax on his 1936 earnings, Owens's friends and one-time track competitors, Russell Brown and Willis Ward, secured Jesse an administrative position representing African American workers at the Ford Motor Company in 1942.

Three months after Owens arrived at the River Rouge Plant, massive interracial riots broke out in Detroit, causing some $2 million in property loss and causing Owens to adopt what biographer William Baker called a "benign corporate image." Owens worked closely with such organizations as the Urban League, YMCA, and NAACP to attempt to improve conditions for Ford workers. Still, for many black workers, Owens's efforts were too little and too late, coming as they did after his earlier efforts to control and mollify black unionists. When Henry Ford II returned from the Navy to take over the family business in 1943, Owens was promptly dismissed in what Ford hoped would be a worker-friendly managerial shake-up.

In 1950, as the Cold War heated up, the Associated Press named Owens the "Greatest Track and Field Athlete of the Past Half Century." The simultaneity of the two events did not go unnoticed by an Eisenhower administration eager to portray the USA as the center of worldwide democracy and civil equality. To reinforce that image, the federal government recognized that it had to do more to improve its domestic racial climate. Jesse Owens, one of a very few well-known black conservatives, fit the bill. Owens, who lived in Chicago at the time, campaigned on behalf of Republican William G. Stratton Governor of Illinois, on the promise that an Illinois Athletic Commission would be formed with Owens as its leader.

In 1952, with the Russians slated to make their first Olympic appearance since the Bolshevik Revolution, the White House asked Owens to attend the Olympic Games in Melbourne, Australia, as the President's personal representative. When it was all over, American-Consul General in Sydney, Orray Taft, wrote in praise of Jesse's "warm and spontaneous" manner and his "keen appreciation for the problems of the youth"—qualities that Owens would later bring to bear in creating the ARCO [Atlantic Richfield Company] Jesse Owens Games, a fitness program for young people.

In 1968, political differences again threatened to overshadow Olympic competition. When the International Olympic Committee announced that Apartheid South Africa would be allowed to compete at the 1968 summer games in Mexico City, thirty-two African teams threatened boycott, as did their African American counterparts. The IOC eventually reversed its decision, but black members of the U.S. Olympic teams remained indignant. Americans that year were seeing, for the first time, footage of Jesse Owens's record-breaking performance in an hour-long television documentary entitled *Jesse Owens Returns to Berlin*. Approximately 180 local television stations broadcast the special. Owens seized the opportunity to retell his Olympic stories while making comparisons between Mexico City and Berlin. Owens maintained that black athletes should make their statement where it mattered most: on the field.

By encouraging competition regardless of politics, Owens had shown his conservative card. The differences between Owens and a new generation of African American athletes would be highlighted when American sprinters Tommie Smith and John Carlos raised black-gloved fists on the medal stand in Mexico City. Also at the 1968 Olympics, Bob Beamon leapt more than twenty-nine feet in the long jump, smashing Owens's record in that event.

Vexed by an inability to communicate with black demonstrators, Owens collaborated with ghostwriter Paul Neimark to produce *Blackthink: My Life as Black Man and White Man* in 1970. In what was considered the last straw by many African Americans, Owens declared, "If the Negro doesn't succeed in today's America, it is because he has chosen to fail." This statement, seemingly ridiculous in the wake of Martin Luther King's death, caused even Owens's politically moderate barber to refuse to cut the former track star's hair. Owens's daughter Marlene defends her father, saying "He really believed it's how you do what you do and not the color that makes a difference. As he got older, though, and got further up the social, economic ladder, he found more obstacles. His celebrity status didn't really matter. He became frustrated, even angry."

Owens's mounting frustration resulted in the 1973 publication of another book *I Have Changed,* a stunning reversal of his earlier Horatio Algerisms. In it, Owens acknowledged the legitimacy of protest and admitted that blacks received inferior education, housing, and job opportunities. Still, Owens's core argument—that effort largely deter-mined socioeconomic success—remained consistent.

⁜

Even in death, Jesse Owens proved political. His passing in 1980 was immediately seized upon by Chicago media, who opposed the U.S.

government's proposed boycott of the Moscow Olympics. David Condon of the Chicago *Tribune* opposed the boycott because, he argued, it would prevent black athletes from electrifying the world as Owens had done in the 1936 summer games. Soon, trustees at The Ohio State University announced plans for the Jesse Owens Memorial Plaza. In an attempt to justify the $1.4 million project, which would include a new synthetic track and recreation center that would bear Owens's name, supporters referred to Owens—who had failed to complete his degree at OSU despite repeated attempts—as one of their "most illustrious sons."

In his boyhood hometown of Oakville, Alabama—where, according to biographer William Baker, Owens had once returned owing $100,000 in back taxes and contemplating suicide—a controversy was brewing that was meaner than north Alabama moonshine. Representative Roger Dutton—whose family, like Owens's kin, had sharecropped in Lawrence County—spearheaded a move to honor

Illustration by Melissa Louise Jack

Jesse Owens

Owens with a monument on the Lawrence County Courthouse lawn in Moulton. This proposal seemed like an attractive idea to some Lawrence County officials and a politically expedient idea to a repentant Governor George Wallace, who gave $2300 to the project from his discretionary fund.

The County Commissions eventual denial of Dutton's proposal made national headlines. Speaking on behalf of the Commission, Chairman Clyde Cameron cited Dutton's heavy-handed methods as the reason for the rejection of the already-created memorial obelisk. Perhaps if the Commission had had more notice, Cameron suggested, the outcome might have been different. Newspapers at the time quoted the Chairman as saying, "We just have a little turf of our own, and we don't like it trampled." County Commissioner Oakley Lanier further explained, "The courthouse lawn is not designed to accommodate an individual," adding that he feared a flood of similar requests. Previous courthouse monuments in Lawrence County had been dedicated collectively to veterans of past wars, including Confederate General Joe Wheeler.

Dutton seized on the irony. While only an annual county marathon had been named after Jesse Owens, "Joe Wheeler's got about everything there is around here named for him—a highway, a dam, a wildlife preserve, a park," Dutton said. Following the logic offered by the County Commission, Dutton asked rhetorically if there would be room to accommodate an individual if that individual was a future U.S. President born in Lawrence County.

In the end, black residents in nearby Oakville, led by Owens's cousin Marvin Fitzgerald, quietly began clearing a vacant half-acre lot next to the Methodist church and Masonic Lodge, with intentions of adopting the orphaned obelisk. Sixty-three residents signed a petition in favor of erecting the hand-me-down monument that read:

> He inspired a world enslaved in tyranny and brought
> hope to his fellow man...from the cotton field of

Oakville to the acclaim of the entire world, he made us all proud to be called Lawrence Countians.

Apart from a subsequent vigilante attempt to pull the obelisk down with a pick-up truck, all remained quiet in Oakville.

❊

In 1991, Therman White, an African American who had recently returned to his native Oakville after retiring from the Navy, looked across County Road 203 from the modest Jesse Owens Memorial toward an adjacent field of weeds and wild onions where Owens's childhood home used to be, and White saw a vision.

James Pinion, then Lawrence County Extension Agent, still isn't clear why White did what he did. "He's not that big of a track fan," Pinion said. Perhaps White, who now serves as volunteer groundskeeper, envisioned it as a retirement project. Or maybe, as Pinion suspects, White just thought it ought to be done. To the roughly $15,000 in unused funding originally earmarked for the Jesse Owens memorial in Moulton, White added over $2,000 of his own pocket-money, buying the property outright.

Pinion, a native Alabamian and a passionate supporter of Auburn University athletics, agreed to help White make Oakville the locus of the Jesse Owens legend. The story of how White, Pinion, and Pinion's fellow county extension agents turned White's pastoral vision into the beginnings of a multi-million dollar park—eventually to incorporate a museum, a visitor center, and a sports complex—is a wholly American tale. More than a few observers have noted the uncanny similarities between White and Pinion's idea and that of Kevin Costner and James Earl Jones's mantra in the 1989 film *Field of Dreams*: "If you build it, they will come."

Indeed they have come—from as far away as Russia and Eastern Europe, and from every state in the nation. A tour of the grounds reveals the eternal flame, which was dedicated and lit by Jesse's widow Ruth Owens when, while the torch was being carried to Atlanta in 1996, the International Olympic Committee rerouted the Olympic torch through Oakville. Also on the grounds of the Owens memorial site in Oakville —officially known as the Jesse Owens Memorial Park and Visitor Center—is a statue of the athlete leaping through the Olympic rings, which appears so life-like that it caused Mel Walker, Owens's teammate at Ohio State, to do a double take at its dedication. Branko Medenica, the statue's Birmingham-based sculptor, sought but was denied approval from a notoriously conservative Olympic Committee to produce a statue that would feature shattered, stylized Olympic rings. According to Pinion, the Committee, horrified by the proposed bastardization of the Olympic design, would only allow Medenica to reproduce the traditional five rings.

The so-called eternal flame is now only burned on "special events." At times during recent years, the park could not afford the propane to fuel it.

❧

A quick glance around the grounds on this overcast, fall day shows that the park, which survived a bomb threat in 1996 from a white citizen, belies a less-than-golden financial reality. Funding for the all-weather track drafted into the original site plan—the track that would help the park be financially self-sufficient by hosting events and reaping concessions—never came to pass. One can still make out its tentative outline in the sod. If built today, the track would cost upwards of $500,000, says Pinion, who estimates the same project would have been built for $300,000 in the early 1990s, if things had gone as planned. East of the unrealized track and south of the grove of trees where Jesse Owens was born, Pinion points to the site of a proposed amphitheater that was also in the park's original plan and is still awaiting groundbreaking.

Inside the museum, Pinion and his part-time assistants—local matrons who earn about $900 a year to field research queries and visitor questions—name Lowe's and Home Depot as possible future donors. Coca-Cola, which gave $15,000 to the Owens park at its dedication, has dropped its support, according to Pinion, who complains the soft drink giant won't "even let me in the door."

According to Pinion, in the past couple of years the park has survived on an annual $12,500 grant from the United Way and a $9,000 utilities stipend from the Lawrence County. Still, the museum, built with the initial infusion of some $1.3 million, is impressive. "They just can't believe how nice it is," Marilyn Moats says of visitors that come to the museum, a brick-walled, steel-roofed structure that commands the park's southern boundary.

The museum houses considerable Owens memorabilia, much of it donated by a willing Owens family and by corporate entities like the Atlantic Richfield Company (ARCO), sponsor of the ARCO Jesse Owens Games and one-time owner of the Jesse Owens name. ARCO, bought out by British Petroleum, has given the museum much of its Owens paraphernalia, including oil paintings showing Owens in his various roles as athlete, emissary, and businessman.

On the visitor center porch this gloomy September day, Alabama 7th District Democrat Jody Letson reminds a mixed-race crowd of Owens's superhuman feats in Berlin and his humble origins in Oakville. Sadly for Hoyt Cagle, Chairman of the County Historical Society and an earnest man who calls the project his "baby," the promised media does not show up for the roadside historical marker dedication. A soft-voiced woman introducing herself as Rose documents the event on a camcorder, stopping to wipe raindrops from the lens.

Still, despite the cold rain, despite the netless basketball hoops and the standing water on the Coca-Cola baseball field, the mood is festive, the dream is alive. Therman White, clad in overalls and wearing a John Deere cap, leaves the porch to erect the new plaque. Pinion, offering rides from the visitor's center to the museum at the top of the hill, hopes that the park's designation as an historical site will entitle it to a sign on nearby I-65.

As White and a small cadre of helpers disappear into the road ditch, the crowd moves to the museum, where they gather at a small theater showing Bud Greenspan's *Jesse Owens Returns to Berlin*, the hour-long documentary film that in the late 1960s brought Owens's Olympic achievements to the attention of a new generation of Americans. The group of about ten people gathered around the screen includes a proud Elsie Fitzgerald, who says it would have been nice for her cousin Jesse Owens to experience this moment. "God bless this park," she says, remembering how, on his rare, whirlwind trips through the South, she would sometimes get to see Owens in nearby Decatur, Alabama.

Whistling quietly at footage of Owens's gazelle-like grace, the small but reverent crowd agrees with Elsie's sentiments. Pinion, now retired from county extension and working for a local chicken processor, watches proudly. Like so many others involved in the park, he donates his time. When the movie reel shows blond German long jumper Lutz Long embracing Jesse Owens under the disapproving stare of Adolf Hitler, Pinion confides that he'd like to bring Lutz Long's son to Oakville, to let him see for himself how Alabama has honored its native son.

My Mother's Hands

by Jo Angela Edwins

My mother's hands were broader than a man's,
splinter-scarred from swinging hickory switches, brooms,
shovels and hoes, sometimes a baseball bat.

My mother's hands were tipped with nails the color
of autumn rust, thick as Kentucky bourbon,
the hard stuff she grew up with and would not touch.

My mother's hands learned in 1948
to find faint pulses, to work a cruel syringe
with quick finesse, like a threaded needle.

My mother's hands cracked with psoriasis,
burned each day in isopropyl alcohol,
each night in wet diapers and lemon-fresh Joy.

My mother's hands grew sinew-strong
like amber stems uplifting in August
tomato vines for one last brilliant month.

My mother's hands held me tightest,
let go in a rush when I begged to run,
clenched in silence, poised to catch the fall.

My mother's hands the last time I saw them
were folded like kerchiefs, antiseptically white.
How hard they would have pounded, had she known.

Going to the Mountain:
Vincent Parker's Last Wagon Train

BY THERESA LLOYD

It was drizzling the morning that Vincent Parker rode on his last wagon train, which pulled out of town a little later than Vincent would have liked. As the long-time president and lead wagon driver of the Western North Carolina Wagon Train Association, Vincent was a man who believed that any self-respecting teamster ought to hit the trail by 7 A.M. But Vincent wasn't in charge that morning. In fact, some people might have said that this wasn't a wagon train at all, for there was just a single wagon, one of Vincent's iron-tired models, driven by his son Jerry Parker and his grandson Lynn Haas. Alone, they plodded the long miles from the Andrews, North Carolina, funeral home to the Parker family cemetery, located on a hill above Parker Branch and the farm where Vincent's family had lived for six generations. Vincent had died three days earlier, and they were carrying his body back home.

I first encountered Vincent Parker four years earlier, during the Summer of 1997, when I began doing documentary fieldwork with recreational wagon trains. As a folklorist, I was intrigued by the wagon train's quirky synthesis of Southern tradition with television Western. Driving covered wagons on trail rides that ran from a day to a week, teamsters modeled themselves, as Vincent and others would point out, partly on Ward Bond, the heroic wagon master who led hardy pioneers across the prairie each week during the 1950s series *Wagon Train*, and partly on their own grandfathers or fathers or younger selves—farmers who worked the land with a team of mules or horses that had become obsolete, thanks to the tractor, during the very decade that Ward Bond led wagon trains across TV screens. It was no coincidence that recreational wagon training arose in the 1950s: group rides were a way to get retired teams and wagons out of the barn, enjoy increased leisure time, and emulate the heroism that television brought into the living room each week.

While it is 1500 miles east of Ward Bond's prairies, the Upper South has been a seedbed of recreational wagon train activity since the 1950s, and in this part of the South, Vincent Parker ranks with such legendary figures as Curtis Hussey, Frank Hemming, Charlie Hall, and Frank Swan—teamsters and riders who helped develop the sport as it is practiced today. Although Vincent drove on rides as far away as Florida, his passion was the Western North Carolina Wagon Train, which since 1958 has roamed the mountains for a week or more each year around the Fourth of July. One of the nation's oldest recreational wagon events, the Western North Carolina ride is particularly steeped in tradition, a tradition that is no less deep for being relatively new. Over the years, as the oldest teamsters died out, Vincent came to be seen as the guardian of that tradition. Unofficial historian, consultant on matters of authenticity, general wagon guru—Vincent became, in a way, the wagon train's spiritual center.

Born in 1922, Vincent was one of those senior teamsters who had grown up working with teams. When twelve years old, he did his first plowing with a team of mules, and after that he was always working with mules and horses. Not long after Vincent returned from World War II, tractors were ousting teams from North Carolina mountain farms, but by then Vincent wasn't farming any more. He played minor league baseball in Florida and worked as a construction foreman. In fact, he was working in Florida at the time of the Western North Carolina Wagon Train's debut trip, which ran from Tellico Plains, Tennessee, to Murphy, North Carolina, in 1958. Vincent did make it to Murphy that year for the big street dance held when the wagon train pulled into town. After he moved back to the family farm south of the Great Smokies, he never missed a trip.

Vincent was well aware of his role as guardian of wagon train tradition. One of the first stories he'd tell any newcomer to the wagon train was how his senior team of mules, the old campaigners Jim and Joe, fit into that tradition. Originally the mules had belonged to Vincent's

Photo by Paul Simmons

Vincent Parker

uncle Harley Thompson, one of the Western North Carolina Wagon Train's founding teamsters and at the time of his death the driver of the lead wagon. Harley died after leading the 1977 wagon train across the Snowbird Mountains, and he left his team to Vincent. Because Harley's mules pulled the lead wagon and had been going on the wagon train since Harley led them along as yearlings in 1964, people felt that it was only proper for those mules to stay out front. So Vincent was appointed lead driver. Tradition had to continue. Vincent figured that by 1999 Jim and Joe had accumulated nearly 5,400 wagon train and parade miles.

The story of Jim and Joe was only one of the many tales in Vincent's repertoire. On the whole, teamsters are inveterate raconteurs, and Vincent was among the finest. You always knew when a tale was about to erupt. He'd grin down at you from beneath the enormous cowboy hat he always wore, his voice would rise and then lower in a certain pitch, and he'd launch forth. Vincent had tales about everything—his aunt's turkey, which wore a bell so that she could locate the free-ranging flock in the days before North Carolina enacted fence laws; the bear cub that had destroyed an irate housewife's boxwoods in a gleeful romp; Vincent's time in the Navy; his playing minor league baseball; his canoeing with his wife Wilma; and, of course, the wagon train.

For Vincent, landscape was story. Take the enormous pecan tree on Fairview Road near Andrews. If you drove by that tree with Vincent, he was likely to tell you the tree's history: Manuel Hardin brought it in a buggy from South Carolina in 1840. Vincent was a man of the mountains—southwestern North Carolina, his home, is a land of countless ridges and peaks with names like Nantahala and Wayah and Chunky Gal—and mountains figured prominently in his stories. He'd tell about heading up into the mountains for a week or more of camping and hunting and trail riding, which he liked to do every autumn. Or about the hard pulls or the dangerous descents the wagon train had made. Or about how, years earlier, when he was coming back home from the Navy, stuffed into a train for what seemed like an endless journey, he looked up one morning and saw the mountains on the horizon. That was when Vincent knew that he was home.

Like most wagon trainers, Vincent particularly enjoyed stories about wagon train hardship. Wagon trainers pride themselves on the difficulty of their sport. Broken axles on the trail, marauding hornets that make a nightmare out of an August ride, runaway teams, overturned wagons—teamsters eat these things for breakfast, spit out the rinds, and then munch on the good old days, back when recreational wagon training was *tough*—when there weren't RVs and hot showers, when a day's ride was long and really tested your mettle, and at the end you still had to make camp.

To make the ordeal more bearable, most wagon trains these days maintain one base camp, to which they return after each day's ride. The Western North Carolina Wagon Train, ever mindful of tradition, still believes a wagon train ought to *go* somewhere and thus moves camp with each day's ride, a practice that makes it no place for the faint-hearted. But Vincent—who always spent the trip in a rarified state of exaltation that his son Jerry and his grandson Lynn dubbed his "wagon train high"—took privation several steps further. Like the pioneers, or boys at summer camp, Vincent felt that the wagon train was a good time for participants to forego little amenities such as bathing, eating regular meals, and shucking off work clothes at bedtime. He also felt that bringing an RV on a wagon train showed a distinct lapse of character, and that customizing a wagon with car seats and pneumatic tires, which alleviate the bone-cracking jounce of a traditional wagon's wooden seats and iron tires, was just this side of mortal sin. As a result, riding on the Western North Carolina Wagon Train with Vincent Parker took recreational suffering to unexpected heights. Yet there was something bracing about it, too. You found yourself drawn to the high moral ground that Vincent occupied. You came to feel that there *was* something wrong with those comfortable seats and rubber tires. As Vincent would mutter, they just weren't authentic.

Authenticity was Vincent's mantra. It was his firm conviction that the wagon train had an almost sacred duty to show people the way things used to be. In part, the past that Vincent, like many old teamsters, wanted to recover was that of the nineteenth-century wagon trains heading West. Some of Vincent's ancestors had ridden on a wagon train as they migrated from North Carolina to Oklahoma. But he also wanted people to remember North Carolina's local wagon train tradition. As he explained, before the days of paved roads and big trucks, merchants in remote villages drove their wagons to large market towns for supplies. Because of the ever-present threat of a breakdown, the merchants usually made the trip in convoys of up to fifteen wagons. Vincent remembered that his grandfather hauled goods from Walhalla, South Carolina, to Andrews, North Carolina. Paying homage to that tradition, Vincent carried his grandfather's watch the year the Western North Carolina Wagon Train traveled to Walhalla.

For all his strictness of principle, Vincent had a boundless enthusiasm for his fellow teamsters, even those erring souls who insisted on sleeping in RVs, and he loved to welcome new members into the fold. Valerie Millar, of Jasper, Georgia, vividly remembers her first encounter with him. She had just bought two draft mules, Bonnie and Clyde, but she knew nothing about driving them. When at the suggestion of a business acquaintance she called Vincent, he immediately offered to meet her in Jasper and evaluate her mules, which he pronounced as being top-notch. That summer, he loaned her one of his wagons to hitch them to, and over the next winter, he built a wagon for her (iron-tired, of course). The fact that women teamsters are almost as rare as dogs walking on their hind legs was irrelevant to Vincent. For him, the main thing was a person's seriousness about wagon training.

During the wagon train, Vincent seemed to be present everywhere, always ready to impart his knowledge to other people. That knowledge was truly encyclopedic. He could look at the running gears of a wagon, tell you its make, and give you a good estimate of the year it was produced. In addition, he had an unusual and effective teaching method: when he gave instructions, he often left out the last little detail, forcing pupils to think for themselves and thus learn the lesson more thoroughly than if he had spelled out everything. He also taught by silently demonstrating something. One of his favorite tricks, for example, involved braking an iron-tired wagon while going downhill on pavement. On a steep, paved road, iron tires will sometimes skid out of control, even when the brakes are locked down. To prevent an accident, Vincent, like other savvy old teamsters, eased the right tires off the pavement onto the road shoulder, where they could find some purchase. Less experienced teamsters driving behind him quickly learned his trick.

But there are some things that even a master cannot control. In 1999, Vincent was involved in a nearly fatal accident on the second day of the wagon train. A car hurled around a blind curve and barreled straight at Vincent's lead wagon. With a line of cars parked in the opposite lane and a bank on the other shoulder, neither the car nor the wagon had any place else to go. I was riding with Vincent that day, and I'm not ashamed to admit that when I saw a car hurling toward us at fifty

Photo by Theresa Lloyd

Wagons in line

miles per hour, my only response was to ponder how to best face eternity—gripping the wagon seat, or clinging to Vincent's arm. Vincent, on the other hand, was busy figuring out a way to buy us a little more time in the temporal world, and as a result he saved both our lives. As he explained later, he decided to back the mules up. In the act of backing up, the mules turned and raised the tongue of the wagon slightly. Thus, instead of plowing headfirst into the wagon and ramming several thousand pounds of mules and metal into Vincent and me, the car slammed sideways into the mules, tossing them around the wagon. Miraculously, both animals remained on their feet, though they were badly bruised, and Joe had an eleven-inch-long gash in his shoulder clear to the bone. Vincent finished the wagon train driving Pete and Pam, his younger mules.

Jim and Joe recovered, but according to Lynn, the accident marked a turning point for Vincent, and he was never quite himself after it. At first the decline was almost imperceptible, but by the Autumn of 1999, when he normally would have pitched his big tent at Fires Creek for a month of backcountry riding and hunting, Vincent felt so ill that he consulted a doctor. Initially the diagnosis was pneumonia; later, the verdict was switched to cancer, which by that time had spread throughout much of Vincent's body. When he entered into chemotherapy, he became so debilitated that he could not get out of bed. His children Jerry and Sandra made up a cot in the living room of his trailer, where he lay on his back week after week.

Yet Vincent was never one to give up, and, despite his condition, he insisted he would go on the 2000 wagon train. With his son Jerry and his grandson Lynn driving Pete and Pam, Vincent lay on a cot in the bed of the lead wagon, eating almost nothing, sometimes drinking a few sips of Ensure or Five-Alive, the names of which now seem rather ironic. At times he would prop himself up on pillows or Jerry would fold up the side of the wagon cover, and a steady stream of teamsters and riders would drop by to pay their respects. Vincent was on everyone's mind, since he was rolling along at the head of the train, suffering no doubt as those iron tires jounced over the rocks and ruts, but never complaining about the pain. We kept remembering that Vincent's very own uncle Harley, from whom Vincent had inherited his mules and his lead position, had died during a past wagon train, and we wondered if Vincent would follow Harley's example. And so the whole train became a cortege of sorts.

Vincent hung on through the entire trip, whether he wanted to or not. Not only hung on, but managed to enjoy himself. "I never knew how pleasurable this ride could be, flat on your back," he said after the third day out. Vincent was still guiding us, and swearing some, too, as he did during one particularly hair-raising ride down the Snowbird Mountains into Tennessee. Along one of those trails so narrow that if a wagon wheel veered too close to the edge you were in real danger of dropping off a nearly vertical precipice, the brakes on Vincent's wagon jammed. Pete and Pam strove mightily, but clearly the mules could not maintain that kind of effort. Jerry, a fine teamster in his own right, allowed as how his nerves were "shot to hell" and stopped the wagon. Several teamsters sprang out to help, as they always do when a fellow driver is in trouble. Vincent, flat on his back, unable to see the brake, knew how to fix it.

Near the end of that same day, the wagon train rolled into its planned campsite on the headwaters of the Tellico River only to be turned away by a forest ranger in a mix-up over a camping permit. From his cot in the wagon bed, Vincent swore a little, rallied the troops, and declared, "Let's take them to Tellico Plains." Tellico Plains was supposed to be the next evening's camp, a good 16 miles away. And so a dozen or more wagons set off at a smart trot down by the wildly rushing Tellico River. It was the purest bliss that a teamster could ever know: cool evening air, a gentle decline, a smooth road, trees arching overhead, mountains rising high above it all. Teams and teamsters found a new reservoir of energy. Sonny Waters, driving the wagon behind Vincent's, said that every now and then Vincent, who was too ill to sit up, would raise his fist in triumph.

Two mornings later, the wagon train pulled out of Tellico Plains and headed back toward North Carolina. Lynn spelled Jerry as driver. Vincent, still lying on his cot, remarked to Lynn and me that in 1958 Claude Angel, the head teamster during the Western North Carolina Wagon Train's early years, had driven the wagon in which we were riding. "This wagon has wore out a bunch of men," Lynn observed. Later, during the lunch break, Vic Campbell, a wagon training buddy whom Vincent had not seen for some years, showed up. Perhaps because Vic is a physician, the dying man felt no obligation to display the hopeful bravado with which he had been encouraging the rest of us. When Vic leaned into the wagon to greet the old teamster, Vincent had tears in his eyes. "I've warmed up the wind; now I'm going in," he said in a broken voice, clasping Vic's hand.

During the Autumn of 2000, Vincent rallied for a short time, but after that he declined steadily. Just before Thanksgiving, Joe, the mule whose shoulder had been torn open in the car accident, died. Jim, his teammate, stood for two days in the exact spot where Joe had gone down, refusing to eat or drink. Jerry kept the news of Joe's death from his father, but Vincent was not long in following. On January 9, 2001, he spoke his last words: "I'm going to the mountain." He died shortly thereafter. Jerry figured that Vincent was probably riding old Joe.

According to an African proverb, when an elder dies, a library is lost. In Vincent's case, the library was enormous. Yet to the family and friends whom Vincent left behind, the legacy is also great. And on that cold, rainy January morning, Jerry and Lynn honored that legacy when they carried Vincent on his last wagon train.

They used Vincent's own wagon, the one with the "Muleskinner's RV" license tag on the back. You could hear it creak as it bounced up the hill to the cemetery. Pete and Pam were pulling; Jim, old and grizzled, walked behind, bearing a riderless saddle with Vincent's boots tied backward in the stirrups. The coffin lay in the same wagon bed where Vincent had regaled his friends with stories and had caught a few hours of sleep during many a wagon train. Over the newly dug grave, a massive hemlock tree rose into the lingering fog. Nearby were the grassy graves of Vincent's kinsmen. The graveside service was short, and after it was over, family and friends trudged silently down the muddy hill.

Vincent Parker had come back to the mountain.

Contributors

Kimberly Greene Angle's work has appeared in *The Chattahoochee Review*, *South Carolina Wildlife*, *The Flannery O'Connor Bulletin*, *Skirt*, and *Weavings: A Journal of Spiritual Growth*. She is currently pursuing a Ph.D. at the University of South Carolina in Columbia.

Ruth Knight Bailey, J.D., is an independent scholar specializing in Appalachian Mormon Studies. This research was supported in part by a grant from the Research Development Committee at East Tennessee State University. A preliminary report was presented at the Annual Conference of the Mormon History Association in Washington, D.C., in May 1998. The author wishes to thank the many people who assisted with information and encouragement, particularly Matthew Heiss and the individuals who shared their personal histories. Special acknowledgement also goes to Sarah Wilhelm, Nancy Fischman, Mike Woodruff, Mark Giesecke, Margaret Maxwell, and Gene Bailey.

Born and raised in upper east Tennessee, Linda Behrend is a librarian at the University of Tennessee, Knoxville. Her work has been published in *Now & Then: The Appalachian Magazine*, *Home and Away: A University Brings Food to the Table*, and *The Lancet*, among others. In 1999 she received the Wilma Dykeman Award for Essays from the Appalachian Writers Association.

Brooks Blevins is Director of Regional Studies at Lyon College in Batesville, Arkansas. He is the author or editor of four books, including *Hill Folks: A History of Arkansas Ozarkers and Their Image* (2002).

A former Baptist minister, Henry A. Buchanan lives in Murray, Kentucky. His writings—seventeen books and a number of articles for various national and regional periodicals—tend to explore four general subject areas: mythology, theology, autobiography, and love and marriage.

James E. Cherry is the author of *Bending the Blues*, published by H & H Press. Cherry's previous work has appeared in *Signifyin' Harlem*, *Langston Hughes Review*, and *DrumVoices Revue*.

Deidra Suwanee Dees, from the Muscogee Nation in Alabama, is a doctoral candidate in Education at Harvard. Her research examines Native American storytelling contributions to American history.

An art historian who specializes in early twentieth century American painting, Mariea Caudill Dennison wrote her dissertation for the University of Illinois on regional art in the Southern states. *The Burlington Magazine*, a London art journal, published two of her articles, while her 2003 article in *Women's Art Journal* documented a 1915 New York art exhibit held at Macbeth Gallery in support of equal suffrage. She has taught at colleges and universities in the Midwest and North Carolina.

G. Wayne Dowdy is the archivist for the History Department at the Memphis/Shelby County Public Library and Information Center. He holds the M.A. degree in History from the University of Arkansas and is a certified archives manager. Dowdy is the author of several articles on twentieth-century Memphis political history, including "'A Business Government by a Business Man': E. H. Crump as a Progressive Mayor, 1910–1915," published in the *Tennessee Historical Quarterly* (Fall 2001).

Jo Angela Edwins was born in Augusta, Georgia. She earned the B.A. degree in English and Journalism at Augusta State University and the M.A. and Ph.D. degrees in English at the University of Tennessee at Knoxville, where she received first prize in the John C. Hodges Graduate Poetry Awards in 1999, 2000, and 2001. She teaches American literature, composition, and creative writing for the University of Tennessee's English Department. "My Mother's Hands" is dedicated to the memory of her mother, Beatrice McCarty Edwins.

A visual artist currently living in Utica, Mississippi, Bart Galloway studied art at the University of Mississippi and at Mississippi State University.

J. D. Graffam Jr. was raised in Farmerville, Louisiana. Since he was of legal working age, he has run fireworks stands, worked on a pipeline, sold life insurance and knives, been a repo man, cooked burgers at McDonald's, bagged groceries, and helped to organize an in-house advertising services department for the Mississippi Choctaw Indians. He is currently a student at Millsaps College in Jackson, Mississippi.

An adjunct professor of Theatre at the University of Illinois at Urbana-Champaign, Allean Hale is a leading Tennessee Williams scholar who also writes fiction and plays. Her introductions to four unknown Tennessee Williams plays were published recently by New Directions Press. Other work has appeared in *Mississippi Quarterly, The Southern Review, The Southern Quarterly, The Missouri Review, Grand Street,* and *Michigan Quarterly Review.* "The Sounds of Friday" is based on her memories of New Orleans in the 1940s.

M. Thomas Inge is the Robert Emory Blackwell Professor of Humanities at Randolph-Macon College in Ashland, Virginia, where he teaches and writes about Southern literature and culture, American humor, animation, film, and William Faulkner. Inge's recent publications include *The Greenwood Guide to American Popular Culture* in four volumes, edited with Dennis Hall; *Conversations with William Faulkner;* and new editions of Mark Twain's *A Connecticut Yankee in King Arthur's Court* for the Oxford World Classics series and of Sam Watkins' Civil War memoir *Company Aytch* for Penguin Books. He is also the editor of the journal *Studies in American Humor.*

Zachary Michael Jack is Assistant Professor of English at Tusculum College in Greeneville, Tennessee.

Theresa Lloyd teaches folklore and Appalachian literature at East Tennessee State University. Originally from the Appalachian foothills of western North Carolina, she is a horsewoman herself and has done extensive fieldwork with recreational wagon trains and the material folk culture of the Upper South.

Dorothy Hampton Marcus, a native of Winston-Salem, North Carolina, is a graduate of Meredith College in Raleigh, which honored her with its Distinguished Alumnae award for her work in race relations. She also holds a master's degree from Temple University in Philadelphia. She currently lives in Teaneck, New Jersey.

Born and raised in the western North Carolina community of Green River, Robert Morgan has taught at Cornell University since 1971. He has published several books of fiction, including the award-winning novels *The Truest Pleasure* (1995) and *Gap Creek* (2000), as well as nine volumes of poetry. Morgan's additional awards and honors include four NEA Fellowships, a Guggenheim Fellowship, a Rockefeller Foundation Bellagio Fellowship, the North Carolina Award for Literature, the James G. Hanes Poetry Award from the Fellowship of Southern Writers, and inclusion in *New Stories from the South* and *Prize Stories: The O. Henry Awards*.

Mendi Lewis Obadike is an interdisciplinary artist whose poetry has appeared recently in such journals as *HOW2*, *Obsidian III*, *Sou'wester*, *Indiana Review*, and *Fence*. Her new media works have been exhibited at the Studio Museum in Harlem, the Whitney Museum of American Art, and the International Center of Photography. A native of California, Mendi grew up in Tennessee. She now lives in Connecticut and teaches at Wesleyan University.

Kevin O'Donnell is Associate Professor of English at East Tennessee State University. He is co-editor of the book *Seekers of Scenery: American*

Travel Writing from Southern Appalachia: circa 1840-1900, published by the University of Tennessee Press in 2004.

Ted Olson holds the Ph.D. in English (1997) from the University of Mississippi. Presently Associate Professor at East Tennessee State University, he also serves as Director of that school's Appalachian, Scottish, and Irish Studies program. Olson is the author of *Blue Ridge Folklife* (the University Press of Mississippi, 1998); the editor of a poetry collection by the late Kentucky author James Still, *From the Mountain, From the Valley: New and Collected Poems* (University Press of Kentucky, 2001); the co-editor (with Charles K. Wolfe) of *The Bristol Sessions: Writings About the Big Bang of Country Music* (McFarland & Company, Inc., 2004); the Music Section editor and associate editor for *The Encyclopedia of Appalachia* (University of Tennessee Press, 2005); and the author of *So Far: Poems* (Creeker Press, 1994). Additionally, Olson is the author of many articles, essays, encyclopedia entries, reviews, oral histories, poems, and creative nonfiction pieces published in a wide variety of books and periodicals.

A native Mississippian, Jon Parrish Peede holds degrees from Vanderbilt University and the University of Mississippi. He lives with his family in Alexandria, Virginia, and serves as aide and speechwriter to the Chairman at the National Endowment for the Arts. His writing has been published most recently in *The New Laurel Review* and *Modern Age: A Quarterly Review*.

James A. Perkins is Professor and Chair of the Department of English and Public Relations at Westminster College in New Wilmington, Pennsylvania. He holds degrees from Centre College, Miami University, and the University of Tennessee at Knoxville. Perkins has written books on Robert Penn Warren, Robert Drake, and other Southern writers. In addition to his scholarly writing and editing, Perkins is a poet and a short story writer. His most recent volume of short stories is *Snakes,*

Butterbeans & the Discovery of Electricity. In 1998, he was a Fulbright Senior Lecturer at Seoul National University in Korea.

Ron Rash has published three books of poems, two short story collections, and, most recently, the novel *One Foot in Eden.* Henry Holt will publish his second novel *Saints at the River* in 2004. He currently holds the John Parris Chair in Appalachian Studies at Western Carolina University in Cullowhee, North Carolina.

A native of Wellsville, Ohio, Randy Rudder received his B.A. from Mount Union College. Prior to his teaching and writing career, he worked in music publicity in Nashville, Tennessee. He obtained the M.A. degree in Literature from Tennessee State University and is completing an M.F.A. in Creative Writing from the University of Memphis. Rudder is currently teaching at Nashville State Community College and is a contributing writer to such periodicals as *Nashville Scene, Country Music, Country Weekly, Bluegrass Unlimited,* and *The Washington Post.*

Currently living in Columbia, South Carolina, where he earned a Master of Library & Information Science at the University of South Carolina, Jean-Mark Sens was born in France and educated in Paris. He has lived in the American South for several years, and has taught English at the University of Mississippi, Rust College, the University of Southern Mississippi, and U.S.C. Sens has published poems in various U.S. and Canadian magazines. His collection of poems entitled *Appetite* was recently published by Red Hen Press.

Charles D. Thompson Jr. is Education Director of the Center for Documentary Studies and Adjunct Professor of Cultural Anthropology and Religion at Duke University. His most recent book is *The Human Cost of Food: Farmworkers' Lives, Labor, and Advocacy.* His book manuscript, entitled *They Go Quietly: A Story of Faith, Farming, and Change in the Virginia Blue Ridge,* is currently under consideration for publication.

Originally from Guyton, Georgia, Renna Tuten is a photographer and writer.

Jaclyn Weldon White was born, raised, and has lived all her life in the South. She worked in law enforcement and the judicial system for over twenty years until retiring to concentrate on her writing. The author of two true crime books and a biography, White's first novel, *Distant Heart*, was published in early 2004. She and her husband live in Macon, Georgia.

Brenda Witchger grew up in Alabama and currently resides in North Carolina. Her fiction generally reflects her Southern heritage. Witchger writes literary fiction and mysteries under the pseudonym Brynn Bonner.